ONE HUNDRED YEARS OF GREEK–TURKISH RELATIONS

ONE HUNDRED YEARS OF GREEK–TURKISH RELATIONS

The Human Dimension of an Ongoing Conflict

Samim Akgönül

With the participation of Tiphaine Delenda

EDINBURGH
University Press

Edinburgh University Press is one of the leading university presses in the UK. We publish academic books and journals in our selected subject areas across the humanities and social sciences, combining cutting-edge scholarship with high editorial and production values to produce academic works of lasting importance. For more information visit our website: edinburghuniversitypress.com

Edinburgh University Press Ltd
13 Infirmary Street
Edinburgh EH1 1LT

First published in hardback by Edinburgh University Press 2024

Typeset in 11/15 EB Garamond by
IDSUK (DataConnection) Ltd

A CIP record for this book is available from the British Library

ISBN 978 1 3995 3384 3 (hardback)
ISBN 978 1 3995 3385 0 (paperback)
ISBN 978 1 3995 3386 7 (webready PDF)
ISBN 978 1 3995 3387 4 (epub)

CONTENTS

Introduction   1

1   Turks and Greeks: Of Partition and Separation   11

2   Greek–Turkish War in *Correspondance d'Orient*, an 'Oriental'
Journal published in Paris, 1919–22   26

3   'New Turks': Turkey's 1923 *Muhacirs*   47

4   A Peculiar Group: *Polites*   66

5   A Specific Branch of Turkish Diaspora and Transnationality:
Greece's Muslims   126

6   One Hundred Years of Greek–Turkish Relations: Breaking Points,
Evolutions and Continuity   157

Conclusion: Turkey, Greece and Complex Interdependence   185

Bibliography   200
Index   210

INTRODUCTION

Tempora mutantur
nos et mutamur in illis

During the summer of 2022, exactly 100 years after the Greek–Turkish war, called *Μικρασιατική καταστροφή* (Catastrophe of Asia Minor) in Greek historiography and *Kurtuluş savaşı* (War of Independence) in Turkish national historiography, tension between the two countries again came to a boil over the Aegean. Previously, in July 2020, conservative Muslims in Turkey had celebrated the conversion of the Greek Orthodox Hagia Sophia Cathedral into a mosque. Then, on 9 September 2022, secular Turks heralded the expulsion of Greeks from Izmir with a large concert featuring the Turkish pop star Tarkan. Despite these events, many Turkish tourists – mostly middle-class – visited Greek islands and praised the benefits of Greek tourism that same summer. The Greek–Turkish relationship remains complex and multi-faceted, with feelings that oscillate between love and hate.

The relationship has been fraught with tension for a century over a range of issues, including territorial disputes and cultural and political differences. Despite being NATO allies and neighbours, the two nations have a long history of conflict and mistrust, but also a sense of similarity and mutual admiration. In the twenty-first century, the situation has become increasingly complex, with a resurgence of nationalist sentiment on both sides, as well as an active engagement between the two nations through common initiatives, tourism, media and social science.

This book explores the human dimension of Greek–Turkish relations, using three fieldwork studies conducted in the 1990s, 2000s and 2020s, as well as a comprehensive archive study. It focuses specifically on the topic of compulsory exchange of populations and its consequences, as well as the Greek minority in Turkey, the Turkish minority in Greece and contemporary developments in the mutual, yet paradoxical, relationships between the two nations.

The human dimension of a conflict encompasses the profound impact that war and other forms of strife have on individuals and communities. In the case of Greek–Turkish relations, the impact of historical and ongoing conflicts can be particularly profound for both minorities and majorities. This includes not only physical harm, such as death and injury, but also emotional and psychological trauma, displacement, as well as loss of homes, livelihoods and loved ones.

Additionally, the forced exchange of populations and its lingering memory has created a traumatic root for the contemporary discord between Greece and Turkey. Greek historiography emphasises the role of fighting against the Turks in the country's independence war, and Turkish historiography emphasises the role of fighting against the Greeks in the country's transition to independence a century later. This ongoing disagreement and tension further exacerbate the human dimension of the conflict.

The human dimension of a conflict also encompasses its broader social, economic and cultural consequences, such as the transmission of history through popular media or political discourse. The existence of nationalist sentiment is often exploited by populist politicians to mobilise the public against the perceived 'other', and to redirect attention away from actual issues and towards irrational emotions. This can further deepen divisions and exacerbate the human dimension of the conflict.

In the midst of a conflict, individuals and communities are often forced to make difficult choices and sacrifices, such as fleeing their homes or taking up arms to defend themselves. They may also experience a range of emotions, including fear, anger and grief, as well as feelings of hopelessness, isolation and despair.

The human dimension of a conflict also extends to the aftermath of the fighting, when individuals and communities are left to rebuild their lives. This is particularly relevant in the case of the groups that were forcibly exchanged in Greece and Turkey. This process can include dealing with the physical and emotional scars of war, as well as rebuilding homes, businesses and infrastructure.

It can also include the process of reconciliation and healing, as individuals and communities attempt to come to terms with the past and move forward. This process can be challenging and may take a long time to achieve, but it is vital for the healing and reconciliation of the affected communities.

It is important to consider the human dimension as a cultural interaction, not just in terms of conflict. This book takes into consideration, especially through narratives, not only the perception of radical otherness, but also those of similarities and sameness.

Cultural interaction between Greeks and Turks has been shaped by centuries of historical, political and social ties. Throughout history, the two cultures have influenced each other through trade, migration and cultural exchanges. The Greeks and the Turks have shared common cultural elements, such as cuisine, music and art, and have also borrowed and adapted elements from each other. Greek and Turkish literature, for example, have been influenced by one another's language, mythology and storytelling traditions. Even though the two countries have had their fair share of conflicts, today, cultural exchange is alive and well with both countries enjoying each other's food, music and art. The Greek and Turkish film industries have collaborated and their music stars have performed in each other's countries. Tourism is also an important dimension of cultural exchange, as many people from both countries visit each other's countries as tourists.

This book is based on original data collected during six different field research phases, conducted in:

- 1996 and 1998 (22 interviews in Istanbul, Bursa, Komoti, Xanthi, Echinos)
- 1998–2001 (98 interviews in Istanbul, Imbros, Izmir, Athens, Thessaloniki)
- 2008–10 (18 interviews in Istanbul, Izmir, Athens, Strasbourg, Boston, Adelaide)
- 2020–2 (28 interviews in Istanbul, Paris, Athens, online)

These were mainly face-to-face interviews, except during the Covid-19 period (2020–1), and participant observation of everyday life events of Turks of Greece, Greeks of Turkey and exchanged populations and their descendants.

The author's research sites included Istanbul, the Imbros and Tenedos Islands, Izmir, Athens, Thessaloniki, Komotini, Xanthi and Echinos, as well as in Europe, mainly in France and Germany, among diasporas of both countries and both minorities. The primary data is supported by the analysis of documents and publications by civil society organisations in the form of pamphlets, reports, newsletters, websites and social media accounts, as well as Turkish and Greek national newspapers and newspapers of both minorities.

For the purpose of different chapters of this book, digital archives (mainly Gallica https://gallica.bnf.fr/accueil/fr/content/accueil-fr?mode=desktop) and physical archives of the following journals and reviews were used. For the physical archives, I would like to thank the Turkish National Library (Ankara), the archives of the Turkish Prime Minister (Istanbul) and the archives of the Centre for Asia Minor Studies.

In France

Correspondance d'Orient 1918–23

In Turkey

Turkish national newspapers

Türkiye, January 1990 – December 1999
Tercüman, July 1955 – September 1955 / December 1963 – December 1964
Son Havadis, December 1963 – December 1964
Akşam, December 1963 – December 1964
Hürriyet, December 1963 – December 1964 / January 1990 – December 1999
Ulus, December 1963 – December 1964
Milliyet, December 1963 – December 1964

Newspaper of Greek minority

Apoyevmatini, January 1955 – December 2018

Monthly magazine of the Turkish minority in Greece

Batı Trakya'nın Sesi, January 1991 – December 2001

In Greece

Greek national newspapers

To Vima, January 1993 – December 1999
Kathimerini, January 1993 – December 1999
Athinaiki, December 1963 – December 1964

Newspapers of Turkish minority of Greece

Azınlıkça, January 2013 – December 2022
Trakya, July 1955 – September 1955 / December 1963 – December 1964
Trakya'nın Sesi, December 1981 – December 1996
Gerçek, December 1984 – December 1991
Akın, December 1984 – December 1992
İleri, January 1989 – December 1990

This book is composed of six chapters, each of which focuses on the identity-based approaches of Greek–Turkish relations over the course of a century. They primarily focus on the 'human' aspects of these relations rather than technical or purely political ones. They analyse the cultural, social and personal dimensions of the relationship between the two nations, exploring how identities are shaped, perceived and interacted with over time. The book is an attempt to understand the complexities of the Greek–Turkish relationship through a different lens, one that is centred around the people and their experiences.

Therefore, my analysis focuses on the concept of identity groups, such as minorities, elites, or migrants, and how they influence the perception and representation of relations between those who identify themselves as Greeks and Turks. Through this examination, it becomes clear that exclusive national constructions have led to a strong sense of 'otherness' between the two groups. However, this phenomenon is closely tied to imagination, and can sometimes be overcome, allowing a shared identity, fraternity and solidarity to emerge. This book offers an examination of the ways in which identity and representation shape and are shaped by the relationship between Greece and Turkey, highlighting the complexities and nuances of this connection.

The first chapter is a sociological and historical approach, attempting to decipher the notion of 'partition' between Greeks and Turks – a partition of territory but also of culture. Even if competing historiographies have built them up as enemies, both nations are close, sometimes even too much so. Understanding the relationships between two nations that have long portrayed each other as the ultimate 'other' can be a challenging task. Both nations have developed relatively short, but also longer, national narratives that are integral parts of this construction process. These narratives have been manipulated, reinterpreted, reinvented and sometimes invented.

The following chapter is an external view. The Greek–Turkish war (1920–2) was followed by all Ottoman subjects and beyond because it was the last battle of the First World War that was already finished in the Western Europe, and the result of this battle would affect the entire post-Ottoman area. Thus, two Syrians living in Paris who published a very intriguing newspaper, the *Correspondance d'Orient*, reported on the war to the French public, always keeping the Syrian (and Lebanese) issue in mind. Thanks to reports directly from Asia Minor, we see how the Greek–Turkish war was, in some aspects, a civil war between two autochthonous groups of Anatolia. As it is explained in detail in the following pages, for this chapter, the main primary source that I used is the Journal *Correspondance D'Orient*, published in Paris between 1908 and 1945. For the purpose of this chapter, I followed the journal between 1918 and 1923, in order to scrutinise an original and almost neutral point of view – almost neutral because the journal's main focus was the Syrian question but still biased in that the publishers and most of the writers of the journal were from the Ottoman Empire. The main challenge in the analysis of this primary source was glossing over the rich content (culture, fashion, middle Eastern politics and so on) of the journal in order to concentrate on the Greek–Turkish war.

The third chapter goes back to the sources of the Greco-Turkish dispute, to the shared trauma concerning the compulsory exchange of populations in 1923, analysed through the lens of Muslim refugees in the newly founded Turkey. What is constructed here is the concept of the forced identity shift that these populations endured, through their language, their religion and even their physical appearance . . . How to 'make Turks' out of them? In addition to secondary sources, this chapter draws on three corpuses of interviews. The first is a collection of interviews conducted by Kemal Yalçın in the 1980s for the purposes of his book Yalçın Kemal, *Emanet çeyiz: Mübadele insanları*, Istanbul, Bir Zamanlar Yayınları, 1989. The second contains interviews conducted by Leyla Keskiner in the 1990s and used in her chapter in Tolga Köker, Köker Tolga, Keskiner Leyla, 'Lessons in Refugeehood: The Experience of Forced Migrants in Turkey' (Hirschon Renee (ed.), *Crossing the Aegean: Assessing the Consequences of the 1923 Exchange of Populations, Between Greece and Turkey*, Oxford, Berghahn Books, 2003, p. 193–208). Finally, I used 12 out of 98 interviews that I conducted in Athens, Thessaloniki and Istanbul between 1998 and 2001. All three corpuses have been remobilised for the purposes of this book and reinterpreted in order to illustrate the memory and impact of the exchange in the identity building process.

The fourth chapter studies one of two remnants of a common Turkish–Greek life, examining the human aspects of the Greek minority in Turkey throughout the twentieth century. The life of this minority evolved along with the bilateral relationship of these two countries. However, Ankara's effort to diminish the extent and quality of this relationship has remained a constant. The chapter analyses the different episodes of the extinction of this minority, from 1923 to today, highlighting some improvements towards the end. For this chapter dealing with the Greeks of Turkey, apart from classic and recent secondary sources (since the 1990s, the Greeks of Turkey have become a popular topic among researchers), I used, as primary sources, demographic statistics of Turkey published in the collection of *Nüfus ve Demografi*, daily newspapers in Turkey around significant events, such as 1955 or 1964 (*Tercüman, Son Havadis, Aksam, Ulus, Milliyet*), as well as eighteen interviews that I conducted between 2008 and 2010 in Athens, Thessaloniki, Istanbul, Izmir, Boston and Adelaide and twenty-eight other interviews that I conducted in the 2020s in Athens and Istanbul.

Following this theme, Chapter 5 focuses on the analysis of the Muslim Turkish minority of Western Thrace in Greece. The Muslim minority of Western Thrace in Greece is a significant and distinct community with a rich history and cultural heritage. The minority is primarily made up of ethnic Turks and Pomaks (Bulgarian-speaking Muslims) and Muslim Roma. The minority, vestiges of the Ottoman Empire, is concentrated in the northeastern region of Greece, specifically in the Xanthi, Rhodope and Evros prefectures.

It is estimated that the Muslim minority of Western Thrace includes around 140,000 people, representing about 3 per cent of the Greek population. The minority has its own culture and traditions, including language, customs and religious practices. The Turkish language is widely spoken among the community, and the vast majority of the minority adheres to Sunni Islam, with some small fringes following the Bektashi order.

Throughout the twentieth century, the minority has faced challenges and discrimination, particularly after the population exchange between Greece and Turkey in 1923 and the subsequent forced assimilation policies of the Greek state. Despite these challenges, the minority has managed to maintain its cultural and linguistic identity and has made significant contributions to the region's economy and society.

In recent years, the Greek government has taken steps to recognise the minority's unique status and to improve the community's rights and well-being. This includes the recognition of the minority's language and religious rights, the establishment of minority schools and the promotion of cultural and economic development in the region. But problems remain, especially regarding the issue of religious leadership.

Chapter 5 places this minority not only in the 'Greek' context but also in a network of common affiliations with Turkey and the Turkish diaspora. It draws mainly on seventeen interviews conducted in Thessaloniki and Komotini and seventeen interviews in Istanbul and Bursa in 2020–2 and on the websites of Turkish organisations in Muslim Thrace. The chapter also draws extensively on minority newspapers from the 1990s (personal archive) and the 2020s (*Gündem*, *Azinlikça* websites).

The final chapter of this work, Chapter 6, examines the human dimension in Greek–Turkish relations, analysing structural aspects of the Greek–Turkish dispute as 'continuities' and presenting ruptures and breaking points that demonstrate the dynamic nature of the bilateral conflict. It begins by examining the impact of the post-1990 new world order on minorities and the perception of majorities. It then focuses on the end of the century and the Öcalan affair, which had a significant impact on bilateral relations. The capture of Kurdish rebel leader Abdullah Öcalan by Turkish special forces on 15 February 1999 in Nairobi, Kenya, while he was using a Cypriot passport, following his transit through Greece and Italy, marked a significant turning point in the Kurdish–Turkish conflict, as the Kurdistan Workers' Party (PKK) had been one of the most active and violent groups in the region. It also left an important mark on Greek–Turkish relations because it cemented the mistrust of Turks towards Greeks, given that some Greek political leaders were suspected of assisting the fugitive.

The negative breaking points in Greek–Turkish relations are partially offset by the 'seism diplomacy' that emerged after the İzmit earthquake in 1999. A magnitude 7.4 earthquake struck the city of İzmit and the surrounding region in northwest Turkey on 17 August 1999. It was one of the deadliest earthquakes in Turkey's history, killing over 17,000 people and injuring more than 50,000. The disaster response was slow and inadequate, leading to widespread public criticism and the resignation of the government. However, the disaster also prompted an unprecedented genuine solidarity movement from all over the world, with Greece playing a particularly prominent role. This led to a sentimental yet sincere rapprochement between the two countries.

The chapter also analyses slower evolutions in the human dimension of Greek–Turkish relations, such as the situation of minorities and the role of the Ecumenical Greek Orthodox Patriarchate. The role of civil society, rather than the states, is emphasised in this primarily positive evolution. However, there are some ossifications in the human dimension of Greek–Turkish relations where continuity is more visible than ruptures. Issues such as Cyprus, the Aegean and aspects of the minority situation, such as muftiates, are discussed in the chapter. The chapter relies heavily on classic and recent secondary sources, as well as Greek and Turkish national media, both in print and online.

Throughout the writing process, I received valuable assistance from Tiphaine Delanda, a student at the prestigious Sciences Po in Bordeaux who completed her internship at the Department of Turkish Studies at the University of Strasbourg and worked on this text. Her contribution was invaluable. I thank a lot Erdem Sander who checked the footnotes and formal consistency of the text. Furthermore, my working conditions at the DRES (Droit, religion, entreprise et société) research centre of the French National Centre for Scientific Research (CNRS) were excellent. At MISHA (Maison Inter-universitaire de Science de l'Homme-Alsace), not only I could organise several conferences and seminars on this topic but also Jean Yves

Bar provided precious proofreading with very important suggestions that improved the quality of the text.

Naturally and as always, during archive work in Istanbul, Athens and Paris and the field research, Eda and Luka were very understanding and supportive. The reader must keep in mind that I wrote these pages by using their love as a sustainable, perpetual, endless energy.

1

TURKS AND GREEKS:
OF PARTITION AND SEPARATION

Introduction: Peace and Conflict in the Nation-building Era

How can we grasp relations between two nations that have depicted each other as the ultimate 'other', especially over a long period of time? This is the history of two national constructions, one relatively short and one longer, an integral part of this construction process, manipulated, reinterpreted, reinvented, sometimes invented. The Greeks' *Turkokratia* is as much a *presentist* construction as the Turks' *Pax Ottomana*. The *Mikrasiatiki Katastrofi* is as much the cornerstone of Greekness as *Kurtuluş Savaşı* is of Turkishness. These visions of the past are indispensable, every nation has them, for they are constructed on victories, heroic feats, but also on catastrophes, exiles, hardships and shared suffering. In short, they are built on hostility, rivalry and sometimes hatred. However, this construction cannot erase what they share with the 'opposite' group, especially if this sharing lasts. These partitions create a proximity, a resemblance, sometimes even sameness. Sometimes, Turks and Greeks are identical, share the same identity, despite the surrounding discourse about their differences.

Anthropology and history, as well as literature and art, in all senses of the word, give contradictory insights into these relations, for what is shared divides as much as it unites. It is these contradictions that I wish to briefly examine, before trying to overcome them by proposing complementary interpretation frameworks, along with tested models which define the tradition of the studies of Turkish–Greek relations.

Or . . . Greek–Turkish relations. There is a lack of balance between the perception of these relations from 'Turkish' side and 'Greek' side. The ideological apparatus in Greece still transmits hints of Turkokratia, emphasising the otherness but, especially after the trauma of 1920s, the artificiality of this otherness has step by step been understood by new generations, while in Turkey the same ideological apparatus, especially national education, ignores or dehumanises the Greek element with a certain success. In Greece, the man (and woman) in the street has more idea on the 'Turk' in Greece than the man (and woman) in Turkey about the Greek. The shared space has more meaning in Greece than in Turkey.

A Space That Is Shared, or That We Do Not Want to Share

The Eastern Mediterranean region, which has been historically shared by the Turkish and Greek peoples, comprises a diverse and fragmented landscape that includes the South Balkans, Western Anatolia and various islands and coastlines. Prior to the current designations of these regions, the Eastern Mediterranean served as a unified entity bound together by the Aegean Sea.

'The Anatolian littoral of the Aegean Sea belongs simultaneously to two geopolitical entities: the edge to an insular world seeking great fertile areas and the opening of a continental world to the sea', writes Stefanos Yerasimos.

> The coast is an economic and strategic addition of the islands close to the littoral, while they constitute a defence line and a geological extension of the coast. It is therefore vain to seek a 'natural border between both worlds. [. . .] The territory shared by the Aegean and Anatolian worlds had to particularly feed these societies' irredentism, as they successively occupied these borderland territories'.[1]

In its historical context, this inhabited region can be characterised by three distinct and sometimes conflicting dimensions. It is a space of encounters and exchanges, marked by interactions between diverse cultures and societies. It is also a region of conflicts and tensions, marked by centuries of hostility and animosity. Yet, despite these divisions, it is also a region that is characterised by shared cultural similarities and bonds that transcend geopolitical boundaries.

The existence of these three perspectives, which intersect and overlap, continues to shape contemporary perceptions of relations between Greeks and Turks. Proponents of friendship between Greeks and Turks often emphasise the first interpretation, that of a shared space marked by encounters, exchanges and coexistence, characterised by harmonious cultural polyphony and *convivenza*. These ideals are symbolised by various places, figures and emblematic objects.[2]

This idealised vision and its justification, are rooted in a shared history, a shared way of life, and the shared experience of state-building and domination. Although post-1950s Turkish historiography has associated the Ottoman Empire with 'Turkish' history and the Greek national narrative has long interpreted their Ottoman history as a history of Turkish domination, some scholars argue that the Ottoman Empire was first and foremost an empire of Greeks and Turks, and that 'Ottomanity' represents a common construction of both groups. This perception, although strongly idealised, is anchored in a shared history and lifestyle, and even in the construction and domination of a shared state.[3] It depicts Greeks and Turks as components of the same identity group, sharing more similarities than differences.

This vision of *convivenza* also finds its justification when looking at most cosmopolitan cities of the nineteenth century. Indeed, the world cities of the second half of the nineteenth century and of the first half of the twentieth, before nationalisms and blocs were cemented, were Istanbul, Smyrna, Salonica, Beirut and Alexandria, among others.[4] This made the region a living space that was as real to its inhabitants as it was imagined by Orientalists. The Eastern Mediterranean is 'where the Orient and the Occident coexist'[5], as Albert Camus put it in 1937. He goes on to say that, at this junction, there is no difference in the lives of, say, a Spaniard or an Italian from the Alger docks, or those of the Arabs surrounding them. Similarly, Ottoman cities housed Turks, Greeks and others, with common lifestyles, sharing everyday life spaces in the city even though they first seemed divided because of the millet system. François Georgeon has shown that this interdependence was vital to those cities; people may have appeared to only exist through their group but were individualised in reality through their work and social status.[6]

It was therefore a space of coexistence, not divided between 'Turks' and 'Greeks' but rather between Muslims and non-Muslims. Indeed, it was also the place of religious division and of a slow alteration process, radical at first, between religious groups, which became ethno-religious along the way. This place of tensions, even hatred, that was the Ottoman territory at the beginning of the twentieth century, is best depicted by Ivo Andric in his Sarajevo 1920 letter:

> Whoever lies awake at night in Sarajevo hears the voices of the Sarajevo night. The clock on the Catholic cathedral strikes the hour with weighty confidence: 2 AM. More than a minute pass (to be exact, seventy-five seconds – I counted) and only then with a rather weaker, but piercing sound does the Orthodox church announce the hour, and chime its own 2 AM. A moment after it the tower clock on the Beys' mosque strikes the hour in a hoarse, faraway voice, and that strikes 11, the ghostly Turkish hour, by the strange calculation of distant and alien parts of the world. The Jews have no clock to sound their hour, so God alone knows what time it is for them by the Sephardic reckoning or the Ashkenazy. Thus, at night, while everyone is sleeping, division keeps vigil in the counting of the late, small hours, and separates these sleeping people who, awake, rejoice and mourn, feast and fast by four different and antagonistic calendars, and send all their prayers and wishes to one heaven in four different ecclesiastical languages.

Venezis says, 'The war was over, and the Turks were gone, but nothing had really changed. We had become strangers in our own land'.[7] He still believes, in 1924, that it's 'their own land' that is already completely forgotten by the Turkish propaganda. Thus, the space shared between Greeks and Turks is not only Eros's, but also Eris's, despite the arguments of the defenders of the Greco-Turkish friendship and brotherhood, and the few champions of their sameness. And as soon as national constructions are initiated, Eris overcomes Eros, without, however, slaying him'.[8]

One Nation Needs Another

The Greek and Turkish national constructions are, admittedly, not synchronous, nor do they take the same tears and blood-stained roads. However, both (still ongoing) processes share a vital need for the other. The 'collective other' must be close, similar, comparable, definable and hateful. Our construction depends primarily on the construction of the other, on our definition in opposition to them. The Greek nation's 'other' isn't necessarily the Turk[9]; the other can be Slavic, Muslim or Catholic. Conversely, the Turkish nation's 'other' is not uniquely the Greek people; it is the non-Muslim, particularly Armenians, at times Arabs and even sometimes the 'Ottoman', all used as foils to define what a Turk is. However, the Greco-Turkish alterity remains the most present 'fruitful' opposition.

This self-definition uses similar instruments. Nations are constructed on legends, heroic acts, victories and other evidence of the group's strength.[10] However, they also need shared suffering and catastrophes, genocides, exiles, evidence of the other's alterity and even inhumanity, to be constructed in opposition to them.[11] Thus, in the alteration process, pain becomes a banner or shelters or walls in order to refuse any similarity with them and convince ourselves of their inherent difference. Greek and Turkish literature are filled with accounts that 'irrefutably' demonstrate the other's savagery. These are endlessly retold 'exorcism stories', aimed at preventing these past sufferings from occurring again. I, for one, believe that these narratives are vital to nationalists on both sides, in order to guarantee the continuity of their national construction. This is how a well-liked neighbour can be turned into a rival, how close alterity can become a constitutive enmity.[12]

In order to construct both nations, it was necessary to first separate them, 'unmix' them. This was made possible by the millet system, which had already created a separation between the two groups on the basis of a religious divide. This divide is so fundamental that both national construction processes were founded on religious affiliation, albeit paradoxically in the case of Turkey. The compulsory exchange of 1923 was not made between Turks and Greeks but between Muslims and Orthodox Christians. In a desperate attempt to create a 'pure' nation, assimilation policies targeted Orthodox Christians in Greece, Macedonians, Muslims in Turkey and Kurds. Unlike other observers, I do not believe that there were assimilation policies aimed at Greek Turks or at Turkish Greeks. There were at the most policies designed to make these minorities, which had been spared from the ethnic purification strategy in extremis, more visible. We now know that this mandatory exchange was more of an amputation procedure than a transplant. While the transplant has been partly successful, an amputation is still experienced unconsciously.[13] Eris still dominates, while Eros shows itself now and again, as it did during the earthquake that both nations suffered at the end of the twentieth century, or during concerts held together, where identical songs were sung with the same enthusiasm. Those are the types of initiatives, both humane and realist, which allow for the 'dead zone' created in the 1920s to resuscitate and to become a passageway.[14]

However, the blame should not solely fall on the architects of the nation, manipulating their ignorant people with political acts and speeches. Humanists, defenders of the friendship between Turks and Greeks, always support the idea that this deterioration is caused by political ambition, while both peoples are profoundly pacifists. But sometimes, as Elias Canetti explains so well, the masses are easily transformed into destructive and self-destructive weapons.[15] How else, then, can we explain the night of 6th/7th September 1955?

To make sense of the night of 6th/7th September, one should rewind the film a bit. Three intertwined radical transformations took place during that period, concerning identity, society and politics. The identity transformation is now well known. As a bitter legacy of the millet system, adhering to Islam was considered to be the dominant criterion in the construction of the Turkish national identity, resulting in the elimination of the ancient non-Muslim populations of Anatolia. In the paradigm of Turkish nationalism, a Turk is a Muslim. Non-Turkish Muslims can be assimilated into Turkishness, but Anatolian non-Muslims cannot be included in Turkishness, even if they speak Turkish. Therefore, they must be eliminated. As a result, Armenians and Greeks were removed from Anatolia between 1915 and 1923. The 1923 Treaty of Lausanne on Population Exchange was not applied to Istanbul's Greeks. Therefore, homogenisation was perceived as not fully achieved by nationalists. Three decades later, in the 1950s, a process of creation of an internal enemy developed.[16] This was when the concept of Turkishness became equated with Muslim affiliation. Using practices such as the Wealth Tax (1942) and the Twenty Classes military service decree (1941) during World War II, non-Muslims were pushed to the outskirts of society.

The construction of the Greek nation has been a complex and multifaceted process spanning two centuries. The formation of the modern Greek nation dates back to the idea of Greekness that was relatively independent from ortho-dox identity in the early nineteenth century. The struggle for independence was not only a military endeavour but also a cultural and ideological movement fuelled by a sense of Greek identity, history and language. This 'history' was a paradoxical one, hesitating to include the ancient Greek history praised by the Western Hellenophilia, but seen as pagan by the religious elite.

Greek intellectuals played a crucial role in fostering national consciousness, promoting Greek language and literature and reviving ancient Greek heritage as symbols of national pride. More than the Turkish nation, the Greek nation is built by poets, not generals.

Following independence, the consolidation of the Greek nation involved significant challenges, including territorial disputes, population exchanges and the integration of diverse regional identities into a cohesive whole. Nation-building efforts focused on constructing a unified Greek identity that transcended regional and religious differences by using Turkish otherness. Education played a vital role in this process, with the establishment of a standardised curriculum and the promotion of a shared historical narrative.

In the meantime, in Turkey, the second transformation was social. Beginning in the early 1950s, with the mechanisation of agriculture under the Marshall Plan and the acceleration of industrialisation thanks to a relatively state-controlled capitalism, migration began from rural to urban areas, especially to Istanbul. However, industrialisation could not keep up with the pace of migration. Thus, new villages were formed around the cities. The first *gecekondu* (shantytowns) date back to the mid-1950s. Their residents formed a population that was susceptible to manipulation by nationalist and Islamic discourses. Moreover, it was a suitable environment for a kind hostility towards visible wealth.

The third transformation was undoubtedly political. With the Democrat Party in power, Turkey abandoned its non-aligned foreign policy and literally discovered the Cyprus issue in the 1950s. To be able to have a say on the Cyprus issue, it was necessary to create public opinion, and the only way to do this was through nationalist and racist propaganda. Throughout the summer of 1955, both the Greek Cypriots in Cyprus and Greeks in Turkey were targeted in the press using classic racist rhetoric, with the use of 'name similarity'. In other words, they were selected as scapegoats. Thus, on the eve of the Cyprus conference in London, the new residents of the already hate-filled cities were further incited against the Greeks, and more generally against all non-Muslims. All that was needed was a single spark, which was ignited with the fake 'bomb' placed in Ataturk's house in Thessaloniki by the Turkish state, an event amplified by the *Istanbul Ekspres* newspaper. The Turkish Consulate doorman who placed that tiny explosive at the Thessaloniki consulate ended his career as a governor in Turkey.

Preparations began on the afternoon of 6 September 1955. After Prime Minister Adnan Menderes boarded a train from Istanbul to Ankara, news began to be repeatedly broadcast on Istanbul Radio that a bomb had been placed in Atatürk's house in Thessaloniki, where the consulate was located. Meanwhile, hundreds of people from the suburbs of Istanbul were transported to Taksim and Şişli by truck, carrying sticks in their hands. This crowd was handed out a special edition of *Istanbul Ekspres*. Despite the state monopoly on printing at the time, thousands of special issues had been printed in just a few hours. The newspaper had two different front pages, both claiming that the Greeks had attacked Atatürk's house, which turned out to be false. The crowd began to walk in the Rumeli, Osmanbey, Harbiye, Taksim and Beyoğlu direction, shouting anti-Greek slogans. There were also gatherings in neighbourhoods such as Adalar, Kadikoy, Moda, Kurtuluş and the Izmir Fairgrounds. Shops and houses in the Taksim area began to hang Turkish flags and Atatürk portraits on their front windows. These flags and pictures had been distributed beforehand to Muslim Turkish owned shops and homes. The crowd took to the streets with gasoline canisters and sticks. All night long, looting, burning and, most importantly, pillaging continued amidst cries of 'Cyprus is Turkish and will remain Turkish'. That day, coincidentally, the Interpol meeting was being held at the Hilton Hotel. European journalists, especially the French photographer from Paris Match, were able to capture the night on camera, so that Europe would witness the nightmare Istanbul had experienced that night.

Throughout the night, the police supported the demonstrators, showed them which houses and shops to attack, sometimes standing behind them and watching, sometimes protecting them. When the situation turned into mass hysteria in the morning, with people looting and rioting, Adnan Menderes, who was returning from Ankara, ordered the military to enter the city. Tanks were driven over torn fabrics, broken glass and shoes on Istiklal Avenue. In general, non-Muslims, especially Greeks, had already lost their sense of security since 1941–2. They had been made to feel that they were no longer at home in their own city, where they had lived for hundreds of years. The events of 6/7th September reinforced this perception. Especially for the Greeks, the police, who were the only hope for a liveable city, became an obstacle. However, contrary to popular belief, the Greeks did not leave Istanbul en masse after 6/7th September 1955. The minority notables, especially the charismatic Patriarch Athenagoras and other minority leaders, persuaded the Greeks to stay in Istanbul. Meanwhile, the government attempted to compensate for the damages, at least partially, while looting and vandalism were blamed on leftist groups in the first few months for anti-communist propaganda purposes. On the other hand, Greece, which was the only place they could go, was a poor country that had just emerged from a ten-year occupation and civil war. Thus, Istanbul Greeks were persuaded to stay in their city with a few individual exceptions. The real mass migration began during the 1963–4 Cyprus crisis, when the Inönü government deported the Greek citizens of Istanbul to Greece. When the 12,000 deported Greeks were followed by their families, Istanbul Greeks had crossed the final threshold in the process of extermination.

In the same period, in Greece, the Italian aggression through Albania on 28 October 1940 did not come as a surprise. Greece had placed great reliance on the fortifications along the Greek–Bulgarian border, considering them impenetrable, much like the Maginot Line. However, the German invasion of Yugoslavia in April 1941 bypassed these fortifications. It is worth noting that the fortified zone did not extend to the Greek–Turkish border, indicating that Turkey was not perceived as a threat, nor the minority as its 'fifth column', at least during the war. Additionally, following the Italian attack, Turkey issued an ultimatum to Bulgaria, declaring that it would support Greece in case of a Bulgarian invasion of Thrace.

These promises were not entirely realistic but part of Turkey's 'balancing game'. In the spring of 1941, there was talk of signing a non-aggression pact with Germany. Among the German proposals was the revision of the Turkish–Bulgarian border in Turkey's favour. Despite this bargaining, the condition Turkey put forward for breaking its neutrality in favour of Greece and England was the status of Dodecanese under Italian domination, not Western Thrace.

After the German–Bulgarian invasion in April 1941, Western Thrace fell under Bulgarian control, and the occupiers exerted their authority over the minority population. All minority institutions, including education and religion, were under Bulgarian control. The Pomaks, a Muslim group speaking a Bulgarian dialect, received particular attention from the occupiers. Bulgaria aimed to legitimise their occupation by taking charge of the education of minority children, while local Greeks constantly complained about the closure of Greek schools.

Bulgaria also interfered in religious matters by appointing a Turkish-speaking mufti named Beiski in Xanthi. The appointment of a mufti went beyond religious affairs and held significance as a social and ceremonial leader. Moreover, the Bulgarian occupation disrupted the management of minority properties by Muslim communities.

The challenges faced by the minority during the occupation extended beyond social and religious pressures, which affected the entire region's population. In 1941, as part of a general mobilisation, the Greek army requisitioned all vehicles and draft animals in the region. Additionally, young members of the minority served in the resistance army, particularly in the defense of Thessaloniki, with the 29th Komotini regiment comprising predominantly soldiers of Turkish origin. This regiment suffered heavy losses during the defense of Pindos.

In September 1941, a resistance movement was formed, with trade unions affiliated with the Greek Communist Party, the Socialist Party and the People's Party of Democracy joining forces to establish the National Liberation Front, or EAM. In February 1942, this alliance established an armed force called the ELAS (People's National Liberation Army). However, Churchill and the exiled royal government in Cairo were concerned about the Communist dominance within the EAM. To diminish its influence, they encouraged the formation of other resistance groups like EKKA (National and Social Liberation Movement) and EDES (Greek National Democratic Union), which soon evolved into anti-Communist paramilitary organisations. ELAS, led by its renowned leaders known as *kapetanios*, swiftly united the mountain guerrilla fighters, the *andartes*, following the legacy of the *klephtes* from a century ago.

Throughout the resistance in Macedonia and Western Thrace, guerrilla activities blended heroism with banditry through the regular ransoming of villagers. Their cruelty towards those who refused to help them was notorious. The British wanted to take advantage of the existence of these irregular bands to fight the German occupiers. British intervention transformed the action of these bands into 'manipulated resistance'. As early as 1942, there were attacks on the property and persons of members of the minority.[17]

Following Italy's fall in 1943, Germany intensified its control and unleashed a series of reprisals in northern Greek villages. The situation was further complicated by the EDES, led by Zervas and supported by the British, who decided to impede the advancement of ELAS. The future regime of Greece after liberation was at stake. In December 1944, when Greece was liberated, fierce clashes erupted between communist guerrilla groups, their People's Army or Democratic Army and the regular army of the provisional government led by George Papandreou, under the return of King George II through a plebiscite in September 1946.

The minority aligned themselves with the royal army, although loyalty to the king varied. When EAM militants arrived in Xanthi on 9 September 1944, aiming to 'return the town to its people', they selected three minority members, namely Osman Nuri Fettahoglu, Mestan Secai and Ali Recep, for the town's management committee. The minority was divided into three factions: those who had collaborated with the Bulgarians were anxious, those who sought collaboration with the communists wanted involvement in the city's 'autonomous' leadership and those who remained loyal to the king opposed any collaboration with the rebels. The majority within the minority remained loyal to the royal government, primarily comprising the elite. Consequently, resistance against the guerrilla warfare began, leading to retaliatory actions from the EAM–ELAS against the minority.

These reprisals took the form of surprise attacks on villages. A few dozen *andartes* took over villages for one or two hours, then withdrew, bringing with them new recruits. The regular army used scorched-earth tactics to clear the villages of recruits; an estimated 200,000 peasants were displaced throughout Greece. In June 1947, the democratic army began attacking towns in the north, including Alexandroúpolis in Western Thrace. Members of the minority, most of them Gypsies in Alexandroupolis, were almost forced to take refuge in Turkey. While it's true that emigration was massive in the cities, in the mountainous regions it was not. There are three reasons for this. Firstly, the towns of Western Thrace suffered more than the Rhodope mountains from guerrilla attacks: the largest town in this region, the town of Echinos, was home to a royal army corps, and most of the inhabitants of the remote villages had been moved to this town following the scorched-earth tactics already mentioned. Then, there's the fact that the population of these mountains was almost exclusively Pomak: while Greece and the guerrillas tolerated Turkish emigration from the towns, they strongly discouraged Pomak emigration. Finally, Turkey accepted Turkish refugees more readily than Pomaks.

States and Institutions: Constants but No Calcification

In both countries, the attitude of officials is crucial. One should not neglect the states' role in both the implementation of policies against the opposite government and in shaping public opinion. Sovereignty, in the case of Greek and Turkish States, is the key word. Both states went through traumatic times before their foundation and stabilisation, which explains their fear, sometimes even paranoia, of seeing their sovereignty eroded. This appears first and foremost in purely technical domains, such as the delimitation of territorial waters, continental shelf and airspace, or the possession of islands populated only by crabs. It is clear that, in a way, the issue of sovereignty of one or the other over a rock, lost in the Aegean Sea, is only a way for them to protect (and even extend) their sovereignty and to convince themselves of their strength and longevity. Surely, this cockfight can always be rationalised by putting forward this or that material gain provided by the domination on said rocks, but those disputes are ultimately symbolic.

The fear of losing sovereignty also appears in less 'technical' domains. The era of construction of nation-states was always one of rivalry between the secular state institutions and the religious structures. This is as true for Turkey and Greece as it is for France. In any case, there were either attempts by the state apparatus to control the religious institutions (as happened in Turkey and Greece) or endeavours to eradicate the strength of said institutions (as was the case in France). In these nation-states, regarding the religious institutions, the threat of sharing sovereignty is a dual one: not only can they take over for the state on a number of prerogatives (charity, education, health), they also represent a threat of external intervention because of their supra- or trans-national nature. Thus, we must look at the conflict between the Turkish state and the Patriarchate about its 'oecumenical' qualification and the conflict between the Greek state and its minority about elected muftis, in this sovereignty prism.

Admittedly, sovereignty-related jealousy is a constant in Greco-Turkish relations, but both states have shown an ability to evolve, adapt and even show sincerity. This has sometimes been to fulfil lowly material interests, as was the case in 1988–9 when the Davos wind blew in the wake of Papandreou and Özal's realism. Sometimes, public opinions are the ones driving leaders to waver, for less rational reasons, as happened during the 1999 earthquakes. In both cases, civil societies stepped into the pre-existing breach, and accomplished real results.

As a Conclusion: A Shared Destiny

Once this deterioration process has reached a point of no return, once the 'other' is placed, collectively, on the margin of humanity, individuals can then easily rationalise their violent behaviour and hateful speech. After all, if Turks are convinced that all Greeks pursue the Megali idea and that their attempts at reconciliation are but a trick to fool the Turkish nation, they will not object to eliminating any individual Greek representing 'their' nation in its entirety. If Greeks are convinced that all Turks have but one idea in mind, reinstating *Turkokratia*, that 'the threat does not come from the North but from the East', they are within their right to invoke self-defence, to attack Turks wherever, whenever. Consequently, nations, being an exclusivist categorisation of individuals into 'imagined communities',[18] fade, or at least they do as long as these individuals do not interact in their everyday life. Indeed, these interactions, prevented through the numerous 'dead zones' mentioned above, shatter prejudices, certainties, dogmas. They are not, however, enough to transform these disputed territories into a land of exchanges and serene partitions, to create common interests, to convince both nations of their shared 'fate'. For both nations precisely believe that they are inherently different, opposed and separated. Nonetheless, these interactions can at least forge links, establish networks and develop a common sense of belonging. They can conjure Eros, sleeping under Eris.

Having examined the internal dynamics of Greek–Turkish relations, it is now pertinent to shift our focus to the perspectives of non-Turks and non-Greeks regarding this conflict. Examining these external perspectives provides valuable insights into how this longstanding dispute has been perceived and its broader implications beyond the immediate Greek and Turkish contexts.

Notes

1. Yerasimos, Stefanos, 'Les rapports gréco-turcs, mythes et réalités', *CEMOTI (Cahiers d'études sur la Méditerranée orientale et le monde turco-iranien)*, 1986, no. 2–3, p. 3.

2. I borrow the concept of *convivenza* from Bromberger, Dominique, 'Méditerranée', *Anthropen* (2019-04-23), https://doi.org/10.17184/eac.anthropen.106.

3. See, for example, the ideas of Kitsikis, Dimitri, *L'Empire Ottoman*, Paris: Presses Universitaires de France, 1985.

4. Bromberger, Dominique, 'Méditerranée', Anthropen (2019-04-23), https://doi.org/10.17184/eac.anthropen.106.

5. Lévi-Valensi, Jacqueline, 'La Méditerranée d'Albert Camus: une mythologie du réel', Armignani, Paul, Laurichesse, Jean-Yves, Thomas, Joël (eds), *Rythmes et lumières de la Méditerranée*, Perpignan: Presses Universitaires de Perpignan, 2004, p. 268.

6. Georgeon, François, Dumont, Paul (dir.), *Vivre dans l'Empire Ottoman: Sociabilités et relations intercommunautaires (XVIIIe–XXe siècles)*, Paris: L'Harmattan, 1997.

7. Venezis, Elias, Νούμερο 31328, Athens: Kambana, 1924.

8. In Greek mythology, the children of Eris, goddess of hate and discord are Ponos (Suffer), Limos (Hunger), Léthé (Oversight), Algea (Paine), Hysminai (Melee), Makhai (Fight), Phonoi (Murder), Androktasiai (Assasination), Neikea (Quarel), Pseudis Logos (Lie), Amphilogiai (Dispute), Dysnmia (Anarchy), Até (Disaster), Horkos (Oath). Paradoxically, Eros, who is depicted as an insipid child and not as an adult, does not have children!

9. National categorisation often uses the singular to emphasise the compactness of the enemy: see Schmitt, Karl, *The Concept of the Political*, Chicago: The University of Chicago Press, 2007 (1932).

10. Thiesse, Anne Marie, *The Creation of National Identities: Europe, 18th–20th Centuries*, Leiden: Brill, 2021, pp. 111–14.

11. Venezis says 'the Greeks, as a community, base their identity on these pains' quoted by Pekin, Müfide (ed.), *Yeniden Kurulan Yaşamlar, 1923 Türk-Yunan Zorunlu Nüfus Mübadelesi*, Istanbul: Bilgi Üniversitesi Yayınları, 2005, p. 129. On the dehumanisation of the enemy, see Erik, Erikson's 'pseudospeciation' concept: Erikson, Erik 'Pseudospeciation in the Nuclear Age', *Political Psychology*, 1985, vol. 6, no. 2, pp. 213–17.

12. Lory, Bernard, 'Strates historiques des relations turco-bulgares', *CEMOTI*, vol. 15, 1993, pp. 149–67.

13. Clark, Bruce, *Twice a Stranger: How Mass Expulsion Forged Modern Greece and Turkey*, London: Granta, 2006.

14. Papadakis, Yannis, *Echoes from the Dead Zone, Across the Cyprus Divide*, London: I. B. Tauris, 2005, p. 293.

15. Canetti, Elias, *Crowds and Power*, London: Farrar, Straus and Giroux, 1984.

16. Ağır, Ülkü, *Pogrom in Istanbul, 6./7. September 1955: Die Rolle der türkischen Presse in einer kollektiven Plünderungs- und Vernichtungshysterie*, Berlin: Klaus Schwartz Verlag, 2014.

17. Eudes, Dominique, *Les Kapétanios: la guerre civile grecque de 1943 à 1949*, Paris: Fayard, 1970, p. 29.

18. Anderson, Benedict, *Imagined Communities: Reflections on the Origin and Spread of Nationalism*, London: Verso, 1991.

2

THE GREEK–TURKISH WAR IN *CORRESPONDANCE D'ORIENT*, AN 'ORIENTAL' JOURNAL PUBLISHED IN PARIS, 1919–22

Introduction: *Correspondance d'Orient*, a Singular Newspaper

Correspondance d'Orient was an unusual newspaper, published in Paris during the 1908–45 period by an intriguing personality: Chekri ibn Ibrahim Ganem. The journal, which presented itself as an 'economic, political and literary review' featured articles and news pertaining mainly to the Ottoman Empire, Egypt and India. Around 60 issues were published regularly between 1919 and 1922, showing a careful approach to the Greek–Turkish war.

Chekri Ganem (1861–1929) was a French-speaking Lebanese intellectual. While he left us several literary texts, including novels, plays and poems, his main activity was journalism and he was one of the French authorities' leading sources on the Orient.

Born on 14 September 1861 in Beirut, in the Ottoman Empire, he founded the literary magazine Al Mostaqbal in Beirut and published collections of poetry, including *Ronce des Fleurs* in 1896. At the beginning of the twentieth century, he was one of the most prominent militants for the independence of Lebanon from the Ottoman Empire. Chased from Beirut, he first lived in Alexandria and Tunisia before travelling to Austria and Italy and finally settling in Paris. There, he co-founded and directed with Georges Samné (1877–1938), the *Correspondance d'Orient* in 1908 after the Young Turks revolution in Istanbul, which gave him some hopes for the Arab provinces.

The journal was actually the newsletter of the 'National Ottoman League' or 'The League of Arab Nation'.

Alongside his journalism activities, he continued to be politically involved in the Arab world. He became the vice-president of the Syrian delegation to the first Arab General Congress, which took place in Paris in 1913, aiming to ask the Ottoman authorities for more autonomy. At the beginning of the First World War, he refused enlistment in the Ottoman army and was forbidden from travelling in the Ottoman territories, especially in Beirut, where many of the Arab delegates were hanged.

During the same period, while based in Paris, he published his first novel *Da'ad* (1908), a nostalgic book describing the habits and customs of old Beirut and highlighting Lebanese hospitality,[1] then plays, including the famous *Antar* in 1910, adapted as an opera by Gabriel Dupont in 1921. Another of his pieces, *La Giaour* (The Infidel), was set to music by Marc Delmas in 1914.

As can be expected, the main topic discussed by the *Correspondance d'Orient* was the Arab question.[2] Clearly, the authors Chekri Ganem and his close friend Georges Samné, staunch supporters of an independent (or at least under French mandate[3]) Near East (Syria and Lebanon) did not want to dilute their struggle by getting involved too deeply in another issue such as the Greek–Turkish war of 1919–20. Nevertheless, as they were one of the main sources of information on the Ottoman/post-Ottoman territories in the Near East, they did publish some articles, news and analyses on this war between two non-Arabic nations of the Ottoman Empire.

First of all, in several articles, the big difference between the Balkan nations' struggle for independence from the Ottoman Empire and the struggle of Arab nations is underlined. For example, in February 1919 the author writes that Serbs, Roumanians, Bulgarians and Greeks cooperated in their search for independence because they are '*homogènes dans leur masse et unis par les liens de race et de religion*' (homogeneous in their mass and united in their race and religion) but that the Arabs of Syria are too divided and without a national identity.[4] Of course, this argument of the unity and internal or external homogeneity of the Balkan nations, including Greece, is a deliberate lie, intended to underline the internal divisions of the Ottoman Empire's Arab nations. Nevertheless, indirectly, the newspaper emphasised the rights of Greece in Asia Minor thanks to this 'homogeneity and unity'.

1919–20: From Smyrna to Sèvres, a Political Journey of the *Correspondance d'Orient*

The journal started taking a more active interest in the Greek–Turkish struggle in late February 1919. In a report on various claims from different nations in the Ottoman Empire ahead of the Sèvres Peace conference, Georges Samné, the associate editor-in-chief of the journal, first heaped praise on Venizelos ('an eminent statesman who puts incomparable qualities of judgement, finesse and clairvoyance at the service of Hellenism'[5]) before listing the territorial claims of Greece, justified by the number of Greek inhabitants in several regions such as Thrace or Asia Minor. These figures are provided by Venizelos (730,000 Greeks in Thrace, 1,700,000 in Asia Minor, etc) and are never questioned by the journal. Mr Samné is convinced that Greece should be able to adjust its borders to accommodate these '4,000,000 Greeks living outside of Greece's borders'.[6] He argues that 'the incapacity of the Turkish people and the importance their leaders give to ensuring order have led Turkey's real friends to rally around the thesis of a purely Asian Turkey subject to European control'. Mr Samné adds that if Constantinople, where the 'Greek elements' are equal to 'Turkish Elements', is not given to the League of Nations, it should be under the control of Greece. It is interesting to see how the justification of Arab nations against the Ottoman state involves the interiorisation of Greek claims in Turkey. The conclusion that the journal drew was that the claim of 'foreign mandates' on the entire Ottoman territory and, therefore, Syria ('that the borders are between the Taurus Mountains and Sinaï and between the Mediterranean border and Euphrates river') must be a French mandate. In other words, *Correspondance d'Orient* instrumentalised Greek claims in order to justify Arab claims without a hint of solidarity with 'Turks', if only, for instance, on the grounds of Islamic identity. Moreover, the journal depicts Arabs, Greeks and Armenians as common victims of Union and Progress atrocities.[7]

However, the tone of the newspaper becomes more nuanced with the beginning of the Sèvres conference. The arrogant attitude of Western powers towards Turkey is condemned in March 1920[8]; Greece is accused of having annexed Thrace to Greece 'd'un trait de plume' ('with the stroke of a pen'). In the same issue, Aly El-Ghaiaty only reluctantly conveys the journal's opinion on the Greek claims but states that 'the non-attached Greeks have the same rights of liberation as Armenians or Arabs'.[9] Nevertheless, El-Ghaiaty thinks that Greek demands are somewhat exaggerated ('quelque peu exagérées') compared with those of the other oppressed nations of the Ottoman Empire. In other words, as the Greek claims were parallel to the Arab demands, the journal strongly supported Venizelos: when, during the conference, Greek demands overshadowed the Syrian (Arab) demands, the journal expressed doubts.[10] According to a Parisian journalist quoted by *Correspondance d'Orient*, the Greeks claimed the Provinces of Smyrna and Aidin but 'without this littoral, an exclusively Asian Turkey cannot survive'.[11] The journal also had no qualms about interviewing Prince Sebahattin during his Geneva exile; he dismissed the Greek claims as 'unreasonable'.[12]

Things worsened over time, according to the journal, to the extent that an April 1919 piece was titled 'Dark hours of the Conference'.[13] Of course, the real 'action' began as the Greek army landed in Smyrna on 16th May 1919 while the peace conference was still underway. On the same day, the *Correspondance d'Orient* reproduced a letter previously published in the April 30 issue of *Le Temps* asking Western powers not to prevent the occupation of Smyrna by the Greek army on the grounds that the region had been inhabited by Greece since the most remote periods of history. Rumours of interventions to stop the Greek occupation 'out of sympathy for Turks or jealousy for Greeks' were deemed unacceptable.[14] In the following issue, Georges Samné worried that the existence of Turkey was still being debated at the conference while an impatient Greece occupied Smyrna.[15] Yet he made it clear that this existence was not to be defended in the name of the Caliphate, as the Indian maharajahs had done. He argued that Turks must be subject to the same nationality principle; otherwise, there would be no stability in the Near East. This made the question of Islam secondary. This opinion is understandable because claiming sovereignty from the Sultan in the name of Islam could be understood as a defence of the unity of Muslims. On the contrary, the journal's main preoccupation was the independence (under French control) of Arabs in Syria (and Lebanon).

That is perhaps why the occupation of Smyrna was announced in very neutral terms by the journal:

Occupation of Smyrna

On May 16 Allied forces landed in Smyrna. The Forts of the city were occupied by French troops. Greek forces established themselves in the main districts of Smyrna.

English and Italian contingents occupied certain areas in the vicinity. A large American naval division was stationed in the harbour. The Ottoman government had been informed about the operation by the Allied naval authorities, which was carried out according to article 7 of the Armistice of Mudros, on the day before the operation.

This caused a great commotion in Constantinople and the Grand Vizier resigned. The Turkish government protested on the grounds that no serious incident had occurred. A Turkish detachment attempted to mount a resistance, which was immediately thwarted.

Colonel Zafiriou, who commanded the Greek occupation troops, addressed the following proclamation to the population:

> I bring to your notice that by order of my government acting in concert with the allies, I am proceeding to the military occupation of Smyrna and the surrounding area. The purpose of this occupation is to guarantee the safety of the population.

News of the conference's decision to allow Greece to militarily occupy Smyrna caused indescribable excitement in Athens.[16]

It is interesting to see that by the beginning of the Greek occupation of Smyrna, the tone of the journal changes even more: between the lines, the reader may get a sense that the Turks are unfairly treated, whereas in early 1919, the *Correspondance d'Orient*'s reporters had no mercy for 'the Turk'. Strangely, the writers appeared to have believed that the Indian maharajah played a role in preventing the dismemberment of Turkey. Admittedly, the May 30 issue does not mention the beginning of the Turkish national struggle or the name of Mustapha Kemal; it was too early. However, the following argument was cautiously offered:

> It is said that the landing of the Allied troops at Smyrna and the occupation of Constantinople caused some excitement among the Muslim population. The Ecumenical Patriarchate has received reports from various provinces of the empire where Turkish gangs continue to terrorise the populations.[17]

In June 1919, the subtitle of the *Correspondance d'Orient* changed again and became 'Islam – Levant – Afrique – Syrie'. In June 1919, Aly El-Ghaiaty still thought that the occupation of Smyrna was unfair, or at least came too early. 'The occupation of Smyrna was marked by incidents which highlighted the danger of introducing presumptive heirs into a succession which is not yet open and whose holder has even more vitality than one would like to believe'.[18] According to Saint Brice, this injustice could only be repaired by single rule because 'experience shows that the Orient finds peace only when it is subject to a single power, strong enough to break international plots'. Moreover, Turks, he thinks, connect easily, not with Great Britain (therefore Greece), not with Italy, but with France, mainly because Turks still remembered the pact between Soliman the Magnificent and François 1st.[19] The journal also printed a letter penned by Turks living in Switzerland 'warning humanity' about the consequences of the Greek army's occupation of Smyrna, in a region inhabited by 1,500,000 Turks and 100,000 Greeks'.[20]

In the meantime, the Greek army in Anatolia struggled. Leaving Smyrna behind, the army tried trying to advance further inland but faced a strong reaction by 4,000 Turks led by 'Nahri Pasha',[21] especially around Ödemis. There, the Greek army arrested journalist Haydar Rüstü,[22] the founder of the newspaper Anadolu, who was allegedly preparing to 'burn down Ödemis'.[23] This background on the aborted burning of Ödemis by the Turkish resistance is important when considering the controversy of the Smyrna fire that raged one year later.

In July 1919, the end of the Ottoman Empire was, according to the journal, obvious. While the Empire had not been defeated by its enemies, it had committed suicide by forging an alliance the Germans and by slaughtering 800,000 Armenians and 200,000 Greeks and Arabs.[24] The conclusion was clear and twofold:

1. No non-Turkish nation would want to be under Ottoman administration.
2. Since Turks always mix with other nations everywhere, they must be controlled by a state under a mandate, even in Anatolia where they are in the majority.[25]

If Turks wanted to create their nation on the ashes of the Ottoman Empire, they could, but not east of the Taurus mountains and Sivas where Armenian, Kurdish and Arab territories started. They could, however, do so in Asia Minor and Thrace (instead of Greeks). Thus, according to Pinon, in the Greek–Turkish war, Arabs should tolerate a Turkish victory because were they unable to establish their new nation in Asia Minor, they might be tempted to turn to the eastern territories. 'By the way', said Pinon, 'what the Turks are doing is harming Islam and nothing else'.[26]

The Turkish national struggle, independent from the Istanbul government, is mentioned first in this issue where we learn that the Turkish mission at the peace conference asked delegates to help defeat the 'ultra-nationalist agitation' in Anatolia by placing Constantinople and Thrace under Ottoman rule and having the Arab provinces remain in the Empire as autonomous entities.[27] It is surprising to see that according to the journal this ultra-nationalist agitation was fomented indirectly by the Committee of Union and Progress, which incited the rebellion through the 'Forces of the Nation' (Kuva-ï Milliye). It is historically true that several leaders of the Turkish national resistance, including Mustapha Kemal, were close to Young Turks in the past, but in 1919, these connections had been severed.

In the meantime, the national resistance morphed into a Greek–Turkish war. The journal reported on the Greek Army's setbacks in places such as Pergame, Balikesir, Soma or Salihli.[28] There was a great deal of confusion about the reciprocal massacres. The ecumenical Patriarch Dorotheos accused Turkish national brigands of attacking Christians in Asia Minor and the Turkish resistance accused Greek troops of executing civilians. In late July, partially due to these difficulties, Greece accepted negotiation with the Italians on sharing several occupied territories, including Aydin.[29] The same issue mentions for the first time the 'political' struggle of the Turkish national movement, independent from Istanbul, during the Erzurum congress of 10 July. According to the journal, it was a 'pan-Turkish' congress. Delegations from six oriental provinces participated in the Erzurum congress to discuss and settle on the following issues:

- The situation of Trabzon
- The response to anti-Turkish propaganda
- An inquiry on the Armenian atrocities
- The general political situation
- Measures to prevent the separation of the oriental provinces
- Increasing the forces of the Gendarmery
- A ban on the emigration of Muslims

The journal adds that this initiative was condemned by the Sultan who declared the congress 'anti-constitutional'.[30]

In this issue, for the first time since the beginning of the War, two names are cited as 'leaders of the "so-called nationalists"' who provoked an "interior agitation". They are Moustapha Keimal[31] [*sic*] Pasha and Roouf Bey [*sic*], who were under orders to be arrested by the Istanbul government. It is important to note that the first national leader mentioned by the journal is, alongside Mustafa Kemal, Rauf Bey, then known as Rauf Orbay, who was a member of the last Ottoman parliament and would go on to become the prime minister of the Ankara government in 1923 as a rival of Ismet Pasha.

In September 1919, the West was surprised to find out about the existence of the 'national consciousness' of '15,000,000 Turks who, whether we like it or not, constituted the dominant population of Asia Minor'.[32] This Turkish national movement swayed the *Correspondance d'Orient*'s opinion on the Greek–Turkish war in favour of the Turks:

> The Greeks started attacking the Turks who had the bad taste not to be satis-
> fied that they had just been disturbed at their home. There was still time to
> limit the damage. Instead, the Greeks were allowed to keep pushing on into
> the interior and occupy Aydin. This time the Turks were angry for good and
> as soon as we (Westerners) violated the armistice, they went on the attack too.[33]

The same issue mentions again 'Réouf Bey' and Moustapha Kemal Pasha as the leaders of the 'rebellion' and argues that as former members of the Ottoman military, they posed a threat not only to the Allies but also to the hapless Ottoman government.[34] Aly El Ghaiaty blames this chaos on the Allies, who allowed Greeks to occupy Smyrna 'prematurely', inflaming Turkish national sentiment. Thus, Mustapha Kemal Pasha, who was sent to Amassia as an inspector, secretly reorganised the 'unionists'. He now claimed that the Government of Istanbul had sold the country to the Allies and called friends of the homeland and the religion to join him.[35] The journal makes it obvious that the Allies were now seriously concerned about the national rebellion and made promises to clarify what happened in Smyrna during the Greek occupation to calm down the civil population and prevent them from joining Mustapha Kemal. Surprisingly, even in October 1919, the uprising in Asia Minor and the Greek–Turkish war was seen as the result of Young Turk agitation.[36] The author is surprised to see that the Sultan who declared himself as the leader of the entire Oumma, was uncapable of securing the obedience of his 'own' subjects who revolted against him and the Greek occupation.[37] According to the journal, Mustapha Kemal still wanted to control the Istanbul government and supported the appointment of Djémal Pasha as minister of War. Kémal (and his 'bands') wanted to include the Istanbul government in the war. The solution for peace was simple according to Georges Samné: '*La Turquie aux Turcs, la Syrie aux Syriens, l'Arménie aux Arméniens, le Hedjaz au Hedjaziens, l'internationalisation des détroits, etc*' ('Turkey belong to Turks, Syria to Syrians, Armenia to Armenians, Hedjaz to Hedjazians, and the straits should be under international status, etc'). As one can see, Greeks are in this 'etc'.[38] The very same issue of the *Correspondance d'Orient* underlines the bicephalic nature of the Ottoman regime insofar as Mustapha Kemal demanded and obtained the resignation of Damat Ferit Pasha's government but was presented as the leader of a 'revolutionary government'.[39] After the congresses of Erzurum and Sivas, this 'nationalist movement' 'triumphed' in Malatya and advanced towards Eskisehir. Except for the Greek army, the nationalist army encountered no resistance. For example, when Mustapha Kemal's army took Konya, the Italian army surrounding the city 'preferred not to intervene'.[40]

In late October, Saint-Brice regretted the 'prevarications' of the Allies that led to a resurgence of the Unionists to be reborn under the helm of sympathetic figures such as Mustapha Kemal and Rauf Bey. It was now too late: the Greek occupation of Smyrna and the advance of the Greek army towards Aydin had awakened the national sentiment, and it was now no longer possible to erase Turkey from the map.[41] Henceforth, from Bursa to Edirne, several cities in Western Anatolia and Thrace joined the nationalist movement.[42] Better (or worse), the Istanbul government now negotiated with Mustapha Kemal and accepted abiding by nationalist principles, mainly regarding the Greek invasion of Anatolia. Mustapha Kemal, who had been dismissed from the army, would be reintegrated[43] (this did not happen). In the meantime, the Greek army asked the British army for help to protect the railway between Smyrna and Konya. The British army agreed to take the control of Bursa, but not further south.[44]

By November, winter had settled in and the dream of dividing Turkey into several mandates was gone. Achieving this would have required additional military effort, and no one would commit to such an undertaking anymore.[45]

The Greeks were now alone. Greeks (and Italians in Adalia) still had the appetite but not the stomach. The solution was to keep the Ottoman Empire alive with the help of the Western powers and by disarming the Ottoman army. An Ottoman state (or Turkish state) without an army could keep its sovereignty in Constantinople where the Khalifa would continue to reside.[46] The hope of Athens was to make it through the winter and to count on the exhaustion of the Muslims of Asia Minor, 'who won't support' new battles.[47] In the meantime, for the first time *Le Temps*, of Switzerland, interviewed Mustapha Kemal in his capacity of leader of the nationalist government in November 1919. He declared the unity of the Turkish territory according to the armistice of 1918 and voiced his opposition to a Unionist government.[48] Occasionally, the journal reported on Greek victories, such as in Akhisar where 50 Turkish 'irregulars' were killed. At the same time, the Christian leaders of the Ottoman Empire, including the Ecumenical Greek Orthodox patriarch and the Armenian Patriarchate wrote a letter to French Prime Minister Georges Clemenceau urging allies to immediately occupy Ottoman territories because Turkish nationalists were gaining strength and imposing a 'regime of terror'.[49]

In November 1919, there were still hopes to create an enlarged Armenia with a coast on the Black Sea by incorporating Greek populations of Trabzon,[50] and Lloyd George still argued that the Turkish government should retreat from the territories where Armenians, Greeks and Arabs lived.[51] Yet, at the same time, the commission in charge of investigating the Smyrna occupation (formed by Generals Bristol, USA, Hare, UK, Bunoust, France and Dall'ollio, Italy) delivered its conclusions, which argued that the occupation was unnecessary and that the Greek reaction to the resistance of 'irregulars' exceeded the limits of self-defence. The commission clearly expressed support for an evacuation that Venizelos firmly refused.[52] Despite this, the British government decided to maintain and support the Greek occupation of Smyrna without promising that the region would eventually be attributed to Greece.[53]

The year 1920 saw the journal mark a turning point in the Greek–Turkish war. While throughout 1919, the Arab and French journalists of the *Correspondance d'Orient* had tried to keep a balance between the Western, Greek and Turkish points of view, the language and vocabulary changed substantively in 1920, in favour, but in fear of, the victories of the Turkish nationalist movement. The situation of the Allies in Asia Minor became, according to the journal, untenable in 1920[54]; even Prince Fayçal was impressed by Moustapha Kemal's struggle and tried to emulate him.[55] The Turkish nationalists following Moustapha Kemal and those following the Union and Progress Party gained a new strength in 1920. Their objective was to 'cleanse' Turkey from foreign elements and to establish a 'Great Turkey' where no influences other than 'fanatic Islamism' would be accepted.[56] However, during the winter and spring of 1920, the *Correspondance d'Orient* reported step by step on how the Allies lost Asia Minor, at least politically. In the summer of 1920, the Greek army's manoeuvres in Anatolia are referred to as a costly 'adventure',[57] made possible only thanks to the diplomatic trickery of Venizelos, who had convinced London and Paris that the Greek army could beat Mustapha Kemal in a few days.[58] Following Venizelos's tour of capital cities, the Greek army occupied Bandirma and Balikesir in June with the help of the British but as stated in the journal 'the nationalists are far from defeated'.[59]

Unsurprisingly, the journal did not make much of the Treaty of Sèvres signed on 10 August 1920. The treaty is first mentioned indirectly in October 1920, in a piece that notes that Greece made a promise to the UK, France, Italy and Japan to protect the ethnic minorities remaining in its territories, including those in Asia Minor and Thrace.[60]

The signature of the treaty was announced – a document of considerable importance in the Greek and Turkish historiographies – in the same issue in the following terse terms: 'Signature of the "Turkish Treaty". Four times delayed as a result of the Italo–Greek conflict, the signing of the "Turkish Treaty" took place on 10 August at 4 o'clock in the honour hall of the Sèvres factory'.[61]

Clearly, for the *Correspondance d'Orient*, which reported on the 'Question of the Orient' in painstaking detail, the Sèvres treaty was still-born. It is curious to see that a document that arouses such passions today was at the time seen as so insignificant. A brief item had previously reported on an armed attack on Venizelos on Paris on 12 August 1920 in Paris after the signing of Sèvres Treaty. Although he was hit by seven bullets, his life was not in danger. However, the attack provoked troubles in Athens.[62]

The treaty was, of course, condemned by Mustapha Kemal 'from his parliament in Angora'. He called for the Muslims of Anatolia not to abide by this agreement on the grounds that it had been signed by a slave of the West in Istanbul and declared that Bolsheviks and Germans, who, had actually never been defeated, would help the Turkish national army. In each village of Anatolia, one soldier per twenty households had to be provided, so that the group pays its fixed fees of 30 Turkish Liras.[63] The same issue also featured a hagiographic 'biography' of Mustapha Kemal, in which Kemal called the Turkish treaty 'abominable. . . . I have all Muslims and a huge power behind me (Soviets) . . . We are only at the beginning of great events'.[64] As a premonitory sign, despite victories in the field and in diplomacy arenas such as the Neuilly and Sèvres treaties, Elefterios Venizelos lost the November 1920 elections in Greece and is immediately forgotten by the journal. At the end of 1920, *Correspondance d'Orient* became Kemalist.

1921–3: A Long and Winding Path from War to Peace

The winter of 1921 started in war, with the first large-scale confrontations between the Greek army and the Turkish nationalist army. The Treaty of Sèvres sparked this war, in Georges Samné's view,[65] by dividing Turkey into two different governments, one in Constantinople, docile and impotent, the other in Anatolia, indomitable and fidgety. This grave result was to be predicted.[66]

This 'grave result' effectively materialised as 'Turkish attacks on Greeks'. According to a telegram from Smyrna, Turkish rebels mounted a strong attack on the Greeks. General Papoulos had to leave Smyrna to assist the Greek Army, and officials publicly read a message from King Constantin to Greek soldiers, asking them to not to demobilise and to be patient as desertions rates ran very high.[67] In the meantime, the journal announced a British and Greek propaganda effort against the Kemalist movement, accusing it of being a formal ally of the Bolsheviks.[68] Surprisingly again, a famous victory of the Turkish army against the Greeks in Inönü on 6 January 1921 barely registered in the journal, which simply announced that the Kemalist army had gathered 100,000 soldiers in Bursa and around Smyrna and that Mustapha Kemal was preparing a new Constitution for Turkey.[69]

After the battle of Inönü, the journal relayed a statement by French General Gouraud, who contended that the Turkish nationalist movement had been successful because the Greek occupation of Smyrna in 1919 had led to the explosion of Turkish nationalism. 'The French and English battalions landing at Smyrna would not have produced the commotion produced by the occupation of the Greeks'.[70] In February 2021, the Treaty of Sèvres was already buried, and the journal was firmly claiming revision of the status quo resulting from Sèvres.[71] 'Sèvres sought to impose the domination of its old subjects on Turkey. Such a peace is not viable'.[72] An anonymous writer claimed that the Greek occupation of Smyrna was a mistake, the Treaty of Sèvres was another mistake and that asking Greeks to withdraw their army from Asia Minor would be a third mistake because the Treaty of Sèvres was going to be obsolete and the Allies would no longer have any means of pressure on Ankara.[73] On the field, there was confusion. While Turkish nationalist newspapers reported that the Turkish army had registered a sweeping victory in Inönü that forced General Papoulas to withdraw until Bilecik, the Greek forces declared, in a statement of 20 January (before the second Inönü battle) that the Army pushed back the resistance and came back to its base. While there were some doubts in the spring of 1921 over the Turkish victories in the field, no doubts were expressed at the diplomatic level: *Correspondance d'Orient* reported on several agreements between Kemalists and Italy[74] or Soviets.[75] Even in April 1921, the secular character of the Kemalist insurrection is not clear in the West: the journal suspected Mustapha Kemal of organising a pan-Islamist congress in Ankara against the 'crusade of the Anglicans and the Orthodox'.[76] In late April 1921, doubts were also dispelled on the battlefield. What Turkish historiography would come to call the second Inönü Victory (which would give Ismet Pasha his name) was described by the *Correspondance d'Orient* as a huge failure of the Greek offensive. 'The Turks have their Marne . . .' says the journal[77] without, however, pronouncing the name Ismet Pasha. This victory was followed by several agreements between the nationalist assembly in Ankara and Italians, French and Soviets, nudging the British to declare their neutrality between Greeks and Turks.[78]

In summer 1921, things became clearer. The new Turkey was victorious, and there was a crisis of the Entente, but manly between the British and the French.[79] As a result of this crisis, France and the UK refrained from intervening.[80] The outcome would be decided in Ankara and not in Constantinople. The existence of the two capitals and two governments caused confusion in public opinion, but the real authority was undoubtedly in Ankara.[81] Ankara had a government, a ministerial cabinet, with Mustapha Kemal as the Chief of State and Fevzi Pasha (later Cakmak) acting as Minister for National Defence and Prime Minister. Yusuf Kemal Bey (then Tengirşenk) was the Minister of Foreign Affairs. The army was under the supreme commandment of Mustapha Kemal but the Major General 'the generalissime' was Ismet Pasha.[82] This was the first mention of the name of the victor of Inönü. The government's main plan was to expel Greeks from Smyrna and from Thrace. The UK firmly opposed the arrival of Greeks in Constantinople, which could provoke the same arduous resistance as that in Izmir, or even worse. Curiously, *Correspondance d'Orient* was lucid here while the British (and to some extent the French) were still expecting signs of power from the Ottoman capital.

In October 1921, after the Inönü battles and the Battle of the Sangarios (22 August to 13 September 1921), the journal announced the victory of the Turkish nationalists in the following terms:

> For several weeks Athens and Ankara have flooded the world with triumphant communiqués announcing a questionable victory. It was therefore necessary to wait until the end of the battle to find out on which side the scales had tipped. It was then noted that victory had smiled on the Turks and the retreat of the Greeks had been a complete failure.[83]

This was a huge disappointment for Greece and diaspora Greeks. The Greeks of New York now demanded the abdication of the king. The impossibility of supporting the Greek army with enough supplies in Anatolia would undoubtedly cause the extermination of the Greek army there. The Greeks may have been weak on the battlefield, but they issued grand statements in which they depicted themselves as descendants of Homer. For instance, they claimed to have won a huge victory in Sangarios on 21 September. On 25 September, King Constantin said that he did not allow the Army to continue to Angora after this victory.[84] This could certainly not fool the Turks or international public opinion; the Greeks themselves, as descendants of Ulysses, were too clever to accept these lies.[85] The only thing that the Greeks did is to try to keep the occupied territories under control during the winter and hope that General Papoulas would be able to reorganise his army for the next spring.[86] The same issue featured a new declaration by Mustapha Kemal, who stated that 'Turkey belongs to the Turks' (a sentence that would then become famous among nationalists). He laid claim to oriental Thrace on the grounds that the majority of its population was Turkish and could agree to a referendum on the rest of Thrace. 'Constantinople belongs to us' he added, 'and Turks were fighting the Greeks in Asia Minor. Granted, he had signed an agreement with the Soviets, but the Bolsheviks would never undertake propaganda in [his] country because [their] organisation is completely different'.[87]

The rest of 1921 and the beginning of 1922 was more 'French' than 'Greek': after the Ankara Agreement between Franklin Bouillon and Yusuf Kemal Bey, France gradually left south-eastern Anatolia. As Italians also left Anatolia after the Battle of the Sangarios, the Greek army was left alone with the Turkish nationalist army.

By early 1922, the situation was clear. The French army evacuated all the localities of Cilicia one by one, effectively recognising the sovereignty of Ankara and the strength of the national forces:

> Turkey is called upon to play a capital role for many reasons: because it is the country of the East which has shown for a long time and especially during the war the most vitality. Because she knew how to defend her honour with dignity and effectively by refusing to accept the Treaty of Sèvres. Because it is a military power. Finally, because it is and will remain whatever one says the sole depositary of the Islamic caliphate.[88]

Things turned in favour of Turks in British discourse as well. In a Cannes speech, Lloyd George clearly argued that since the occupation of Constantinople by the British and of Smyrna by the Greeks, Turkish people had been more often victims than perpetrators, and they defended their territory against the Greeks supported by the British.[89]

During the winter of 1922, Western observers began seeing weariness on both sides; both Greeks and Turks were in fact impatient to end the war.[90] Saint-Brice wrote that the British had already abandoned Greeks in favour of the Turks and could ask for the withdrawal of the Greek army if Ankara was a little bit more flexible.[91] The same issue published a Tribute of Ankara Assembly to Pierre Loti, a famous French orientalist and novelist, by offering him a carpet woven by Greek–Turkish war orphans![92] Loti, who attended himself, was moved to tears; he got down on his knees to ask fellow orientalist Claude Farrère to continue the struggle of liberation of Turks because he was now too old to be on the frontline.[93]

During the spring, the journal repeatedly urged the Greeks to come to an agreement with Turks; this was the only condition of peace and prosperity according to Aly EL-Ghaiati.[94] Surprisingly, maybe because pacific resolution was expected, the summer of 1922 was very quiet. Saint-Brice believed that this would not last. This nearly complete three-month standstill was disturbed only by the bombing of Samson Harbor by the Greek fleet in retaliation for Turkish raids in the Black Sea.[95] There were no battles, but there were also no negotiations, which suggested that tensions would again flare up sooner or later.[96] While the Turks prepared to fight back and refused all negotiations, the Greeks were tired of this ruinous adventure and the Gounaris government was condemned to negotiate directly with Turks. Unfortunately, this will be made impossible by London.[97]

As we know, this explosion came in late August. The final Greek–Turkish War lasted exactly one month, from 25 August 1922 with the 'walk of Mustapha Kemal to Kocatepe', a picture of which is one of the famous nationalist icons, to the evacuation of Salihli on 25 September. In the interval, there were two highly controversial events: the abandonment of Smyrna by the Greek army on 9 September and the Smyrna fire on 14 September. The journal followed this with great concern. In September 1922, *Correspondance d'Orient* announced that 'everything is cracking'.[98] The 'lightning offensive' of Turks had blindsided the British.[99] The author suspected that Mustapha Kemal gave this impression of calm deliberately in order to numb his enemies. It is also true that Lloyd George and Poincaré abandoned the Greeks because they understood them to be a lost cause.[100] Thus, the support of the British to the Greek army became an 'act'.[101] They still officially supported them but actually did nothing; the 'lightning victory' of the Turks, ending with the capture of the Greek General Trikoupis was anything but a surprise.[102]

In October 1922, the fighting was over and the situation was characterised by three major developments and matters to be resolved: the debacle of the Greek army, resulting in the Turkish army's march into Smyrna and the resurgence of Turkish nationalism; the need for a new conference that would decide the faith of Turkey; and the situation of the Middle East under the French mandate.[103] If London and Paris had been more courageous, they could have convinced Constantin of evacuating Thrace and Smyrna earlier to avoid fatalities. The Turkish victory gave the final word.[104] But even after the victory, the British were not completely convinced. They again proposed a partition, attributing Thrace to the Greeks and Smyrna to the Turks.[105] The Turks categorically refused; France and Italy immediately accepted this refusal but the British were reluctant. At that time, it was not known that Thrace, the straits and Constantinople would one by one fall under Turkish dominion, which would ultimately be recognised during the Lausanne negotiations (December 1922 to July 1923). Thus, the agreement on the compulsory exchange of populations[106] between Greece and Turkey was reported on in neutral terms while the Treaty itself was presented as the result of an excessively long negotiation and the peace it established as a precarious one.[107]

Conclusion: Greek–Turkish War Seen by the West

The *Correspondance d'Orient* defended Syria and Lebanon: Asia Minor and the Greek–Turkish War were not its leading concerns. Nevertheless, between 1918 and 1922, in the aftermath of the disaster of the First World War, the 'Catastrophe of Asia Minor' loomed so large that the journal was forced to change its focus and step by step, week by week, it began covering the Greek–Turkish War extensively, without of course neglecting the Syrian question and the French interests in the Region. This was, however, not the only change during these five years. By the end of the war, figures such as Chekri Ganem, Georges Samné, Aly El Ghaiaty or Saint-Brice were convinced that there would no longer be an Ottoman Empire (which they occasionally called Turkey). They believed that the dismantling of the Ottoman Empire and the allocation of its former territories to Great Britain, France and Italy were fair and inevitable steps. Thus, initially, the Greek occupation of Smyrna was welcomed prudently because the authors were mainly interested in Syrian issues. Things changed after 1921 when the Greek advance started to put in danger the Syrian struggle and began to provoke a nationalist reaction among Turks. At that point, the tone changed, sources changed and *Correspondance d'Orient* pivoted from a prudent pro-Greek and anti-Turkish position to a clear pro-Turkish stance. The Greek point of view was only rarely relayed, and readers may have struggled to understand why the Greeks called what happened the 'Catastrophe of Asia Minor'. The contemporary reader of the *Correspondance d'Orient* should not forget that the journal's main agenda was Syrian liberation under French mandate, and that its reporting on the Greek–Turkish war was informed by this perspective. One can make one last observation. The official Turkish historiography depicts Mustapha Kemal as the only figure of the 'War of Independence'. Today's alternative historiography shows, on the contrary, that he was one of the many leaders of the national struggle and that he became the 'Single Man' (Tek Adam) afterwards, when he eliminated all his rivals. Reading *Correspondance d'Orient* between 1918 and 1922 shows that the reality lies somewhere in between. Mustapha Kemal was not alone in this national struggle, that much its true, but his name comes up so often that it is obvious that he was much more than a *primus inter pares*.

Notes

1. Baddoura, Rita, 'Chékri Ganem: pionnier et virtuose du verbe', *L'Orient le Jour*, no. 166, April 2020.
2. While the first issues of the journal in 1908 bore the subtitle 'Revue Économique, Politique Et Littéraire', in 1919 the subtitle became 'Islam – Orient – Syrie'.
3. De Cloarec, Vincent, *La France et la question de la Syrie, 1914-1918*, Paris: *CNRS Éditions*, 2010.
4. 'Requête des comités libano-syriens d'Égypte', *Correspondance d'Orient*, no. 207, 15 February 1919, p. 124.
5. Samné, Georges, 'L'Orient devant la conférence de paix', *Correspondance d'Orient*, no. 208, 28 February 1919, p. 153.
6. Ibid. p. 154.
7. Ibid. p. 173.
8. Saint-Brice, 'L'erreur fondamentale de la conférence', *Correspondance d'Orient*, no. 209, 15 March 1919, p. 198.
9. El-Ghaiaty, Aly, 'Les Grecs et leurs revendications', *Correspondance d'Orient*, no. 209, 15 March 1919, p. 208.
10. Saint-Brice, 'Que fait la conférence en Europe et en Orient', *Correspondance d'Orient*, no. 210, 30 March 1919, p. 246.
11. *Correspondance d'Orient*, no. 209, 15 March 1919, p. 208.
12. Ibid. p. 217.
13. Saint-Brice, 'Les heures sombres de la conférence', *Correspondance d'Orient*, no. 212, 15 April 1919, p. 289.
14. *Correspondance d'Orient*, 15 May 1919, no. 213, p. 403.
15. Samné, Georges, 'La liquidation orientale', *Correspondace d'Orient*, no. 214, p. 433.
16. Ibid. pp. 448–9.
17. Ibid. p. 465.

18. El-Ghaiaty, Aly, 'La question d'Orient devant la conférence', *Correspondance d'Orient*, no. 215, 15 June 1919, p. 485.
19. Ibid. p. 487.
20. Ibid. p. 505.
21. I could not identify this 'Nahri Pasha'. He could have been Tahir, one of the organisers of the Ödemis resistance, but by 1919 he was a Lieutenant and not yet a Pasha.
22. Güçlü, Mehmet, 'İzmir'in işgaline tanık bir zatın kaleminden, İzmir'de neler oldu 1336/1920 kitapçığı üzerine', *Çağdaş Türkiye Tarihi Araştırmaları Dergisi*, vol. 10, no. 22, 2011, pp. 65–76.
23. *Correspondance d'Orient*, no. 215, 15 June 1919, p. 509.
24. Pinon, R., 'Plus de Sultan à Constantinople', *Correspondance d'Orient*, no. 217, 15 July 1919, p. 2.
25. Ibid.
26. Ibid. p. 3.
27. Ibid. p. 18.
28. Ibid. p. 26.
29. 'La liquidation orientale', *Correspondance d'Orient*, no. 218, 30 July 1919, p. 77.
30. Ibid. p. 80–1
31. Throughout the years, *Correspondance d'Orient*, uses several spellings of the names of Turkish leaders such as Mustafa Kemal, Ismet or Rauf; we chose to keep original spellings to show that things were far from being fixed in 1920s, and there were hesitations not only on the names but also on the personalities of these leaders.
32. Saint-Brice, 'Le gâchis oriental et la paix future', *Correspondance d'Orient*, no. 221, 15 September 1919, p. 99.
33. Ibid. p. 100.
34. El-Ghaiaty, Aly, 'Le problème Ottoman', *Correspondance d'Orient*, no. 221, 15 September 1919, p. 117.
35. *Correspondance d'Orient*, no. 221, 15 September 1919, p. 137.
36. Samné, Georges, 'La crise Ottomane', *Correspondance d'Orient*, no. 223, 15 October 1919, p. 201.
37. Ibid.
38. Ibid. p. 204.
39. *Correspondance d'Orient*, no. 223, 15 October 1919, p. 225.
40. Ibid. p. 226.
41. Saint-Brice, 'Éternelle Turquie', *Correspondance d'Orient*, no. 224, 30 October 1919, p. 247.
42. Ibid. p. 267.
43. Ibid.

44. Ibid. p. 269.
45. *Correspondance d'Orient*, no. 225, 15 November 1919, p. 291.
46. Ibid. p. 295.
47. Ibid. p. 324.
48. Ibid. p. 325.
49. Ibid. p. 326.
50. *Correspondance d'Orient*, no. 226, 30 November 1919, p. 339.
51. Ibid. p. 373.
52. Ibid. p. 374.
53. Ibid*em*.
54. *Correspondance d'Orient*, no. 229, 15 January 1920, p. 35.
55. *Correspondance d'Orient*, no. 226, 29 February 1920, p. 149.
56. Ibid. p. 151.
57. Saint-Brice, 'Aventure grecque', *Correspondance d'Orient*, no. 241–2, 15–30 July 1920, p. 1.
58. Ibid. p. 3.
59. *Correspondance d'Orient*, no. 247, 15 October 1920, p. 223.
60. Ibid. p. 206.
61. Ibid. p. 221.
62. *Correspondance d'Orient*, no. 243–4, 15–30 August 1920, p. 73.
63. *Correspondance d'Orient*, no. 247, 15 October 1920, p. 225.
64. Ibid. p. 227.
65. Samné, Georges, 'La souveraineté syrienne', *Correspondance d'Orient*, no. 253, 15 January 1921, p. 1.
66. Ibid. p. 3.
67. Ibid. p. 38.
68. Ibid. p. 40.
69. Ibid. p. 87.
70. *Correspondance d'Orient*, no. 255–4, 15 February 1921, p. 109.
71. Samné, George, 'Le Traité de Sèvres et la révision nécessaire', *Correspondance d'Orient*, no. 256, 28 February 1921, p. 145.
72. Ibid. p. 150.
73. J. N., 'Le Traité de Sèvres et sa répercussion en Orient', *Correspondance d'Orient*, no. 256, 28 February 1921, p. 158.
74 *Correspondance d'Orient*, no. 260, 30 April 1921, p. 366.
75. Ibid. p. 377.
76. Ibid. p. 378.
77. Ibid. p. 378.

78. Ibid. p. 183.
79. Saint-Brice, 'La Crise de l'entente et l'Orient', *Correspondance d'Orient*, no. 267–8, 15–30 August 1921, p. 577.
80. Ibid. p. 579.
81. Ibid. p. 587.
82. Ibid. p. 589.
83. *Correspondance d'Orient*, no. 271, 15 October 1921, p. 675.
84. Ibid. p. 680.
85. Ibid.
86. Ibid. p. 684.
87. Ibid. p. 715.
88. Samné, Georges, 'Vers la solution du problème oriental', *Correspondance d'Orient*, no. 278, 30 January 2022, p. 52.
89. Ibid. p. 66.
90. Saint-Brice, 'La Chance de la France', *Correspondance d'Orient*, no. 281–2, 15–30 March 1922.
91. Ibid. p. 149
92. Ibid. p. 158.
93. Ibid. p. 160.
94. *Correspondance d'Orient*, no. 287–8, 15–30 June 1922, p. 329.
95. Saint-Brice, 'L'Orient nous tient', *Correspondance d'Orient*, no. 289–90, 15–30 July 1922, p. 393.
96. Ibid.
97. Ibid. p. 396.
98. 'Tout craque', *Correspondance d'Orient*, no. 293–4, 15–30 September 1922, p. 513
99. Ibid.
100. Ibid. p. 517.
101. Beriner, Edouard, 'La comédie anglo-grecque', *Correspondance d'Orient*, no. 293–4, 15–30 September 1922, p. 527.
102. *Correspondance d'Orient*, no. 293–4, 15–30 September 1922, p. 530.
103. 'Aspect actuel du problème oriental, la paix turque', *Correspondance d'Orient*, no. 295–6, 15–30 October 1922, p. 577.
104. Ibid. p. 581.
105. Ibid. p. 591.
106. 'Un accord entre Grecs et Turcs', *Correspondance d'Orient*, no. 302, February 1923, p. 101.
107. Saint-Brice, 'La paix de Lausanne', *Correspondance d'Orient*, no. 308, August 1923, p. 449.

3

'NEW TURKS': TURKEY'S 1923 *MUHACIRS*

Introduction: Purification as a Nation-building Tool

In the Turkish version of Karagöz (*Καραγκιόζης*), the Ottoman Shadow Theatre that spread over Turkey and also in Greece, the *muhacir* (immigrant) character comes from the Balkan regions of the Empire. He speaks very slowly with a Slavic or Greek accent without pronouncing the 'h'. He is often presented as a wrestler or a cart driver. He speaks constantly about his village with a lot of nostalgia. He is very proud of his physical abilities but, in reality, he usually loses his fights. He always tries to appear intelligent and careful. He is very boastful but is most often the laughing stock of those around him. He represents how in Turkish society, especially in its popular fringes, an immigrant from the Northern or Southern Balkans is perceived, as a part of the Ottoman society, yet not fully legitimate anymore in the second half of the nineteenth century and the beginning of the twentieth century.

The identity of the Ottoman society of that period is hard to define. It is even harder to define the Turkish identity within the Ottoman society after the official end of the 'millet system' with *Tanzimat* while Greek identity is easier to construct (but still needed to be constructed). A simplistic formula is still taught in Turkish schools, claiming that the Turkish nation = a people (Turks) + a territory (*Misak-ı Millî's* Turkey) + a language (Turkish) + a common ideal (this ideal is dynamic according the regime) + a shared past (that is also subject to contradictory approaches between Central Asia and Anatolia, Islam and Western modernity as History is the present of the past).

The Ottoman Empire's populations were used to mass displacements. The central power would decide on specific populations settling in specific regions according to the Empire's demographic and/or defensive needs. In any case, it is difficult to know whether the Muslims from the Empire's European territories were indeed Muslims settled in these regions by the central government or whether the local populations themselves were Islamised forcefully or willingly. The fact is that in 1923 Venizelos and İnönü decided on the compulsory exchange of populations (Muslims in Greece, mainly in Crete and Epirus, and Orthodox Greeks in Asia minor, mainly from the western coast and Thrace, many of whom had already left in 1922, as well as those from Central Anatolia and North Eastern Anatolia), and most exiled felt firmly at home,[1] even if the nationalist propaganda from both sides reached cities (and sometimes rural areas).

The main question of this chapter is to understand, through the study of the exchange's refugees, whether an identity change occurred, and if it did, how and with which tools. Admittedly, according to the meaning we give to the notion of identity, and therefore to the transformation process, the communities that have lived under Ottoman rule and the Turkish Republic are the ones who led this change. The duration and manifestation of this process of identity transformation varies among different sub-groups and communities. The collective identity is often shaped by factors such as language, religion, cultural customs and practices, representation and lifestyle. In this context, it can be argued that a significant shift in identity occurred among various communities within the newly formed Turkish nation during the 1920s and 1930s. It is worth noting that this nation was formed through a centralised process of nation-building. Indeed, the process of nation-building was primarily a cognitive and emotional endeavour, preceding any physical manifestation. This is how the various components of the Turkish population came together to form the present-day Turkish nation, through a variety of processes.

The following chapter is based on a compilation of texts comprising testimonials. It comprises, in part, interviews conducted by Turkish novelist Kemal Yalcin with a literary intent, in the northern region of Turkey, and published in his 1989 book *Emanet Çeyiz*. Additionally, it includes interviews conducted by Turkish scholars Leyla Keskiner and Tolga Köker, which focus on the western region of the country. Furthermore, the corpus includes 12 face-to-face interviews I personally conducted in the cities of Izmir and Istanbul between 1998 and 2001. Additionally, as a member of a third-generation exchanged Cretan family, I was able to access sources through oral family history.

The utilisation of oral sources to depict a complex situation presents certain challenges. The assumption that the individuals interviewed possess accurate recollections of 'true facts' and that they recount these facts in a manner that is faithful to their memories are both foundational premises of this approach. However, given that there is not one objective truth in historical research, the validity of this method is further called into question. Furthermore, the ability of individuals to observe objectively, retain clear-headed perspectives and subsequently lucidly resituate themselves, is also a concern. As Norbert Elias states:

> the perception of events occurring 'in succession in time' presupposes the presence in the world of beings like men, who are capable, of identifying past events in their memory and *mentally constructing* an image associating them with other more recent or unfolding events.[2]

Consequently, the events recounted by those interviewed are also, in part, subjective constructions. However, it is important to consider that these constructions also possess their own history, motivations and ramifications. Moreover, they hold their own significance within the broader context of historical inquiry.

The Origins of the Displacement: 1920 War and 1923 Lausanne Convention

On the populations exchanged in 1923, in order to understand in which extent this identity change occurred and under which conditions, one should first and foremost be reminded of the context. In 1923, in the wake of the 'Asia Minor Catastrophe' (or the 'Liberation War', depending on the national historiography), Turkish and Greek authorities decided on the forced exchange of Greek Orthodox populations of Turkey with the Greek Muslims, exempting those of Istanbul, Imbros and Tenedos Greeks,[3] as well as the Western Thrace Muslims (we will come back to this question in the following chapters).

The first article of the Convention Concerning the Exchange of Greek and Turkish Populations, which was signed on 30 January 1923, six months before the Lausanne Treaty, has particularities.[4] Firstly, we should study the obligatory aspect of this exchange. Both countries' authorities wished to avoid the potential issues connected to maintaining these 'minorities' in their territories. Secondly, and importantly as well, the first article of the convention defines the Greekness and Turkishness in the exchange on a religious basis. While the amalgam between Orthodoxy and Greekness is usual, though debatable,[5] confusing Islam and Turkishness, especially in the Balkans, is much more problematic, at least from the Muslim side. Indeed, from a non-Muslim perspective, Turkishness is more or less equivalent to Muslimness. Among those who came to Turkey between 1923 and 1930, there were Muslims from Macedonia, some of whom converted from Judaism in the seventeenth century, *sabetaycı*,[6] but many of those who came at that time were Greek-speaking Muslim Turks, from the Aegean Islands, especially from Crete.

During the exchange, around 600,000 Muslims from Greece came to Anatolia, in exchange for about 1.5 million Orthodox Greeks. Thus, more than a half million refugees arrived in Turkey, having left behind them their goods and their personal history. Most Greeks had already left their homes in 1922 after the Greek army's defeat, before the signing of the protocol. They were mostly settled in ad hoc refugee camps in the houses of Greece's Muslims while waiting for them to leave.[7] Thus, we can say that a certain number of Muslims of exchanged populations knew the new owners of their property, who were also the old owners of their future homes:

> Laz came from Turkey, there were other Greeks as well. We stayed six months together. They conversed in Turkish and we talked in Greek. We couldn't understand each other. It was the same when we came here. We did not know Turkish. I couldn't even say 'bread' in Turkish. The exchange began. We rented mounts. First we went to Karaferia, then we passed through Thessaloniki by train and we came to Izmir on a boat. We stayed for a week or two in the Tepecik barracks. They were dividing the refugees on a village-to-village basis. We heard they were going to send us to Malatya. Murat Bey intervened and sent people from Kastro and Vrasno to Honaz . . .[8]

The Circumstances of the Exchange

The exchange had been mandatory. It seems there was no resistance from the Turks, except from a few isolated incidents.[9] The pro-Turkish propaganda (defending Kemalist Turkey) in the Balkans, coupled with a rumour of forced conversions to Orthodoxy, favoured the departures.[10] However, the trauma was unavoidable. Abandoning their goods, their jobs, their friends and neighbours, their ancestor's graves, caused deep wounds.

We heard that in Lausanne, they had decided on this exchange. We sold our goats and sheep, but we couldn't sell our houses and lands. Atatürk sent a commission to register our property over there, in order to give us an equivalent here. They gave us certificates, we brought them here, but they didn't even take them into account. There were a few tensions between us and the Greeks who arrived in Kastro from Anatolia. They gave us 20 gendarmes to stay with us. Each house gave, in turn, a meal to the Greeks. We stayed with them for six months.

Then, one day, they told us the exchange had begun. Everyone had rented mules, according to their means, loaded up their goods, and we left our country, our village, our properties, and we followed the road.

We had teary eyes. It was very difficult to be separated from this land. We travelled for four days on foot and mule-back. We went through Greban Kozana, Ianka, and we arrived in Karaferia. We stayed there for a week, then we took the train to Thessaloniki. They settled us in tents, where we waited 15 to 20 days for the boat. We were grouped with the population of 12 or 13 villages. There were maybe 10 000 people. They were boarding us on a region-by-region and village-by-village basis. We had packed our things and they marked our names on them.

The boats were two or three stories high, to be able to transport the animals. . . . We arrived in Izmir after a crossing which lasted two days and two nights. Atatürk had barracks built in Tepecik. It smelled like straw, and was completely new. We stayed for a month in these barracks. Atatürk had free meals served to us three times a day.

The day of the apportionment came. They told us those from Vrasno and Kastro, like us, would be sent to Malatya. But we learned that Suleyman Passa's son, Murat Bey from Vrasno, was in the installation commission. He had previously worked in Tavas and knew the Denizli region well. He sent us to Honaz, a mountainous, high and fertile region, just like Vrasno and Kastro.[11]

This heartbreak, however, should be put in perspective. Indeed, although most Greek Muslims were farmers, more or less impervious to pan-Turkish propaganda, urban populations and Ottoman intellectuals were relieved to hear the news. Reşat Tesal describes, as follows, his sentiment:

> furthermore, the [Lausanne] Treaty envisioned Turkey's Greeks exchange, except for the Istanbul Greeks, with Greece's Turks, except for the Western Thrace Turks. We were all very happy to hear of this exchange, from which we would benefit as well. As for me, I was cheerful and impatient, thinking about finally living in the shadow cast by our glorious flag, and being able to join Turkey, which I only knew from books, images, and the elder's tales.[12]

Depending on the case, the journey could last from a few weeks to a few months, first regrouping people in campsites and tents in harbour towns, then sending people on boats towards Turkish ports and finally transferring these populations to cities and villages designated for each family.[13] In many cases, the voyage did not stop there, either because it was impossible to house the families in the designated villages, or because some of the refugees were back on the road looking for family members, or simply looking for a better life. Upon arrival, an entire community had their geographical location radically changed. This text asks the question, to what extent has this geographical change led to an identity change, and how has such a shift proceeded.

In summary, the forced relocation of an entire community, which also includes internal variations, such as the differences between Crete Muslims and Macedonian Muslims, in a largely inhospitable environment, was the primary catalyst for a shift in socio-cultural identity. However, this displacement does not imply that feelings of otherness were immediately eradicated in the first generation, or that memories of an alternate place of origin were swiftly forgotten by subsequent generations. In fact, members of the second and third generation are aware of their origins beyond the Aegean Sea. Additionally, within the diverse composition of the Turkish population, each community, including those that lived in Anatolia for centuries, possess varying levels of knowledge about their non-local geographical and cultural origins, which is both real and imagined. This phenomenon of identifying with a distant origin is present in other populations as well, but holds particular significance in the Turkish nation, due to historical and historiographical reasons. Thus, it is not surprising to observe third-generation individuals claiming Cretan or Macedonian heritage, despite never having visited these lands or speaking a single word of Greek, while concurrently harbouring strong nationalist sentiments towards Turkey. This shift in identity leads to a form of sentimental irredentism, which is fuelled by the more or less accurate memories passed down by their grandparents. This is evident in the favourable reception of documentaries depicting the idyllic nature of life in Thrace, the Aegean Islands and Macedonia, during their tenure as 'Turkish lands', in popular journals.

Particularly for the Greek Muslim exchange population, I believe that the concept of identity shift is more relevant than that of identity change. Indeed, the former implies a form of cut-off or breaking point, which is hard to associate with *muhacirs* and their descendants. Furthermore, when this population was living in the Empire's European lands or in the Greek borders following their extensions, a feeling of otherness already existed.[14] In other words, one cannot say that they had a Greek identity, which they traded for a Turkish one after the exchange. It is certain that Greece's Turks had a Muslim identity, even Turkish, though it was less certain for them in 1923 than it is today concerning Thrace's Turks.[15] Moreover, this concept allows us to explain the vestiges of identity, which I have just mentioned, from older generations.

Factual Changes

Geography

The initial and most notable transformation is a geographic one, which results in changes to living conditions, climate, cultures and so on. The inquiry that should be considered is whether the physical and collective displacement of a population is sufficient to alter its identity. The examination of international migrations illustrates that, based on the host country's perception of the nation, a reverse process, characterised by a reaffirmation and reinforcement of the identity, can often be observed. However, within the assimilationist and Jacobin model of the Turkish state, cultural, linguistic, and even to some extent, religious distinctiveness, tend to diminish. Therefore, Turkey as a host country does not actively promote the preservation of a distinct collective identity. There are numerous examples of communities having preserved their identity or even having reinforced it. Asians in the United States and Turks in Germany for instance, are far from having lost their identity when their environment and land changed. Their original environments were, to a certain extent, copied, with 'clean' neighbourhoods, communication networks and clan ties, which of course, contributed to this identity preservation.[16]

Muslims who were relocated to Turkey through the population exchange were not able to recreate their living spaces, due to the forced nature of their displacement and settlement. They were settled in certain regions and villages by the Turkish government, based on the pre-existing needs for labour and the availability of housing previously occupied by their Greek counterparts. As a result, while the initial intention was to keep neighbouring villages from Greece together, entire regions and families were dispersed throughout Turkey:

> My father's name was Hüseyin. He was a mason. He died in 1975 at the age of 88. During the exchange, they came on a boat to Samsun. They assigned them a place there. The people from Kayalar and Inelli were settled in the village Hüseyin of Elazığ. At the time, there was the Kurdish problem. Every day, there were confrontations about the sharing of water. My father had decided to bring his family to Amasya. He had to renounce his settlement rights to be able to leave. The Kayalar village is divided. Some are in Dinar, near Denizli, others are in Elazig. There are more in Ferizdağ, Bafra, Tokat and Erbaa. The whole village had been scattered. When the people from Inelli arrived in Amasya, they asked the prefect for some property. The prefect told them that their place of settlement was Elazığ and that there was nothing for them here, and that he was going to send them all back . . . They were only able to stay by renouncing their rights.[17]

Already, before their departure, Muslims from Greece were able to hear, from the refugees' mouths, what regions and villages were favourable for settling and what villages had been entirely destroyed, where they should not go: 'This infidel told my mother: I hope you will go to Kütahya. There is a bridge there. Cross the bridge and you will find a house with new doors. Settle in this house, it is ours'.[18]

Thus, Greece's *muhacirs* found themselves almost isolated amongst the local population. Though this isolation is a vector of identity shift, the confrontation with local populations has an opposite effect. The term 'confrontation' is used on purpose here. Indeed, as soon as the first refugees from Greece arrived, a cultural, linguistic, psychological and even physical confrontation occurred. I will not dwell here on the difficult conditions in which the *muhacirs* arrived in Turkey, but we should not neglect that, in this process of change in identity, the physical displacement under extremely difficult conditions tends to increase the hope for a better life once the final destination is reached. These hopes were all dashed:

> We arrived here with our documents. We did not find what we were hoping for. We stayed in tents, here. We became precarious: one mattress, one blanket. The locals were occupying the houses. We stayed in tents for ten to fifteen days, the time for them to evacuate the houses. (Did they feed you while you were in the tents?). Who had bread to give to others? Turkey was destroyed. They were creating a new order. The government was helping some. They distributed houses, two acres of vine and two acres of fields per person. Twelve people, twenty-four acres of vine, twenty-four acres of fields. The lands they gave were not regrouped. A parcel here, a parcel there.[19]

The refugees were welcomed by a sense of otherness, aggravated by the locals. First because their arrival opposed immediate material interests: Greeks had left Anatolia, following the defeated Greek army, before Muslims had left Greece. This lack of synchronisation led to the lack of occupancy of Greek property, while Turkish authorities failed to do a complete inventory of these goods. Thus, progressively, in 1922–3, these goods, houses, fields, vegetable gardens and so on, were occupied and savagely pillaged by locals, who were in dire economic situations after so many years at war. When the first refugees arrived in Anatolia, deprived of any means of sustenance, the houses and other property that the government intended to give them had actually been occupied for almost a year. Thus, the first confrontation started immediately. In order to settle the first refugees that arrived, there was a need to expel, first, the occupants. For them, the refugees became usurpers who prevented them from owning the property that was rightly theirs:

> There was nothing left. My father started to weep. We had become migrants. We came to Muradiye. In the region where people whose houses had burnt had been settled in the abandoned Greek houses. Muradiye had not been burnt. It

was the Turkish houses which were burning. People from these neighbour-hoods had come to Muradiye on the fourth day of the Manisa fire. We entered Muradiye on the fourth day of the Manisa fire. People from Karaali stayed there for a year. We stayed for two and a half years. My father had obtained the authorisation (to stay) from the State. The government had sent back those who had occupied the Greek houses. And the population exchange had begun. They forced us to leave. My father asked for the authorization to remain, but did not get it. *Muhacirs* were installed in the Greek houses and lands. They devastated all the fields. Now they understand that vines and olive trees are gold. Now they have learned.[20]

It is important to remark that both populations, *muhacirs* and locals, mutu-ally saw each other as inferior people. For the locals, refugees were uneducated people, with no jobs; refugees saw the locals as uncivilised brutes:

they first settled us in a church that the Greeks had abandoned. We dug in the church's floor to find money. There had been a lot of injustice in the house repartition. In any case, all houses had been pillaged, ransacked. Some had even been destroyed in the hope of finding money, or in order to sell the beams. We fixed the houses.

The State fed us for six to nine months. Then we distributed the Greeks' goods, gardens and fields. But there were a lot of injustices. The nine acres they had given us were, in reality, three acres. We were not able to claim what was rightly ours. We were refugees. Some of us still hoped to go home. Others, on the con-trary, feared being sent forcefully back to Greece if they complained. We were shocked, lost. What was going to happen, what were we going to do? We did not know. Some people from Honaz said 'Greeks left, other Greeks came. Where is the difference?' What could we do, we spoke Greek. The locals were getting angry with us. *When we came, there was no civilization in Honaz. There were straw construction that they called toilets, back home every house had toilet inside.*[21]

Moreover, it seems there was clothing differences:

When we came here, there was not one local wearing a jacket. A *şalvar*, a cloth waistband, and a knife on their waist. Those who dressed in goat hair-woven clothes were considered rich. The poor wore cotton undergarments.

We dressed in suits, with a jacket and pants. We appeared as civilised people, through the way we dressed, our lifestyle, the way we worked. There was always a difference among us. They were lazy. They admired us while watching us work.[22]

Language

But more confrontation followed: those newly arrived spoke Greek as those who had left. The sentiment of otherness was reinforced through the crucial issue of language.

> Those who had come to Honaz through the exchange didn't know how to manage a farm or a vegetable patch. As soon as they arrived, they started to die . . . The young ones, the men, died. Graves aligned in the cemetery. After that, they had tombstones with inscriptions made: from Grebena, from Vrasno, etc. The Greeks who had left knew Turkish, the Turks who had arrived only knew Greek. Not one knew how to say 'bread' or 'water'. No house, no refuge. The Greek neighbourhood had been pillaged. What was given to them, as houses, were but four walls.

> At that time, my dad had a grocery store. People from the Ministry of Finance told him to give to the *muhacirs* everything they needed and that the government would pay. There was only the teacher, Ismail Efendi, who knew Greek. We put him in our shop as an interpreter and an accountant. The *muhacirs* shopped there for two or three years.[23]

Greece's Muslims were either descendants of locals converted to Islam during more or less ancient times or descendants from Turks who had settled in these regions under Ottoman rule. In both cases, until the end of the nineteenth century and the beginning of the twentieth, Turkish language was only accessible for those who had received an education. Given that a majority of the exchanged population were Muslim, uneducated farmers, very few were able to speak Turkish, to the point where the commission charged by the government to settle refugees in the towns and villages abandoned by the Greeks had to ask Istanbul Greeks to translate. Indeed, in most testimonies, the issue of language regularly comes up. It seems that the local populations immediately associated those newly arrived with those who had left.

> We arrived in April . . . I was fifteen years old. We did not know Turkish. There were only 3 or 4 people who had been to school who knew this language.

They told us 'there are your houses'. But there were only four walls. All had been pillaged ... Some houses didn't even have windows or doors. We had nothing to eat or drink. The State gave us food for 8 or 9 months ... In the first years, there were a lot of lost in Honaz among the *muhacirs*, even among the younger ones.[24]

Reciprocally, if I may say, among the Greek Orthodox population expelled from Asia Minor to Greece mainly after 1923, there were some groups who could not speak Greek. Indeed, while Rums who followed the Greek army after 1920 identified themselves as Greek and were objects of national propaganda since at least 1821, those included in the compulsory exchange, mainly from central Anatolia but also sometimes from the northeastern Black Sea region, felt only loosely connected to Greek identity or spoke only Turkish (for Karamanlides) or Pontic Greek (for Black Sea Orthodox). But the advantage was the use of the Greek alphabet on both sides of the Aegean.

In Turkey, an important phenomenon of the process of identity change occurred: since the beginning of the Republic, in the momentum of Westernisation of the country, a wide-ranging campaign for learning the Latin alphabet and the Turkish language was launched. One can easily put forward the hypothesis that the 1923 *muhacirs* have greatly benefitted from this campaign to progressively abandon the Greek language and learn the Turkish one, which was going through a mutation (one that was both artificial and natural):

Our local friends complained because we did not speak Turkish. They said 'we don't understand anything, those who left spoke Greek, those who came speak Greek'.

It is said that their complaint reached Atatürk. He asked if we had other faults: theft, treater, etc. They told him that we did not. So, he answered, 'do not worry. A language is like a man. The *muhacirs* will learn Turkish over time. Here, the majority is Turkish. You will speak Greek to their grandchildren, they will answer in Turkish. Do not fear.[25]

In the Turkish definition of the concept of 'nation', the unity of language is crucial. Hoping to reach such unity was a fantasy, and it still is today.

However, for the refugees from Greece at least, the intensive learning of the Turkish language allowed them to partially integrate into the emerging Turkish nation, maybe even more than the diverse linguistic minorities did, who were (and still are) part of the Turkish population. This linguistic barter is paramount. Associating the idea of enemy and that of their language (in this case, Greek) led to a reaction to that language on both sides, that is to say the locals and the refugees. Because of this, the loss (or at least the lack of transmission) of Greek for the children and grandchildren of the refugees was not seen as a bereavement. This phenomenon is less important in the case of refugees from Anatolia in Greece, who were able to more or less keep their linguistic heritage and, to a certain extent, pass it on.

In the span of two generations, if not one, the *muhacirs* from Greece, who only spoke Greek in 1924–5, had almost completely abandoned their language for the benefit of the updated Turkish language. To our knowledge, there are no specific studies on the linguistic input that refugees from Greece had on the current Turkish language. Besides, it would be difficult to measure to what extent the contribution of Greek in this language comes from Anatolian Greeks and to what extent it comes from the refugees from Greece. In any case, learning Greek did not seem indispensable to the *muhacirs'* descendants.

Lifestyles

A third change, indissociable from the first two, is that of the change in lifestyle, in the practical sense of the term. Though the Turkish authorities' naïve hope was to settle the *muhacirs* in a socio-professional environment resembling their initial environment, this wish was quickly abandoned before the immediate imperatives of the situation. The analysis of the interviews conducted with the exchanged populations shows that most of them were farmers,[26] whereas among the Greeks that were exchanged, a lot of them practised liberal professions. In this context, it was impossible to give olive trees to all the refugees that used to cultivate them, tobacco fields to those working in the cultivation of tobacco and so on.

Furthermore, given the absence or lack of hosting structures in Anatolia's remote areas, especially in the north and the northeast of the region, and given the difficulty of settling in a new life, some of the refugees decided to leave the villages to migrate to cities or other villages. This was a sub-phase of mass population displacement, that is to say a migration within the migration, with all the material and psychological difficulties it supposes.

> They led us to a village in the mountains. The terrain was dry. A vine here and there, with a few grapes on them. We could not stay. We fled. I stayed there three years. I came here because the people from my village were here. Here the soil is fertile. Here, a vine produces three times more grapes.[27]

Let's not forget that, during the first years of the Republic, and even later, rural and internal exodus was frequent. It is not surprising to see, in this flux, elements of the *muhacirs*. This double displacement, from Greece to Turkey, from the village to city, resulted in entire families finding themselves, after a few years, in living conditions that were completely foreign to them:

> They first sent those who came from Kozlu to Yozgar-Maden. We went to Maden. But our fathers and grandfathers did not like Maden. We fled to Erbaa. The Erbaa prefect spread us out in villages. In this village ten homes, in that one fifty, etc. Our family was sent to Kuşluk. Everything was destroyed in the villages . . . We stayed one year in Kuşluk. The houses they gave us were Greek houses. But all the houses were destroyed, ransacked. Even the beams had been snatched. They gave us some money and distributed the lands.

> Over there, we had everything, we were rich, we came here and had nothing left. No house, no land, no goods, nothing.

> We had always thought that we would go back. We used to say that if we gave our daughter to a local, she would stay here. That is why we didn't marry our daughters with locals for at least ten years.[28]

It is perfectly normal that adapting to these new practical lifestyles resulted in a change in the representation and self-representation grid, through which the communal and individual identity is drawn: 'The climate was different. The terrain and the products were different, and the local population did not have a friendly approach in general. They called us names: bitli macir, pis macir, çıplak macir, etc'.[29]

Conclusion: The Graft is Also an Amputation

Identity is a construct. However, it is reliant on memory. If we accept that memory, that is to say the individual and collective history, is also a construct, we understand the complexity of trying to grasp the process of identity shift. Memory evolves, it does not simply record, it adapts. This adjustment significantly and inevitably impacts our self-representation, therefore our identity. Almost all testimonies reveal that the exchanged populations thought that life before the displacement was wonderful, at least much more that it was *here*. They were all rich and became poor, the climate was better, the neighbourhood more agreeable, life in general was easier:

> We are farmers. Our land was so fertile. We could grow anything there. There was an abundance in everything. There were two lakes. One in the East and the other in the West. My uncle was a hunter, he hunted game, ducks, he fished. There was an abundance in food. Here, we cannot find anything. There, there was a lot of food.

> Of course, I miss my country. What I miss most are my lands. There, we had 2,500 acres of fields. Here, they gave us two acres per person. We were four people, my two sisters, my mother and I. As one says in Turkish: 'mal canın yongasıdır.[30]

However, exceptions exist. That is to say, there were some who were convinced that, on the contrary, life was impossible 'over there' and that the only place to live was 'here':

> We were at the border between Greece and Bulgaria. We suffered much cruelty. Much cruelty. By the grace of God, we are in Turkish lands and Muslim lands. Who would want to live in the country of the infidels? The infidels cannot be friends. Thank God who led us here. May God protect us from living like we did in the old days. May God protect us from seeing again what we have seen. (Allah yaşadıklarımızı yaşatmasın, Allah gördüklerimizi göstermesin). How we suffered! (neler çektik neler . . .).[31]

In any case, the opinions are always sharp. It is either black or white. The median position, that is to say recognising the inconveniences of life back in the village of origin, as well as its advantages, and similarly for the city or village of arrival, is non-existent. Here, we mean that one of the consequences of the identity shift is a very decided view over the phenomenon of the forced exchange of population between Greece and Turkey, including in the following generations. This exchange is analysed by its first- or second-degree actors as a bad (in most cases) or a good event. It is normal that, in extremely sensitive conditions, the analysis of this or that event is rooted in passion and not reason. However, surprisingly, these feelings towards the host country did not transform into actions, at least not as much as that of the Greeks of Anatolia in Greece. Indeed, the Greeks who were exchanged or who took refuge in Greece express the Anatolian aspect of their personality in a much stronger and militant way than their Turkish counterparts. Organisation networks, such as associations and other forms of regrouping are much denser in Greece than they are in Turkey for the *muhacirs*. This phenomenon had several roots. Firstly, one can put forward their numerical superiority. The share of people of Anatolian origin within the total Greek population is much more important than *muhacirs* in the Turkish population. Secondly, the role of Minor Asia in the Greek identity journey is comparatively more crucial than the few European provinces of the Ottoman Empire are to today's Anatolian Turks. Proportionally, Anatolia, for Greeks, can be compared to what Central Asia represents to Turks. Furthermore, the Turkish people remain much less organised, as a whole, than Western people, which means that the associative life is much less important there. Finally, the virtues of the Turkish integrationist model are to be praised in the success of the integration of all Muslim groups of the population into the Turkish nation, with the exception of the Kurdish people. In this model, based on schools, school books, press and one-track thinking, particularities are erased, to the benefit of commonalities, forming the nation in its entirety. While individual identity feelings exist, the manifestation of collective particularities are poorly looked upon. Union of the 1923 *muhacirs* is not mentioned in any of the interviews. There are only two cases of a couple of *muhacirs* reuniting to visit their old village:

> When we came to Honaz in 1924, we did not want to stay here. It was very difficult to bear. There were no jobs. We became impoverished. Like a lot of other *muhacirs*, I went to Izmir to work. I worked there for two or three years.

My real trade is hunting. I used to hunt boars and foxes. I missed my country, my village, very much. In 1970 we went to Kastro with a friend. Kastro had been destroyed. The village was almost abandoned. We found our houses. I found the Aga's kids next to whom I used to work. We knew the language. We were very well received. They invited us to eat. They had made a lot of progress compared to us.[32]

Moreover, it is surprising to see that most *muhacirs*, now very old, think of their village or house as material concepts, as if having feelings towards Greece was not acceptable. It is unnecessary to specify that they always remember their abandoned goods exaggeratedly:

Behind our Vrasno house, we had a vegetable garden of 5–6 acres. All the fruit trees were in it . . . The taste of our plums was the sweetest. There are no such plums here. I have travelled a lot in my 93 years-long life, but I have never seen such plums.[33]

The most important conclusion to draw from these testimonies confirms, in a way, our first hypothesis, that is to say that there was, indeed, an identity shift in the first generation, and an identity change in the second and third generation. Indeed, we can conclude that, 100 years after the exchange, the idea of belonging to the Turkish nation seems to be complete.

Notes

1. 'Home was there, not here', Interview with Stavros, A., 12 May 1998, Athens.
2. Elias, Norbert, *Time: An Essay*, Oxford: Blackwell Publishers, 1992, p. 47. Emphasis added.
3. For the specific status of Greeks of Imbros and Tenedos, close to an autonomy, never provided, see Akbulut, Olgun, 'Legal Background of Autonomy Arrangements in Turkey from Historical Perspectives', Akbulut, Olgun, Aktoprak, Elçin (eds), *Minority Self-Government in Europe and the Middle East*, Leiden: Brill, 2021, pp. 228–45.
4. https://mjp.univ-perp.fr/traites/1923lausanne4.htm.
5. Among Orthodox populations who had to leave Turkey, there were *Karamanlides*, Turkish-speaking Christians from central Anatolia. See Balta, Evangelia, *Beyond the Language Frontier: Studies on Karamanlis and Karamanlidika Printing*, Istanbul:

Isis, 2010, mainly chapter II 'Gerçi Rum isekde rumca bilmeyiz. The Adventures of an Identity in the Triptych: Vatan, Religion and Language', pp. 49–66.

6. Baer, Marc David, 'An Enemy Old and New: The Dönme, Anti-Semitism, and Conspiracy Theories in the Ottoman Empire and Turkish Republic', *Jewish Quarterly Review*, vol. 103 no. 4, 2013, pp. 523–55.

7. Interview with Maria, A., 14 May 1998 in Thessaloniki.

8. Yalçın, Kemal, *Emanet çeyiz: Mübadele insanları*, Istanbul: Bir Zamanlar Yayınları, 1989, p. 201.

9. Köker, Tolga, Kekiner, Leyla, 'Lessons in Refugeehood: The Experience of Forced Migrants in Turkey', pp. 193–208.

10. On these (false) rumours, see for example Tesal, Reşat, *Selanik'ten Istanbul'a*, Istanbul: İletişim, 1998.

11. Yalçın, *Emanet çeyiz: Mübadele insanları*, pp. 184–5.

12. Tesal, *Selanik'ten Istanbul'a*, p. 66.

13. 'We knew but we were scared', interview with Maria, A., 16 May 1998 in Thessaloniki.

14. Abdülkadir, A. A refugee from Rethymno in Crete to Ayvalık says, 'In Crete we were at home but already strangers', interview on 12 April 1997 in Izmir.

15. 'I remember my mother, who couldn't speak in Turkish but was a good Muslim. As a good Muslim, she used to say that she was a good Turkish', interview with Ayten, C., 16 January 2005 in Istanbul.

16. For the concept of 'Territorial continuity' see Ma Mung Emmanuel, *La Diaspora chinoise, géographie d'une migration*, Paris: Ophrys, 2000.

17. Interview with Ibadullah Inelli, Yalçın, *Emanet çeyiz: Mübadele insanları*, p. 207.

18. Interview with Necmiye, Ögreten in Muradiye by Keskiner, Leyla, 'Lessons in Refugeehood: The Experience of Forced Migrants in Turkey', p. 196.

19. Interview with Ahmet Kumrular in Ayvalık, 17 April 1999, in Ayvalık.

20. Interview with Haci Ahmet de Karaali, by Keskiner, Leyla, 'Lessons in Refugeehood: The Experience of Forced Migrants in Turkey', p. 202.

21. Interview with Muhitin Yavuz, Yalçın, *Emanet çeyiz: Mübadele insanları*, p. 199. Emphasis added.

22. Interview with Tahsin Özkan, Yalçın, *Emanet çeyiz: Mübadele insanları*, p. 120.

23. Interview with Ramazan, Yalçın, 19 May 2000, in Izmir.

24. Interview with Murtaza Acar, Yalçın, *Emanet çeyiz: Mübadele insanları*, p. 186.

25. Interview with Murtaza Acar, Yalçın, *Emanet çeyiz: Mübadele insanları*, p. 188.

26. Interview with Hasan Kavalalı, second generation of refugees from Yanina, in Izmir, 2 May 1998.

27. Interview with Ismail Özcan, first generation of refugees from Filorina, in Izmir-Ayvalık, 1 March 1996.
28. Interview with Nazmi Önal, Yalçın, Emanet çeyiz: Mübadele insanları, p. 217.
29. Interview with Ismail Özcan in Istanbul, 18 May 2000.
30. Ibid.
31. Interview with İzzet Burgazlı, in Istanbul, 18 May 2000, in Istanbul.
32. Interview with Abbas Barut, Yalçın, *Emanet çeyiz: Mübadele insanları*, p. 203.
33. Interview with Muhittin Yavuz, Yalçın, *Emanet çeyiz: Mübadele insanları*, p. 200.

4

A PECULIAR GROUP: *POLITES*

Introduction: Greeks of Istanbul at Home

Among several serious issues that exist between Turkey and Greece, there is a more constant and important one, in its historical and human dimension: the issue of reciprocal minorities, a perverse notion. While the Cyprus issue emerged in the late 1950s, the Aegean dispute in the 1970s and, finally, the Kurdish conflict in the 1990s, the issue of minorities has existed since the foundation of modern Turkey in 1923 at least, if not since the Greek independence in 1831. Thus, among the concrete bilateral issues, that of minorities is the most ancient. I shall study the question of Western Thrace Muslims in another chapter and focus here on Turkey's Greeks, more specifically on *Polites*, Istanbul's (former) *Rum* inhabitants. This Greek-speaking Christian Orthodox community has even been brought to the brink of disappearance in their home city. Scattered around the world as a result of the homogenising policies of Turkey, the *Rum Polites* in the diaspora continue to identify with its cosmopolitan legacy.[1]

The concept of 'reciprocity'[2] summarises the destiny of the Greek community in Turkey, that is to say Greeks[3] from Istanbul (*Polites*) and from the two islands at the entry of the Dardanelles: Imbros and Tenedos (Bozcaada and Gökçeada in Turkish).[4] This community, which was 'allowed' by the Lausanne exchange convention of January 1923 to stay in the country, contrary

66

to other Greek Orthodox communities living in Asia Minor, shared that right with Muslims living in Greek Thrace. It is important to note that such reciprocity (*mütekabiliyet* in ancient Turkish, *karşılıklılık* in modern Turkish, *αμοιβαιοτητα* in Greek) was abundantly used during the entire Turkish Republic history, to the point where it is now associated with the notion of retaliation (as it was in Greece for Western Thrace Muslims). Thus, Greeks of Turkey were never accepted as integral parts of the Turkish nation (in regards to citizenship) and were suspected of being a Trojan horse serving the interests of Greece. Moreover, one cannot only say that they were the counterparts of Greece's Muslims and, for this reason, suffered the retaliation when the Greek government mistreated them, but they also were hostages, in the hands of the Turkish government in crises such as the Cyprus issue. Thus, for 100 years, this community's destiny was dependent not only on the situation of Greek Muslims but also on all bilateral issues and further. In this chapter, I will attempt to present every key date in this minority's history, before focusing on the ongoing situation.

The Beginnings of the Minority Situation

It is anachronistic to classify non-Muslim communities of the Ottoman Empire into a 'minority status', at least before the nineteenth century. In this chapter, the Lausanne population exchange protocol, which was signed between Greece and Turkey six months prior to the Lausanne Treaty, is my starting point. This protocol planned for the mandatory exchange of the Greek Orthodox populations (in the religious sense of the designation) who were living within Turkey's new borders, ten months before the proclamation of the Turkish Republic, with the Muslim population living in Greece. Muslims of Western Thrace and the Istanbul Greek Orthodox community who were established in the city since before 1918, as well as the Greeks from the islands of Imbros and Tenedos, were all excluded from this protocol. Both communities were, from the onset, viewed as parallels, and this reciprocity was institutionalised during the Lausanne Treaty on 23 July 1923. Indeed, the third section of the Treaty's first part, entitled 'Minority Protection', specifies the status of non-Muslim minorities in Turkey and grants certain rights to these minorities through articles 37 to 44. Article 45 indicated that these resolutions would be applied similarly to Greece on the matter of its Muslim minority. Besides, Turkey would only accept these resolutions if they were reciprocal to Greece:

Convention Concerning the Exchange of Greek and Turkish Populations Signed at Lausanne, January 30, 1923.[5]

The Government of the Grand National Assembly of Turkey and the Greek Government have agreed upon the following provisions:

Article 1: As from the 1st May, 1923, there shall take place a compulsory exchange of Turkish nationals of the Greek Orthodox religion established in Turkish territory, and of Greek nationals of the Moslem [*sic*] religion established in Greek territory.

These persons shall not return to live in Turkey or Greece respectively without the authorisation of the Turkish Government or of the Greek Government respectively.

Article 2: The following persons shall not be included in the exchange provided for in Article 1:

    a) The Greek inhabitants of Constantinople.
    b) The Moslem inhabitants of Western Thrace.

All Greeks who were already established before the 30th October, 1918, within the areas under the Prefecture of the City of Constantinople, as defined by the law of 1912, shall be considered as Greek inhabitants of Constantinople.

Moslems established in the region to the east of the frontier line laid down in 1918 by the Treaty of Bucharest shall be considered as Moslem inhabitants of Western Thrace.

Article 3: Those Greeks and Moslems who have already, and since the 18th October, 1912, left the territories the Greek and Turkish inhabitants of which are to be respectively exchanged, shall be considered as included in the exchange provided for in Article 1.

The expression 'emigrant' in the present Convention includes all physical and juridical persons who have been obliged to emigrate or have emigrated since the 18th October, 1912.

TREATY OF PEACE WITH TURKEY SIGNED AT LAUSANNE
JULY 24, 1923
ARTICLE 14: The islands of Imbros and Tenedos, remaining under Turkish sovereignty, shall enjoy a special administrative organisation composed of local elements and furnishing every guarantee for the native non-Moslem population in so far as concerns local administration and the protection of persons and property. The maintenance of order will be assured therein by a police force recruited from amongst the local population by the local administration above provided for and placed under its orders.

The agreements which have been, or may be, concluded between Greece and Turkey relating to the exchange of the Greek and Turkish populations will not be applied to the inhabitants of the islands of Imbros and Tenedos.

These provisions show first and foremost the distinction made in the rights granted to the non-Muslim minority members. One the one hand, these provisions warranty equality between non-Muslim and Muslim citizens of the Turkish State ('negative rights' as articles 38 and 39 state), and on the other hand, they grant special rights to this minority, for its members to be able to preserve their identity ('positive rights', as defended by articles 40 to 43). It is important to note that no group or region is specifically named here. These rights concern all people living in Turkey, as well as Turkish nationals, non-Muslim nationals and Turkish nationals whose native language is not Turkish.

SECTION III.
PROTECTION OF MINORITIES.

ARTICLE 37: Turkey undertakes that the stipulations contained in Articles 38 to 44 shall be recognized as fundamental laws, and that no law, no regulation, nor official action shall conflict or interfere with these stipulations, nor shall any law, regulation, nor official action prevail over them.

ARTICLE 38: The Turkish Government undertakes to assure full and complete protection of life and liberty to all inhabitants of Turkey without distinction of birth, nationality, language, race or religion.

All inhabitants of Turkey shall be entitled to free exercise, whether in public or private, of any creed, religion or belief, the observance of which shall not be incompatible with public order and good morals.

Non-Moslem minorities will enjoy full freedom of movement and of emigration, subject to the measures applied, on the whole or on part of the territory, to all Turkish nationals, and which may be taken by the Turkish Government for national defense, or for the maintenance of public order.

ARTICLE 39: Turkish nationals belonging to non-Moslem minorities will enjoy the same civil and political rights as Moslems.

All the inhabitants of Turkey, without distinction of religion, shall be equal before the law.

Differences of religion, creed or confession shall not prejudice any Turkish national in matters relating to the enjoyment of civil or political rights, as, for instance, admission to public employments, functions and honors, or the exercise of professions and industries.

No restrictions shall be imposed on the free use by any Turkish national of any language in private intercourse, in commerce, religion, in the press, or in publications of any kind or at public meetings.

Notwithstanding the existence of the official language, adequate facilities shall be given to Turkish nationals of non-Turkish speech for the oral use of their own language before the Courts.

ARTICLE 40: Turkish nationals belonging to non-Moslem minorities shall enjoy the same treatment and security in law and in fact as other Turkish nationals. In particular, they shall have an equal right to establish, manage and control at their own expense, any charitable, religious and social institutions, any schools and other establishments for instruction and education, with the right to use their own language and to exercise their own religion freely therein.

ARTICLE 41: As regards public instruction, the Turkish Government will grant in those towns and districts, where a considerable proportion of non-Moslem nationals are resident, adequate facilities for ensuring that in the primary schools the instruction shall be given to the children of such Turkish nationals through the medium of their own language. This provision will not prevent the Turkish Government from making the teaching of the Turkish language obligatory in the said schools.

In towns and districts where there is a considerable proportion of Turkish nationals belonging to non-Moslem minorities, these minorities shall be assured an equitable share in the enjoyment and application of the sums which may be provided out of public funds under the State, municipal or other budgets for educational, religious, or charitable purposes. The sums in question shall be paid to the qualified representatives of the establishments and institutions concerned.

ARTICLE 42: The Turkish Government undertakes to take, as regards non-Moslem minorities, in so far as concerns their family law or personal status, measures permitting the settlement of these questions in accordance with the customs of those minorities.

These measures will be elaborated by special Commissions composed of representatives of the Turkish Government and of representatives of each of the minorities concerned in equal number. In case of divergence, the Turkish Government and the Council of the League of Nations will appoint in agreement an umpire chosen from amongst European lawyers.

The Turkish Government undertakes to grant full protection to the churches, synagogues, cemeteries, and other religious establishments of the above-mentioned minorities. All facilities and authorisation will be granted to the pious foundations, and to the religious and charitable institutions of the said minorities at present existing in Turkey, and the Turkish Government will not refuse, for the formation of new religious and charitable institutions, any of the necessary facilities which are guaranteed to other private institutions of that nature.

ARTICLE 43: Turkish nationals belonging to non-Moslem minorities shall not be compelled to perform any act which constitutes a violation of their faith or religious observances, and shall not be placed under any disability by reason of their refusal to attend Courts of Law or to perform any legal business on their weekly day of rest.

This provision, however, shall not exempt such Turkish nationals from such obligations as shall be imposed upon all other Turkish nationals for the preservation of public order.

ARTICLE 44: Turkey agrees that, in so far as the preceding Articles of this Section affect non-Moslem nationals of Turkey, these provisions constitute obligations of international concern and shall be placed under the guarantee of the League of Nations. They shall not be modified without the assent of the majority of the Council of the League of Nations. The British Empire, France, Italy and Japan hereby agree not to withhold their assent to any modification in these Articles which is in due form assented to by a majority of the Council of the League of Nations.

Turkey agrees that any Member of the Council of the League of Nations shall have the right to bring to the attention of the Council any infraction or danger of infraction of any of these obligations, and that the Council may thereupon take such action and give such directions as it may deem proper and effective in the circumstances.

Turkey further agrees that any difference of opinion as to questions of law or of fact arising out of these Articles between the Turkish Government and any one of the other Signatory Powers or any other Power, a member of the Council of the League of Nations, shall be held to be a dispute of an international character under Article 14 of the Covenant of the League of Nations. The Turkish Government hereby consents that any such dispute shall, if the other party thereto demands, be referred to the Permanent Court of International Justice. The decision of the Permanent Court shall be final and shall have the same force and effect as an award under Article 13 of the Covenant.

ARTICLE 45: The rights conferred by the provisions of the present Section on the non-Moslem minorities of Turkey will be similarly conferred by Greece on the Moslem minority in her territory.

However, since Mustafa Kemal's secularisation reforms, there is a polemic around the religious legal rights of the community according to the first paragraph of Article 42. Though the Lausanne Treaty envisions a family jurisdiction specific to the Orthodox community, this right could no longer be applied following the Turkish State's laicisation. That is to say, in matters of marriage, heritage, divorce and other family jurisdiction issues, civil law took over religious law since non-Muslim minorities, including Greeks, were forced to declare in 1926 that they would give up their rights arising from the article 42, following the acceptation of the Swiss Civil Code in Turkey.[6]

In any case, following the international recognition of the Turkish Republic, and according to a 1927 Istanbul population census, the city counted 700,000 inhabitants out of whom 100,000 declared being Greek Orthodox (in the religious sense of the designation), and 90,000 whose native language was Greek. Those of Greek Orthodox denomination who were not Greek-speaking spoke Albanian and Turkish. Furthermore, there were 26,500 Greek nationals in the city, and the Imbros and Tenedos Greeks were estimated to be 8,200.

There is no need to specify that the Greek minority's living conditions in Turkey depended much on Greco-Turkish relations. Thus, the reconciliation between the two countries, which occurred in the first two decades of the Turkish Republic, immediately impacted the minorities.

The Greco-Turkish reconciliation started with the return of Venizelos to power in 1928. Indeed, in the first years that followed the Lausanne Treaty, a great political instability afflicted Greece.[7] Three governments took turns, followed by two military coups. Despite the 1 December 1926 agreement, concerning *established* goods, that is to say those exempted from the exchange, Greco-Turkish relations remained tense, and both sides were arming themselves rapidly.[8] In this context, we can better understand the pressure exerted on Istanbul Greeks, viewed as potential traitors. However, the return to power of Venizelos from the Island of Crete, appeased the relationship. This rapprochement was necessary because both Venizelos and Atatürk sought to consolidate their power, even more so since both countries attempted to transition into republic after long monarchical eras. Thus, as soon as he came to power, Venizelos declared that he wished to establish friendly relations with Turkey. His message addressed to Ismet Pasha on 30 August 1928 highlights this wish[9]:

> At a time when the Hellenic people have only just entrusted me, through a strong majority, its government leadership for a four-year mandate, I wish to affirm my strong desire to contribute to settling our two countries' relations, contributing to a close friendship which would be consecrated through a friendship, non-aggression and arbitration pact, with as wide a range as possible.

I am fully aware that Turkey has no views on our territories, and I have been able, several times during my election period, to publicly declare that Greece has no view on Turkish territories and that it accepts peace treaties sincerely and without any restriction. I can therefore have no doubt that settling our relations, such as I understand it, matches your Excellency's desires. For this shared desire to be achieved, there is no obstacle but the question pending between our two countries about the population exchange convention and the following agreements.

Thus, here is the text that characterises the Greco-Turkish relations in the 1930s. This reconciliation is not only caused by internal and bilateral preoccupations. The international conjuncture, to use an anachronistic term, pushed both countries to a *cordial entente*. Greece feared Bulgarian revisionist views and the rise of fascism in Italy. As for Turkey, they wished to escape the Soviet Union's growing zone of influence under Stalin's rule. In this context, the signing of a friendship agreement was profitable. During the official visit of the Greek Prime Minister E. Venizelos to Ankara from 27–31 October 1930, Turkey and Greece signed three agreements: a friendship and neutrality pact, a treaty of limitation of armed navy forces and a convention of residence, commerce and maritime commerce. Among these agreements, the first and last one directly impact the subject we focus on in this chapter. Indeed, while the first agreement settled disputes around the *established ones*, heirs to the population exchange, the third agreement opened doors to an Istanbul residence for Istanbul Greeks who had opted for the Hellenic nationality at one point or another. Following these agreements, the 1935 census showed that, in Istanbul, there were 125,000 Greek Orthodox persons, including 18,000 who were of Greek nationality.

World War II and its Consequences

An era of relative calm in Greco-Turkish relations started in 1930. Turkey's Greeks took advantage of this era and were emancipated both economically and culturally. Retrospectively, the 1930s can be considered one of the happiest decades for this minority. With the start of World War II, however, difficulties arose. Though Turkey was able to stay somehow out of the war's armed confrontations, it was fully impacted by the economic and ideological consequences of the conflict.

Despite the limited number of (non-Muslim) minorities and the more serene bilateral relations between the two countries, the war stirred up old obsessions among Turkish leaders and in public opinion. In the political and public agenda theory,[10] it is hard to know whether public opinion led governmental decisions or if it was leaders who created a public opinion adverse to minorities. In any case, there was a suspicious climate surrounding the non-Muslim minorities. Once more, non-Muslim minority members, Greeks in particular, were suspected of forming a fifth column.

Anti-Greek 'preventive' measures were not long in coming. As soon as 1941, young Greeks were mobilised, not into the regular army corps, but into a special corps created at the time, called *amele taburu*. There were about twenty, in remote areas of Anatolia. Some Istanbul Greek memoirs speak of it.[11] It would seem that the treatment of minorities was not bad. However, the minorities who had been through the experience claimed that the authorities frightened them and that they suffered mostly from psychological pressure. Even if they were not mistreated, such a measure shows how complex the situation was for Greeks in Turkey. Furthermore, a year later, a new measure even less acceptable and with even more devastating consequences was carried out, a 'wealth tax', the *varlık vergisi*.

We believe there are three things overlapping that allowed for the establishment of such a discriminatory measure:

1. The indecision from the Inönü government in its policy to stay out of the war, its wish to neither quarrel with the Allies nor the Axis, in order to be able to choose the best time to join the war on the winning side.
2. The country's disastrous economic situation due to the international conjuncture but also due to structural issues, such as the delay in industrialisation of Turkey. Moreover, the absence of a Turkish bourgeois class dominating the world of business was an issue in the eyes of Turkish leaders.[12]
3. Finally, the strong climate of suspicion around minorities and their loyalty to the Turkish State.

The combination of these three cyclical and structural causes led Rüştü Saraçoğlu's government (head of government under Ismet Inönü, who was the president since 1938; Atatürk had died in 1938) to vote on law number 4305, called *varlık vergisi*, to tax the fortune (not revenues) of the bourgeoisie, only applicable once.

At first, the reason cited for such a measure was the Turkish state's need for financing and the 'overflow of money in circulation'. However, it was clearly carried out and enforced against minorities. Indeed, though it is not explicitly written as such in the law, there are four taxable categories: Muslims, converts, non-Muslims and foreigners, taxed differently. Furthermore, the rates applied were left for the members of the 'commissions' created for this instance to decide. These commissions were composed of the members of the People's Republican Party (at the time, Turkey's single party), who were exclusively Muslims.

The members of the commission of a department determined the tax an individual owed, and gave them 15 days to pay it. Given that the sums required were often exorbitant, a great part of those taxable could not pay them in such a short time. Among non-Muslims, a limited number of those who were not able to pay their debt were sent to 'work camps' (*çalışma kampları*) for short periods of time (a few weeks). The plan was, in fact, to have them work in road construction (and other similar) projects in the east of the country. Moreover, almost 800 real estate properties were confiscated by the state in exchange for unpaid debts.

Before the unpopularity of such a measure, before the domestic and foreign criticism and before the weakening of the German ideology in Europe, the decree on fortune was abolished 16 months after it was first carried out, on 15 March 1944. Beyond the Turkification of the economy, one of the most important consequences of this era was the start of the Greek community's erosion in Turkey. Admittedly, the great exodus had not yet started, but Turkey's Greeks lost their faith in the future they could have in Turkey. The two following tables demonstrate this erosion starting.[13]

Istanbul's population according to native language

Language	1935	1950
Turkish	692,460	827,860
Greek	79,920	66,106
Armenian	39,821	42,207
Judeo-Spanish	26,435	28,140

Turkey's population according to native language

Language	1935	1950
Total	13,899,073	20,947,188
Greek	108,725	89,472
Armenian	57,599	52,776
Judeo-Spanish	42,607	35,786

Multiple remarks were made on these statistics. First, we can indeed observe a decline of 13,000 people in the Greek-speaking population of Istanbul and 19,000 in the entire country (which respectively represent 17 per cent and 18 per cent of the total Greek population), while the Istanbul population rose by 19 per cent and Turkey's by almost 50 per cent. Thus, the decline of the Greek population is important, although it appears moderate at first. Let's not forget that Turkey's Greeks did not have many places to go in 1942. European countries were in the middle of a violent conflict, and Greece was no exception. Furthermore, when World War II ended, Greece remained in the chaos of a civil war until at least 1951. In this context, the departure of 20,000 Greeks within fifteen years becomes a much more significant figure. Moreover, the analysis of the statistics above confirms that Greeks were much more concerned by this episode of emigration than other minorities in Turkey.[14] However, it is true that Greeks could emigrate to Greece although it was at war, while Armenians and Istanbul Jews' only homeland was Turkey. Nevertheless, following the economic, physical and psychological pressure (the tax of fortune paralleled a campaign of 'Turkification' of everyday language called 'Compatriot, speak Turkish!'), the members of the Greek community no longer envisioned a serene future in Turkey for their children. Lastly, to conclude on the subject of anti-minority and anti-Greek humiliations, it is important to note that the rule of reciprocity was not applied in these cases. Although the measures concerning Turkey's Greeks in the following years were related to other Greco-Turkish issues (Thrace Muslims, Cyprus, etc.), the establishment of *varlık vergisi* and the different measures surrounding it were not linked to a specific bilateral issue. On the contrary, relations between Greece, at war, and Turkey, trying to stay out of it, were rather cordial at the time. We should not forget that the tax on fortune did not 'aim' at the Greek population, but rather, initially, the country's Jewish population and other minorities.

The Greek–Turkish Reconciliation and 6/7 September 1955

The Greco-Turkish relation is full of twists, with periods of tension followed by a reconciliation, and eras of cordial relations ending in disputes. Loyal to that pattern, the ten years that followed the end of World War II were 'happy' ones for the Greek minority in Turkey. The Greco-Turkish rapprochement, which had started in the 1930s, was reinforced, despite the 1942 episode.

The civil war in Greece was perceived, in Turkey, as a communist revolt, and, as such, was watched with great worry.[15] The threat of a pro-Soviet power in Athens caused great worry in Ankara. The end of the civil war, with the victory of the royal forces, thus greatly relieved Turkey. The period that followed the Greek civil war was one of a relative political stabilisation in both countries, which created a reconciliation, beneficial to both minorities.

This rapprochement is easily explained. First, there is the role of the United States, which saw Turkey and Greece as the best defenders of the Eastern Mediterranean against Stalinism. The wish of both capitals to become NATO members led them to cooperate, in order to prove to Washington that they were indispensable in the Aegean Sea in the resistance against the rising Soviet Union. The best proof of this military cooperation lies in their participation in the Korean War. Both countries officially integrated the Atlantic Alliance on 15 February 1952. On the other hand, Greece was still very much affected by the aftermath of the civil war and increasingly feared Bulgarian communism. Thus, cooperating with Turkey and treating its Muslim minority, who was living in a region directly affected by this fear, well, became indispensable.

Other, more calculated reasons, were put forward by the press of the Turkish minority living in Greece. A radical change in the Greek policy concerning Cyprus had occurred under the government of Marshal Papagos, who officially brought the issue to the UN. In this internationalisation policy, Athens officials did not wish to see Turkey and Cypriot Turks opposing them and wished to prove to the US and to England that the treatment of the island's Turks would be a fair one, as with the treatment of the Muslim minority in Western Thrace. On the other hand, Turkey's worries about the Dodecanese sovereignty transfer from Italy to Greece during the 1947 Paris Treaty had lessened before the decision to demilitarise the twelve islands.

Thus, all conditions for a political, military and cultural rapprochement were there. On 26 April 1952, a Turkish delegation led by Prime Minister Adnan Menderes, which included Minister of Foreign Affairs Fuat Köprülü and Head General Şükrü Kanatlı, arrived in Athens for an official visit.[16] Greek Prime Minister Sophocles Venizelos had come to Ankara in February. The aim of these visits was to decide on the specific nature of the countries' military cooperation following their NATO membership. The most significant diplomatic exchange in this period was King Paul and Queen Frederica's visit to Turkey in June 1952. King Paul was the first Greek monarch to set foot on Turkish soil since the Byzantine era. Moreover, it was the King's first official travel abroad since his accession to the throne. In October 1952, the Turkish President Celal Bayar came to Athens by train, cutting across the entire Western Thrace region. This journey is still, to this day, recalled by the members of the minority as a symbol of happier days, especially since Celal Bayar took advantage of this passage to inaugurate the Komotini minority's first secondary school, which would bear his name. The negotiations of the 1952–3 winter led to an alliance treaty between Greece and Turkey, signed in Ankara in February 1953, but also in Yugoslavia.

Beyond these political and military reconciliations, some cooperation could also be observed in the cultural domain. It is from this domain that the Greek minority profited most. Following many negotiations, a cultural treaty was signed on 20 April 1951. The content of this treaty of 20 April 1951 is very important, in the sense that most negotiations and disputes to come would refer to this text.

The treaty's provisions around the school books and student exchanges directly impacted the Greek minority in Turkey, especially since, following this treaty, the first secular secondary school of the Muslim minority in Western Thrace would be established, in Komotini. It is the Celal Bayar high school, named after the Turkish President who inaugurated the school.

This climate, favourable to both minorities, was interrupted because of the bilateral tensions related to the deterioration of the Cyprus issue. Unusually, the events of 6 and 7 September 1955 in Istanbul (and Izmir) are not related to the issue of reciprocal minorities, but to the degradation of

Greco-Turkish relations in Cyprus and to the rise of nationalism on both sides. As early as September 1954, Turkish public opinion criticised the Ecumenical Patriarchate for its passivity in controlling the Orthodox clergy in Cyprus. In 1955, the Turkish press repeatedly appealed to Patriarch Athenagoras to call the Cypriot archbishop, Monsignor Makarios, to reason.[17] Unlike previous requests for the restriction of the Patriarchate's powers, the public opinion now demanded its direct intervention in the Cyprus conflict. Of course, the support Makarios had obtained in Greece and in the United States' Greek community, prevented any direct intervention. *Tercüman*'s and *Hürriyet*'s campaigns grew, soon joined by *Cumhuriyet*. A rumour, launched from a bulletin of the *İstanbul Ekspres* radio on 6 September at 4pm, announcing that a bomb attack had struck the birthplace of Mustafa Kemal Atatürk in Thessaloniki was the last straw. The night of the 6th to 7th September is one of the darkest ones of Turkey's contemporary history, where thousands of *Stanbuliotes*, protected by the passivity of police forces, followed agents provocateurs in breaking, ransacking and destroying stores, houses, schools and other places belonging to Istanbul Greeks.

The programmed and calculated nature of these vandalism events needs no further proof since the *Yassıada* trial, during which Adnan Menderes, then the Prime Minister of the government of the Democratic Party, was judged, among other people. On this matter, we should note an oddity concerning the electoral behaviour of Turkey's Greeks. Since the foundation of the Republic and during the single-party regime era, this minority had always been diffident towards the decisions of the People's Republican Party. Moreover, the humiliations directed at the minority during World War II had further distanced the Greek electorate from the People's Republican Party. Thus, as soon as the regime became one of multipartyism, minority members brought support, on mass, to the new hope of the moment: the Democratic Party. Furthermore, the liberal visions of this group seduced the mercantile bourgeois minority of Istanbul. Yet, there is no longer any doubt about the fact that it is that very political party, which orchestrated the riots and sackings on 6 to 7 September. Despite this undeniable fact, even after 1955, Turkey's Greeks continued to support the Democratic Party and Adnan Menderes, until the coup of 27 May 1960 ended the Party's deviations.

Turks in Western Thrace became very afraid following these events. The minority feared retaliation, which became, afterwards, a common reality concerning the issue of minorities between both countries. It would however seem that, immediately after the night of 6 to 7 December, no retaliation took place.[18]

These events naturally affected Istanbul's Greeks. First and foremost, there was enormous material damage. However, this damage was compensated for, at least partially, by the Turkish government. The true injuries, which would be hard to heal, were psychological and sentimental ones. The first reaction was to turn inward, to no longer mention this sad episode, either in newspapers or in discussions, to opt for an attitude of 'what is done is done, let us now move on'. It was only later that we finally grasped the depth of the wound. In the Istanbul Greeks' collective memory, especially for those who emigrated to Greece or elsewhere, this event was magnified and is, today, considered one of the principal causes for the exodus. However, it would seem that despite the fear caused by the events, the Patriarchate and the minority's elite succeeded in preventing a massive emigration of the community. The statistics indeed support the idea that, although there was an erosion, the minority's massive emigration from the city had not yet started.[19]

In 1935, 14 per cent of Turkish citizens had a native language which was not Turkish. In 1960, they represented 10 per cent of the population. In Istanbul, those whose native language was Turkish represented 9 per cent of the city's population in 1935 and 2.5 per cent in 1960. Furthermore, it is important to note that in 1935, 73.5 per cent of Turkish citizens whose native language was Greek lived in Istanbul, versus 78 per cent in 1960.[20]

Expulsion of Greeks in 1964

From the mid-1950s, Greco-Turkish relations entered a new era. The deterioration of the Cyprus issue began to seriously aggravate bilateral relations and endanger the situation of their reciprocal minorities. From the 1960s to today, the life of Istanbul's Greek minority has been indexed on the Cypriot situation. They were viewed as linked to the events that occurred on the island; even worse, they were sometimes perceived as responsible for these events.

The expulsion of the Greeks (of Greek nationality) from Turkey in 1964 is the best example of this retaliation policy. Indeed, Turkey's Greeks were not only punished for the actions of Greek Cypriots but also served as currency with Greece.

In Cyprus, following the Zurich and London agreements of 1959, a Republic was founded, dependent on Great Britain, Greece and Turkey. Strategically and psychologically, Turkey viewed the isle as its weak spot, its 'underbelly'. Thus, when the President of the Cypriot Republic, Archbishop Makarios, decided, in 1963, to amend the fragile Constitution of 1960, Ismet Inönü's government, which had returned to power in Turkey in 1961, attempted to react, with the intent to use armed force if necessary. This intervention turned out to be impossible to carry out because of both the incapacity of the Turkish armed forces and the US threatening opposition. This powerlessness, or the feeling of it, led the Turkish government to carry out a striking blow to demonstrate to its public and to the Greek government – held responsible for the Cyprian events – that Turkey had leverage. That is why, on 17 March 1964, Turkey unilaterally cancelled the free residence treaty for citizens from both Greece and Turkey living in the opposite country, which had allowed, in 1930, many Istanbul Greeks who had opted for Greek nationality to stay back and settle in the city.

Thus, in the year 1964, Istanbul Greeks were forcefully expelled from Turkey. This expulsion was, inevitably, followed by an exodus of Greek of Turkish nationality, for, since 1930, the Greek community of the city had organised outside of concerns about nationality. The 'mixed' marriages between Greeks of both nationalities were very common, and, naturally, every Greek citizen expelled had Turkish citizens in their close family, who followed them in their exodus.

Already, in the late 1950s, with the degradation of the Cyprus issue, an anti-Greek (and, by extension, anti-Rum[21]) discourse had re-emerged in public opinion, through political statements and media propaganda. Especially in ordinary law infractions, the press emphasised the Greek origins of the suspects. Here are a few newspaper titles from popular journals around the time of the decision of 16 March 1964:

'Trafficker of Greek nationality arrested'.[22]
'A Greek murderer and trafficker has been arrested'.[23]
'Counterfeiters who cooperated with the Rums have been arrested'.[24]

'A restaurant owner was involved in tax evasion'.[25]

'A rum woman who was involved in tax evasion was arrested'.[26]

'Three young Rums beat up a young Turk. The motive is unknown'.[27]

'Two Greek currency traffickers were arrested. A drug addict named Hristofaros Tolga killed a Turk who refused to give him money'.[28]

'A Rum currency trafficker was arrested'.[29]

'Undeclared watches were found in the store of a Rum'.[30]

'A Greek mage who gave discounts to lovers was arrested'.[31]

'A Rum fired three shots and injured a Turk'.[32]

'The Greeks who were fishing in our territorial waters fired shots. The thugs who fled leaving their nets were not able to injure anyone'.[33]

'An assassin, Greek national, wanted, was apprehended while engaged in dubious trafficking'.[34]

'A pimp named Maria Dodogi was expelled from the territory'.[35]

'Five Greek revue artists will be deported'.[36]

The basis for the discourse was established. The re-emergence of anti-Greek manifestations in 1964, therefore, easily took place and was little opposed. The aggravation of nationalism and popular euphoria, fed by the press and statements from political figures, limited the negative reactions to the abolition of the 1930 treaty. On the contrary, the press stirred old resentments from the 1919–22 war, the 1942 tax on fortune and the night of 6 to 7 September 1955. The discourse on minorities holding key functions and that of the Turkification of the economy re-appeared. The press seemed very conscious of the drama that would ensue and based its commentary on a 'cost-benefit' assessment. When, on 16 March 1964, on the 44th anniversary of Istanbul's liberation, the government decided not to renew Greek nationals' visas, *Milliyet* announced the decision by stipulating that 'we will not have any loss'.[37] Greeks started leaving the country as soon as late March, that is to say two weeks after the governmental decision to abolish the 1930 treaty, to the complete indifference of the Turkish public opinion.[38] In reality, according to Article 36 of the treaty, Turkey had to warn Greece six months ahead of the expulsion, but given that the Turkish government wished to use Istanbul Greeks as a lever in the Cyprus dispute, they could not wait six months. Thus, invoking article 16 of the treaty, which stipulates that the terms of the treaty could be overridden in the case of national safety, Inönü's government quickly carried out its decision. Throughout 1964 and 1965, Istanbul Greeks left Turkey. A pressure put on the city's minority Greek schools paralleled their departure, as well as an umpteenth reconsideration of the Patriarchate's status. When the execution of the expulsion ended, Istanbul had lost not only its 12,000 Greek nationals but also the Greek Turkish citizens who had family and economic and sentimental ties to them.

Anti-Greek and anti-Rum measures of the 1960s did not stop at Istanbul Greeks. The Greek community living in the two isles in the Dardanelles, Imbros and Tenedos, were also affected by governmental actions. The Turkification of the isles began at that time and is still ongoing. In the anti-Greek discourse, Imbros and Tenedos (Gökçeada and Bozcaada) had a special place. Imbros had an almost completely Greek population, apart from the state officials in charge there, and Tenedos had as many Turkish inhabitants as Greek ones. In 1964, both isles' population was estimated at 70,000 people. These two isles are of capital importance to Turkey on a military and strategic level, but also on a psychological one.

Following the Cyprian events, the minority schools of the islands were re-attached to the National Education Ministry, as retaliation. A series of articles from *Akşam* can give us clues as to the public opinion surrounding the two isles[39]:

> 'In Imbros, the economic domination of the Rums is increasing every day'.
> 'The Turkish flag flies here, but they don't speak Turkish . . . Its name is Turkish but its soul is still Greek'.
> 'The Turks are far surpassed in terms of economics'.
> 'The shopkeepers, the dentist, the doctors of the island are from their country'.
> 'They ask for films and coins in Greek for underhand activities'.
> 'Priests are walking in the streets with their religious clothes'.
> 'The representatives of all political parties are Greeks'.

Turkish authorities feared that, one day, the isles' inhabitants would ask for a referendum to be re-attached to Greece (following the example of Cyprus). Thus, the government ordered the settlement of 6,000 Turks across both islands. They would give advantageous credit to the new inhabitants for them to take root there.[40] This evolution of the education and settlement policies in the isles was brought to UNESCO by Greece.[41] Turkey, according to the rule of reciprocity, asked for the matter of pressures exerted on Turkish schools in Western Thrace to be discussed as well.[42]

In 1965, a battalion of Balıkesir policemen was sent and settled on both isles. Thereafter, the militarisation of this land, as well as the construction of a prison, led to a strong increase in the Turkish share of the population, since the Greeks progressively left their island.[43]

According to a 1960 census, there were 106,000 Greek Orthodox persons (of Turkish nationality) living in Turkey. Five years later, a 1965 census showed that already 30,000 of them had left, following the expulsion of the 12,000 Greek nationals from Istanbul. However, the exodus did not stop there. From 1964 to today, the departures are regular, though more voluntary.[44]

It seems unnecessary to mention that the impact of the 1964 events is still very strong in the collective memory of the Greek community of Istanbul. Better (or worse) yet, the remembrance of this year is maintained, perhaps even amplified. There is no use in highlighting the fact that uprooted communities need points of reference. The year 1964 is the main reference for the Greek community of Istanbul, especially for those who now live in Greece. The minority newspapers constantly recall these events, publishing programmes and regularly producing broadcasts about them. Finally, the children born after 1964 have a very gloomy image, perhaps even darker than the reality was, of this expulsion from the city. Though the minority elite, supported by the Patriarchate, was able to avoid a mass exodus after 1942, and especially after 1955,[45] 1964 was the last straw for them. Entire families left Istanbul to never come back.

To these retaliation measures carried out by Ankara against Turkey's Greeks, Athens responded immediately with similar measures against its Muslim minority. An anti-Turkish press propaganda started as soon as 1964.[46] Bomb attacks aimed at mosques and Muslim cemeteries.[47] A very important part of the pressures concentrated on the domain of education,[48] notably during the nomination of teachers of Turkish nationality.[49] On 7 October 1964, a royal decree (decree number 649) complicated the committee elections for the *vakıfs* and cancelled the elections for village committees (*Encümen*).

Last Exodus of Istanbul Greeks and the 1974 Intervention in Cyprus

The ten years that followed the events of 1964 were extremely tense between Greece and Turkey. On the standpoint of domestic policy, both countries suffered two military interventions of totalitarian forces against the progressive forces. In Greece, the colonels took power in 1967, and in Turkey the military took control of the government in 1971. Even if both military powers started a reconciliation, the Cyprian events prevented a durable *entente*.

According to some observers, the diffident reconciliation between the Greek junta and Turkey in the late 1960s (for instance, with the 1968 Greco-Turkish cultural agreement[50]) was, in part, due to the lobbying of Istanbul Greeks and of both isles, settled in important Greek cities, most certainly in order to be able to get a hold of their abandoned properties, with the hope of maybe coming back some day. However, the eternal apple of discord that is Cyprus, always interfered in such reconciliation.

Some events led to the complication of both reciprocal minorities. In 1967, Süleyman Demirel's government almost intervened in Cyprus, and this escalation greatly impacted minorities in Istanbul and in Thrace. Admittedly, the 1967 crisis was settled during the conference of Keşan-Alexandropolis, where both Prime Ministers met and after which the Greek delegation (M. Oikonomou-Gouras and Colonel Papadopoulos) were accused of making concessions on Turkey's Greek minority.[51] The true blow to optimism on the issue of minorities came in August 1971, with the shutdown of the Halki theological school, which was not only the Patriarchate's recruitment pool, but also one of the most important institutions of the community.

Throughout the 1970s, the issue of minorities became a background issue. First because Turkey's Greeks were considerably less numerous than they used to be and therefore no longer presenting a 'danger' but more particularly because other, more technical, issues were added to the Greco-Turkish dispute. Beyond Cyprus, which became deadlocked in 1974, the conflicts related to the Aegean Sea emerged: territorial waters, the continental shelf, demilitarisation of the Aegean Isles, the Flight Information Region and so on.

It is hard to measure the impact of the Turkish intervention in Cyprus on minorities. If 1974 is a pivot date for the Thrace Muslims, because of the fall of the junta and not because of the intervention in itself, no such direct impact can be observed for Turkey's Greeks. The emigration continued, no longer motivated by political decisions causing a mass exodus, but caused by more psychological, and certainly economic, reasons.

Twenty-first Century, a Possible Upsurge?

From the moment where Turkey's Greeks, as a united minority, no longer believed in their future in Turkey, the erosion became inevitable. That is even more true considering that the living standards in Greece were continuously rising, with the return of economic and political stability, while, in Turkey, crises followed one another. The end of the junta in Greece paralleled a rise in political violence in Turkey. The 1980 military coup in Turkey, particularly severe, was followed one year later by Greece's admission to the EU in 1981. Thus, life became more attractive in Greece than in Turkey. The defenders of the official Turkish hypothesis promote the idea that Istanbul Greeks did not leave because of the diverse pressures exerted on them (explicit and implicit) but because of the economic and social attraction of foreign countries, including Greece. They add that this departure did not only concern Greeks but the whole Turkish population, citing the departure of Western Europe Turks. Admittedly, this simplistic explanation holds up, at least for the post-1980 era. Indeed, from the moment that parents ceased to see a future for their children in Turkey, when minority schools could no longer dispense an acceptable education while preserving the minority identity, when most of their family had already settled in Greece, when their expectations of a better life were higher in Kallithéa than in Nea Smyrni, in Palaio Phaliron than in Kurtuluş, in Moda, or in Pera, why stay? To these rational reasons were added a sentiment of rejection, of feeling excluded from the nation:

> The great majority of people in this society sees us as foreigners. During my entire schooling and beyond, they always asked me the same questions: where are you from? Why did you come? Are you from Greece? Are you a migrant? Why did you settle in Turkey? As a member of a family that has been living in this country for seven generations, encountering these types of questions made me feel as if the entire nation did not see us as one of its essential elements. Recently, I have been answering these questions with: Us, we have always been here. And you, where did you come from?[52]

Often, the children leave before the parents do. The parents wait for the children to graduate high school (at 17–18 years old) and send them to Greece for university. After university, it is much easier to find a job in Greece (or else-where) than in Turkey. Moreover, the young people, having spent their young adulthood in Greece, feel reluctant to come back to Turkey, even though they feel a certain nostalgia thereafter. Once the children are settled in Greece, the parents only have to follow. First starting with recurring trips, then settling definitively when they retire.

This erosion in the younger population leads to another problem related to marriage. The parents of young women often complain that there are no longer enough young Greeks in Istanbul to start a family. Let's not forget that we are talking about a community of a few thousand people who wish to preserve at all cost the unity and identity of the minority. The danger in the eyes of the parents and minority elite is that the young woman would live in Istanbul, old enough to flirt and date, and end up in mixed marriages with Armenians, Arab-speaking Orthodox or, especially, Turks. The children born of these marriages, who cannot be reclaimed by the community, notably on the matter of education, and the young Greek woman and her children will be seen as 'lost' to the community. Therefore, only one solution remains for traditionalist families: sending their daughters to Greece before they are old enough to marry. We will circle back to the issue of the Arab-speaking Orthodox population.

Numbers and Structure of the Community

In order to talk about the Greek Orthodox population in Turkey, we must first assess its numbers. Admittedly, there is no consensus, neither for the Turkish authorities nor among the minority members (whether they live in Turkey or Greece), on the number of those remaining in Turkey. These numbers vary, from 2,000 to 10,000, according to the point of view that one wants to defend and on the definition of 'Greek Orthodox'. The minimal estimates only count the Greek-speaking Orthodox population, that is to say that the hundreds of Turkish-speaking Orthodox persons are not counted, nor are the few thousand from Antakya – who, despite their 'ethnic' background and Arabic language are classified by Turkish authorities as religiously Greek Orthodox. This is the implicit result of the millet system of the Ottoman Empire, which placed religious affiliation above ethnicity, language or residence. Thus, there are four possibilities for counting the population:

1. Only Greek-speaking Greek Orthodox from Istanbul: they are estimated at 2,000.
2. The Greek-speaking Greek Orthodox from Istanbul and Greek Orthodox from Tenedos and Imbros: 2,500 to 3,500 people.
3. Adding the Arab-speaking Orthodox, which emigrated and are now settled in Istanbul: numbers vary from 4,000 to 5,000.
4. Finally, with the total count of all Turkish citizens with the *rum-ortodoks* inscription on their ID card (living in Istanbul, Imbros, Tenedos and Antakya), the number amounts to 8,000 to 10,000 people.

For the whole of the Orthodox population in Turkey, the most reliable number seems to be that of 8,000 people.[53] It is clear that, whether we trust the low or high estimate, the community remains very small in Turkey, with its 61 million inhabitants, and in Istanbul, with its population of 12 million. However, beyond these small numbers, the Greek community in Turkey is important on a political (with the reciprocity with Thrace's Turks), symbolic and historical (with the role of Constantinople in the Greek identitary discourse) standpoints.

The previous considerations on the numbers of this minority would be incomplete without the mention of the polemic surrounding the Arab-speaking Orthodox population. The attitudes of the minority elite, and to a greater extent, of the minority members, are contradictory and complex on the issue of the arrival and integration of the Antakya Orthodox population in Istanbul. Given that these people have, officially and administratively, the *rum-ortodoks* identity, they are allowed to send their children to minority schools, to go to the community's churches and, most importantly, have a say in the management of community goods (through the religious foundations, *vakıfs*).

This intrusion of the Antakya Orthodox population in the small world of Istanbul Greeks is not without positive impacts. As the numbers of the community grow, so does its importance. The arrival of more working force is appreciated, especially in the religious and school domains. Indeed, the community had difficulties in making them function smoothly, not only because of the lack of followers and students, but also because of the lack of personnel, especially those to manage everyday tasks. Furthermore, the children of the Arab-speaking Orthodox population started to go to minority schools, which would be otherwise under the threat of shutting down. Finally, with the number of the young Arab-speaking Orthodox population being more important, marriage opportunities become more frequent.

All these positive impacts are seen, for a part of the minority elite, as negative, 'dangerous'. Indeed, those who do not accept the Arab-speaking Orthodox population as a true part of the community are afraid of mixed marriages. They view the arrival of these children who do not speak Greek as a considerable weight on the schooling of the minority's children. Because of this issue, the intellectuals of the minority faced a dilemma: while defending the idea of systematically sending Greek children to minority schools and not foreign and private schools (usually French) in order to preserve their Greek identity, they complained about the very low level of the teaching in these schools. 'Should we sacrifice our own children to save the schools and the minority?'[54] Some people propose classes, or even special schools, for Arab-speaking children, to separate them from Greek children.[55] The most common fear is that of Arab-speaking people being, one day, in charge of the management of *vakıfs*: 'they came to take possession of the *vakıfs*. Us, we soon won't be here anymore, it is *them* who will take our goods'.[56] The distinction between 'us' and 'them' is very revealing. There is the feeling of loss (of death? of departure?) and being represented only by usurpers.

Institutions and Bodies

Witnesses of a glorious past, the minority institutions have, today, a disproportionate importance. Despite the spectacular decrease of minority members, the prestige of these institutions remains intact, if not being even greater. For more than vestiges of a bygone era, they still have a national, and even international, role.

The Valoukli Hospital (Balıklı)

The Valoukli Hospital (Balıklı) is a prestigious institution of the minority of the Foundation of the Greek (*rum*) Hospital of Balıklı. Founded in the fifteenth century in a building near the Golden Horn (Karaköy, Büyük Balıklı Han), the Hospital settled in its current premises (in Zeytinburnu on a 160,000 m² area) in 1753. It is a very big hospital, which functions perfectly in almost every medical domain. The patients, as well as the personnel, are mostly Turkish (in 2012, only four out of sixteen clinic directors were Greeks, and one was Armenian. However, by 2024, all clinic directors were ethnically

Turkish). Though the patients of diverse sections of the hospital are almost exclusively Turkish (there are not enough Greeks in Istanbul for such an establishment to function anyway), the retirement home that is attached to it is the one where Greeks and Istanbul Greeks retire to. Currently, the 300 places of this retirement and nursing home are occupied. According to the procedure, when an elderly person wishes to settle in the hospital for their last years, instead of paying a certain sum for the lodging and care, they leave their goods (house, commerce, etc.) to the foundation. These inheritances are more or less strict, depending on the case. The income from these goods is managed by the foundation and, according to their importance, part of them can be given to the children. When the person dies, the foundation collects their assets.

The hospital is the property of a *vakıf* (religious foundation) and, as such, is administered and dealt with by the community itself while being attached, for the care it provides, to the Ministry of Health. The direction committee of the foundation elects its president and a hospital administrator. After Dimitri Karayani, the current president of the Foundation Council is Konstantin Yuvanidis, a businessman. The president of the foundation, elected by the members of the community, is not a member of the medical personnel. Indeed, his function is one of management of hospital assets and business. In 2022, Mr Yuvanidis was very controversial because of his support to the Islamist regime and his pro-government attitude during the fire that burned down an important part of the historical building in August 2022.

Churches

Besides this strong and prestigious institution, the minority possesses a flourishing internal organisation network, a legacy from a time when they were more numerous. Although churches no longer have enough followers to fill them, nor enough priests, they continue to function sporadically. Without material means or enough followers these churches remain empty most of the time. Usually, these churches are open at least on the day of the saint they bear the name of. That is to say both priests and followers travel on each Sunday to another church. The church, however, remains an important place of socialisation, with holy days being particularly important days. Let's not forget that this is a pretty traditional community, mostly composed of older people, who wish to preserve their Orthodox identity. Even the rare younger minority members that we were able to encounter assert that they try not to miss mass, at least to have the feeling of being part of a defined community. The presence of the Patriarchate as a power place and ultimate protector, communicating through the priests, should not be overlooked in the analysis of the religious life of the community.

The names of the parishes, at least those bearing the name of an Istanbul neighbourhood, are supposed to give us an insight on the geographical distribution of the minority. Of course, this map is no longer relevant today, as the number of Greeks, in the strict sense of the term, is down to approximately 2,000. A few places where the minority population is concentrated can still be established. Firstly, the *Balıklı* hospital: the 300 elders living in the nursing home of the hospital make it the main point of population concentration. Then, the Patriarchate and its surroundings. In the Patriarchate, between the personnel and the priests, we can estimate the number of people living there at around 300. Many of the Patriarchate personnel are Greek nationals. Apart from these two sectors, we can establish the following neighbourhoods as privileged places of living for Istanbul Greeks: Beyoğlu and Kurtuluş on the city's European side, Kadıköy on the Asian coast and the Princes islands.

Schools

Another vital institution for the minority is, of course, schools. The issue of schools is rather a complex one. Indeed, in all teaching domains there are intertwined issues. A lack of students, of teachers, of books, lack of quality of the materials and of the teaching, cohabitation between Greek and Turkish teachers and so on. To a larger extent, we can observe that these issues are born of the narrow application of the reciprocity principle with Western Thrace schools. The same type of issue exists in the Muslim minority in Thrace.

Among these problems, the lack of students might be the most important. Indeed, not only is the minority very reduced, but students moreover represent a very small portion of it, because of the marriages and emigration issues. This leads to most schools threatening to shut down. Those that are functioning are forced to regroup several age groups with sometimes Arab-speaking children. This situation significantly diminishes the quality of the teaching and the minority elite hesitates to put its few children in the secondary minority schools. Among the secondary schools, the three most important that currently function are the Phanar Patriarchal High School, the Pera Zographeion

High School for boys and the Pera Zographeion High School for girls. There are numerous elementary schools and these mostly function thanks to the contribution of Arab-speaking Orthodox children who, in certain schools, represent the majority of students. As the school problem is at the heart of the survival of Greeks of Istanbul, we can analyse it in depth.

As we mentioned above, it was in 1964 that the fate of the community was sealed. After Cyprus gained independence (1960), inter-community clashes multiplied to the point that Cypriot President Monsignor Makarios was tempted to change the Constitution. Ankara, fearing a Greek takeover of the island, was brandishing the threat, initially, of military intervention in Cyprus, using its status as 'guarantor'. But faced with the opposition, even the disguised threat of the United States barely emerging from the Cuban crisis and the assassination of John F. Kennedy, Ankara had to swallow its anger. It was redirected to the usual scapegoats: the Greeks of Istanbul. It was then that their expulsion was decided. The government unilaterally suspended the 1930 agreement and expelled the 12,000 Greeks with Hellenic citizenship. This was done to put pressure on Greece but also in order to complete the annihilation of the Greeks of the country, begun forty years before. Therefore, the Greek schools that were an important part of the educational panorama of Istanbul started to face the danger of shutting down or, worse, becoming ghost schools.

The fear of abuses after 1964 was not completely unfounded. Above all, the main bilateral problem, the one that had brought so much suffering to the minority, Cyprus, remained. And because of the experiences of 1955 and 1964, in each bilateral crisis the minority felt targeted, as for example during the crisis of 1967. But instead of spectacular measures, there were more diffuse applications affecting the structures of the minority. Already with the departure of 30,000 members of the community, many schools had to close.

Year	Pupils and students	Pre-schools	Primary schools	Middle and high schools
1923	16,123	70	85	8
1964	6,002	4	42	6
1970	4,412	–	52	6
1978	1,147	–	22	6

To these shortages of students (and teachers) must be added the attempts of the Turkish government to take control of these minority schools considered as 'breeding grounds for treachery'. To do this, in 1967, a decree promulgated in 1963 (number 246/7) was applied in order to appoint, in a compulsory way, a Turkish deputy director in all minority schools. These deputy directors were invested with such power that any school action became impossible without their agreement. When a Greek director retired or died, he was not replaced and thus the management of these schools passed directly to the control of the Turkish deputy directors appointed by the Ministry of Education. In some cases, the school was kept open on paper despite the absence of students to allow a Turkish deputy director to keep his position of convenience. In this way, not only a Turkish director was kept in his position but also the Turkish government did not attract the anger of its Western partners because of the closure of one more Greek school.

Moreover, from 1964 the difficulties in the recruitment of Greek teachers in minority schools began. From this time, an aptitude test in the Turkish language became compulsory, immediately eliminating several candidates. At the same time, inspections of minority schools were becoming extremely frequent and harsh. It was during the same period that the difficulties began for the repair and expansion of school buildings, as with other public buildings belonging to the minority elsewhere.

All these interventions in minority schools were possible thanks to a law passed in 1961 (number 222), which henceforth considered minority schools as 'private schools' and not as 'community schools'. In March 1964, a government decree (number 410/16) prohibited members of the Orthodox clergy from entering minority schools. In September 1964, another decree (number 3885) prohibited Orthodox prayers in courses as well as school books.[57] Thus, a kind of 'secularisation' from the top down took place at the end of the 1960s. All these educational restrictions considerably disturbed the minority. Not only were the schools threatened with closure because of the drop in population, but moreover their control passed gradually into the hands of the central state, putting an end to a communitarianism to which the minority had been accustomed for centuries.

These direct pressures on minority schools were followed by another application that indirectly affected minority education. In 1971, given the disastrous situation of universities where gangs of armed students clashed every day, the government of the time decided to close all private universities. And the Theological School of Halki, which depended directly on the Patriarchate and which was the cradle of Greek Orthodoxy, also closed. This closure was not forced, but the patriarchal authorities preferred to put an end to the activities of the Academy rather than let it become a school dependent on the Turkish Ministry of National Education. Let us understand that the 1971 decision was not a measure against the minority in general or against minority education in particular, but it was a measure of general application for the whole country. It was later, when the opening of other private universities was allowed and the reopening of the Halki Theological School was not that this became a real minority problem. The Theological School of Halki is still closed in 2024.

How Many Greeks Remain in Turkey?

As one can see immediately, there are today two main problems that the Greek minority schools face in Turkey. The first one is obvious, as the Greeks of Istanbul are still not seen as first class citizens but as means of pressure on Greece, Greek schools are constantly objects of policy implementations related not to the Greek children of Turkish citizenship but related to bilateral relations! The second problem is naturally related to demographics. Today, depending on how one defines the 'Greekness' of Turkey, there are only between 3,000 and 10,000 'Greeks' of Turkish citizenship living in Turkey. According to several surveys, those who are named 'Polites' (i.e., Greeks of Istanbul) are around 3,000 and most are elderly.[58] To them, one may add around 2,000 other Greeks of Turkey mainly from the two Aegean islands, Imbros and Tenedos. Greeks from these two islands migrated, mostly to Greece and elsewhere, but those who remain in Turkey live in Istanbul and partially on the islands, especially in summertime.

There is another group. In 1923, when the compulsory exchange of populations was decided in Lausanne, the city of Antioch was in Syria under French mandate. Thus, the Arabic-speaking orthodox community of the city remained at home. Therefore, when Antioch was reattached to Turkey in 1939, around 15,000 Christians automatically became Turkish citizens. During several decades, these Christians left Turkey, mainly for Europe, especially Scandinavian countries. Nevertheless, after 1990s, the Arabic-speaking orthodox

population of the city that could remain in Turkey despite harsh life conditions started to emigrate to Istanbul. And as the perception of the Turkish
republic is still related to religious belonging (and not ethnicity of language),
they have been considered as 'Rum' (i.e., Greek Orthodox). Consequently,
they have the 'right' to use the Greek minority's institutions, including schools
(and foundations). Their number disputed, but in total they are believed to be
5,000, with 2,000 of these in Istanbul.[59] This addition makes, at best, a Greek
Orthodox population of 10,000 in a country of 82,000,0000!

And How Many Students and Teachers?

The automatic consequence of this demographic collapse is easy to understand. While in 1922 there were 1245 Greek schools in the Ottoman territories, in 2022, exactly one century later, there were only seven that remained
open.[60] These schools are Zapeion, Zografeion, Fener, Langa and Prinkipos
(Büyükada) in Istanbul and two schools in Imbros (Gökçeada) attended by
around 300 pupils of all ages. Each year, there are five to ten students who
are enrolled in these schools, with the basic requirement being that the student must be Greek Orthodox of Turkish citizenship. This requirement was
introduced by the Ministry of National Education in 1968. This requirement
means that not only non-Orthodox families cannot send their children to
these schools but in addition (and this is the most important point) children of
Greek Orthodox families, diplomats, businessmen and women, teachers, and
so on, who are not Turkish citizens cannot either.

In addition, it is not only Greeks who are very few in number; some families do not send their children to minority schools for several reasons, such as
the reputation of bad quality, the fear of being labelled and because many of
the Arabic-speaking Orthodox population attend these schools. We will come
back to this question.

The quality of the education in these schools suffers mainly because of
the misuse of the principle of reciprocity between Greece and Turkey. In this
framework, sixteen contingent teachers can be appointed in these schools. In
1973, it was decided that teachers could be appointed for the courses where
there might be a quota deficit in schools. Within the framework of reciprocity,
it was decided that sixteen teachers would go to Western Thrace, while sixteen
teachers would come to schools in Istanbul and Gökçeada. Normally, in line

with human rights legislation, such reciprocity cannot be applied to the citizens of a state; in other words, the use of reciprocity on minority rights is unlawful and unethical. The same principle is also used for schoolbooks in Greek schools. Books coming from Greece are tightly controlled and specifically not appropriate for Greek language learning students. Students who receive education in the mother tongue (Greek) in schools that have the curriculum of the Ministry of National Education and have the status of private minority school use both Turkish textbooks and Greek textbooks from Greece. This is done in order to impose books and curriculum from Turkey in Western Thrace. This treats a minority always as a 'minority', not as adults, the other meaning of the word in French, who remain under the strict control of the state, under the cover of protection.

Another issue preventing Greek families from sending their children to these schools is the issue of the Turkish deputy director acting like a nanny to control and scold. The position, which was started in 1937, ended in 1948–9 and re-established in 1962, previously referred to as the Turkish Deputy Director, and now as the Chief Deputy Director, is also included in the new regulation. The word 'Turkish' disappeared in the reform of education in 2012 but de facto it's still the case.

And finally, one can mention the financial problems of the minority schools. Most of the buildings are old constructions from the nineteenth century needing constant maintenance and repair. Foundations that own these buildings do not have enough resources, and they are not allowed to receive donations. As is the case, for example, of the Phanar Greek school dating back to 1881–3.

How to Save Greek Schools of Istanbul?

The situation of Greek schools of Istanbul is critical and requires urgent solutions. Three main ongoing processes and their combination are capable of guaranteeing the survival of these schools.

First of all, one must mention the 'Arabisation', which comes from the Arabic-speaking Orthodox population, mainly from Antioch, creating a minority within the minority, at least sociologically speaking. Unlike the remaining bourgeois Greek families of Polis, Arabs who immigrated to Istanbul do not hesitate to send their children to minority schools. The result is very paradoxical. In many classes, children from Arabic-speaking families are in majority as for example at the Phanar Greek school. Nevertheless, we should emphasise the fact that the Arabic-speaking Orthodox population in Istanbul has lived in the city for at least twenty years now, and most of the children are initiated into the Greek language since kindergarten. The attitude of *Polites* (Greeks of Istanbul) towards these children at Greek schools is very ambiguous. While many families think that the presence of these Arab children at Greek schools is a problem, degenerating the *Polites* identity, others, on the contrary, consider that their presence saves not only the schools but all minority institutions that are otherwise threatened with closure.

The second option for survival is immigration. This has two different aspects. On the one hand, following the 2008 economic crisis in Greece, in a relatively peaceful atmosphere of Greek–Turkish relations, several Greek citizens, some of them being the descendants of former *Polites* but also other young Greeks in search of economic dynamism, came to settle in Turkey, mainly in Istanbul.[61] In 2024, approximately 2,800 Greek citizens (including students) live in Turkey, and some of them send their children to Greek minority schools even if these children cannot obtain their graduation because they are not Turkish citizens! These 'guest students' comprise, for example, around 15 to 50 students of the Zografeion school. Another example is in Imbros. The Private Gökçeada Greek Primary School, which started its educational life in 1951 under the name of Aya Theodori, was closed in 1964 due to the tense Cyprus policies. It was reopened in 2012 after forty-eight years, and the school started its first lesson with four students. Noting that most of the students at the school were residents of Gökçeada, the children of quota teachers from Greece were also educated. If the settlement of Greek citizens in Turkey becomes stable, and if foreign citizens obtain the right to graduate from minority schools, the Greek schools of Turkey may find a new lease of life.

The second aspect of immigration is related to Syrians. In 2022, according to several statistics, around 5,000,000 Syrians live in Turkey under the temporary protection of the UNCHR. In Syria, 10 per cent of the population is Christian (Orthodox or Nestorian),[62] but there is no data about the percentage of Christians among 'refugees'. Nevertheless, it would not be a surprise to see Syrian Arabic-speaking Orthodox families' children in the Greek Schools of Istanbul. This additional population may also allow the survival of minority schools if the Greek minority of Turkey does not fall into the trap of racism that shakes Turkish society in 2022.

There is a third option, which is also an ongoing process. This process can be called 'folklorisation' because schools are not used anymore only for educational purposes but serve as venues for exhibitions, conferences, concerts and so on. For example, Galata Greek Primary School was built at the end of the nineteenth century in order to contribute to the education and training of Greek children. Located in Galata, one of the oldest districts of Istanbul, with its neo-classical architectural style, the school had to cease its activities in September 1988 due to the demographic problems that arose, especially since the 1960s and 1970s. The school, which started to serve as a kindergarten in 2001, was closed once again in 2007 due to the lack of pupils. Galata Greek Primary School reopened its doors in 2012 for 'Adhocracy', one of the two main exhibitions of the Istanbul Design Biennial and curated by Joseph Grima.

Similarly, The Yoakimion Greek Girls' School started to be used as an exhibition space, like the Galata Greek School. The first exhibition in the school building was the sculpture exhibition titled 'Me, me, between worlds and between heavens', of the Greek artist Kalliopi Lemos (describes male violence).

The Greek schools of Turkey, especially in Istanbul, cannot only be seen as educational institutions. They represent at the very same time the glorious and rich past of the community and its uncertain future. Thus, their protection is not only an issue of the transmission of the knowledge. It is about interiorising and legitimation of the Greek past of the city, which means the rich and diverse heritage of the Ottoman Empire. Therefore, the existence of the Greek schools of Istanbul, their educational and cultural activities, is not only a problem of the Greek minority. It is directly related to the entire Turkish society and the state.

The Patriarchate: From Human Dimension to Institutional Strength

Before delving into the analysis of the history of the Patriarchate during the early decades of the Republic of Turkey, we need to geographically locate this institution. The Patriarchate is located in Istanbul, situated in the historic peninsula of the city, on the European coast, more precisely in one of the oldest neighbourhoods of the city on the shores of the Golden Horn (*Haliç*): the Phanar (*Fener/Fanarion*).

This has been an important concentration area for Greeks in Istanbul since Byzantine times. The name of the neighbourhood comes from the Greek word 'fanarion', which means a lighthouse. From this word, the adjective 'Phanariotes' was derived, which refers to the Greek aristocracy of the Ottoman period.[63] The name of the neighbourhood is certainly due to the presence of a gate in the Byzantine walls, Porta Phanari, which has now disappeared. But the name of the neighbourhood is still the same today.

The importance and renown of the neighbourhood undoubtedly come from the presence of the Patriarchate and the influential Greek community that was there. In the seventeenth century, it was a residential district with its stone houses and richly decorated facades. Some educated Greek Phanariotes served in the Ottoman diplomacy. Travellers in the nineteenth century indicated that it was a rich, chic and quiet neighbourhood.[64]

It was in the eighteenth and nineteenth centuries that aristocratic Greek families began to build villas around the Patriarchate. These were luxurious stone or brick houses, with two or three floors. During the second half of the nineteenth century, wealthy families left the neighbourhood for the shores of the Bosphorus, while middle-class families settled there. Until the 1960s, the neighbourhood retained its Greek character. Since then, it has become one of the most dilapidated old neighbourhoods, with a population of immigrants from rural areas (mainly from the Black Sea region)[65] until the spectacular urban transformation of 2010 and the settlement of new conservative bourgeoisie.

It is in this highly colourful neighbourhood that the Patriarchate is located, on a small street starting from the ancient Porta Fanari, Sadrazam Ali Paşa Caddesi. The Patriarchate has been there since 1601. Before that date, the institution had other locations: first the Church of Saint Irene, then the Cathedral of Saint Sophia (315–1453) and then the Church of the Holy Apostles of Nicaea during the Latin occupation (1205–62) before returning to Istanbul at the Church of the Holy Apostles of Istanbul (1453–6), then at the Church of Pammakaristhos (1456–1587); following the conversion of this church into a mosque (Fethiye Camii), it was transferred to the Palace of Blachernae (1587–97) and finally it was located in the Church of Saint Demetrius of Ksiloporta (1597–1600).[66]

The construction of the core of the current building dates back to the time of Patriarch Ioachim III (1901–12), while the other sections were built during the Patriarchate of Yermanos V (1913–18). The central building is located in a courtyard that can be entered through three arched doors. The middle door has not been used since the hanging of Patriarch Grigorios V at this location in 1821. Access to the Patriarchate is through the two adjacent doors.

There are several buildings in the Patriarchate courtyard. Through the southern annex door, one enters the patriarchal church, while the northern door (the usual access to the Patriarchate) leads to the patriarchal building. This building, as well as the other structures of the Patriarchate, are backed by the Byzantine walls of Constantinople. The clergy dormitories, offices and library are located in this elongated section. This part of the Patriarchate was devastated by a fire in 1941. Turkey was then in a very delicate economic, political and social situation. A climate of suspicion towards non-Muslims prevailed. Thus, economic difficulties combined with this climate prevented the reconstruction of the Patriarchate during the war years. Although Greek–Turkish relations were good during the decade following World War II, the patriarchal building remained in ruins. The institution remained confined to a few intact buildings. From the late 1950s onwards, all hope of authorisation to rebuild disappeared. Indeed, from the second half of the 1950s, Greco-Turkish relations were affected by the Cyprus issue, and the Patriarchate, as well as the Greek minority as a whole, played the role of hostages in the hands of various Turkish governments and were used against the Greek authorities; this was despite the view of the Turkish authorities and general Turkish public opinion that Greek identity was taken into consideration as a whole without differentiation. This means that Greeks in Turkey, Greeks in Cyprus, Greeks in the United States, as well as all institutions related to this Greek identity (through language or religion, such as the Patriarchate) are considered to be an integral part of Greece. Thus, disagreements or even rivalries within the Orthodox Greek world are never taken into account. Therefore, treating the Greek minority in Turkey well is equivalent to a gesture towards Greece, and allowing a restoration of the Patriarchate would be an even more significant action. However, this is a double mistake. Not only is there a historical rivalry between the Patriarchate of Istanbul and the Church of Greece,[67] but the minority does not necessarily identify with the Patriarchate either.

Thus, the authorisation for the reconstruction of the Patriarchate depended on the municipality of Fatih (District of Istanbul under whose jurisdiction the patriarchal building is located), the municipality of Istanbul, as well as the Ministry of Foreign Affairs. It can therefore be said that patriarchal affairs depend on two paradoxical powers: a micro-dependence (municipality of a neighbourhood for an institution that claims to be ecumenical) and a macro-dependence (Ministry of Foreign Affairs, while the Turkish Republic considers the Patriarchate as the religious leader of a few thousand Greeks remaining in Turkey). Under these conditions, it is not surprising that this authorisation did not come quickly, as the parameters are complex and intertwined and not necessarily logical.

The atmosphere of mistrust has never dissipated, even after the separation of Cyprus in 1974. Over the last thirty years, there have been three official requests for authorisation for reconstruction: in 1978, 1979 and 1985.[68] All three requests were refused by the governments of the time within the framework of the prohibition for minority foundations to possess new properties. Thus, it took until 1987 for authorisation to be granted.

Lausanne: The New Turkey No Longer Wants the Patriarchate

World War I, as well as the Greek-Turkish War that followed, left multiple wounds in the Turkish psyche. These wars worked as a catalyst to create a nation that would adapt to the newly established Turkish state. One of these wounds was, of course, the loss of trust in the nations surrounding Turkey, some of which were even within its borders. As the construction of a nation can only be achieved through differentiation from other nations, the Turkish nation also created enemies both externally and internally. Among the enemies within, the 'Rum millet', or the Greek nation, holds a particular place. Turkish historiography accuses Greeks of three distinct evils:

- Of irredentism: since the creation of the Greek state, Greek populations in the Ottoman Empire have risen up or supported the Greek state to expand its territory.
- Of collaboration: Greeks in the Ottoman Empire welcomed the defeat of the Ottoman Empire, the occupation of cities, such as Istanbul and Izmir, by the Allies and subsequently actively collaborated with Greek armies that invaded western Anatolia.
- Of plotting, notably through Greek institutions in the Empire, associations and schools, but primarily through the Church.

This is how the idea of the Greeks in the Empire as a compact and institutionalised body, pledging allegiance more to Greece than to the Sublime Porte
and later to Ankara, was born. At the beginning of World War I, Ottoman
authorities pointed the finger at the various millets accused of collaboration.[69]
The Arabs were accused of aiding the British, the Armenians of aiding the
Russians, and so on. In this configuration, the Patriarchate was seen as a leader
of treachery, being the largest minority institution in the Empire.

But it should be remembered that at the beginning of the war, Greece was
not yet explicitly involved. Despite pressure from both sides, perhaps because
of this pressure, Greek leaders were divided on what approach to take. While
King Constantine seemed pro-German, Prime Minister Eleftherios Venizelos
had a pro-Entente attitude. It was only in June 1917, after bitter internal
debates and schisms, that Greece finally decided to join the war with the Allied
countries and therefore against Germany and the Ottoman Empire. It should
be noted that Greek and Ottoman armies did not confront each other during the last two years of the war, but it would not be wrong to say that the
Greek populations in the Empire (but also obviously the Armenian populations) were constantly and strongly accused of betraying the state, or having
the potential for betrayal. This suspicion reached its peak with the mass depor-
tation quickly becoming a genocide of Armenians in 1915. Other suspicions,
justified or not, of espionage, aid to the enemy, and so on, became common-
place. In any case, the Greek Patriarchate was considered the nest of all betray-
als. It cannot be said that the armistice of Mudros and the Treaty of Sèvres of
1920, which sealed the complete dismantling of the Empire,[70] greatly saddened
the Greeks of Istanbul, who welcomed the Allies warmly.

The end of the Greek–Turkish war marks the beginning of a long period
of negotiations between Greece and Turkey on the one hand, and between
Turkey and the Allies on the other. The delegations met for over six months
in the Swiss city of Lausanne. The Turkish delegation was led by Ismet Pasha,
the victor of the Inönü battle and one of Mustafa Kemal's most loyal collaborators. Paul Dumont describes him as follows:

On this occasion, he was promoted to Minister of Foreign Affairs. As a career soldier, it was not with great enthusiasm that he donned the diplomat's mantle. But
he is well-suited to this new role. Intelligent and tenacious, yet flexible enough to

concede on minor points, he has already demonstrated his negotiating skills in Mudanya. His firmness, his persistence, and his agility of mind have proven to be highly effective.[71]

During the Lausanne negotiations, what Paul Dumont refers to as 'minor points' means the maintenance of a Greek community and the Patriarch-ate in Istanbul, among other things. In his memoirs, Ismet Pasha himself recounts how he was forced to give in to Eleftherios Venizelos and George Curzon's insistence on the issue of this maintenance, which goes hand in hand with the maintenance of the Patriarchate.[72] Indeed, that was the real issue. What mattered to Greece and partly to the Western powers was, more than the maintenance of a Greek community in Turkey, the maintenance of the Patriarchate in Istanbul. For the Turks, the starting point of the negotia-tions was to exempt the Muslims of Western Thrace from the exchange, but to integrate the Rums of Istanbul and especially the Patriarchate.[73] But as any negotiation implies a compromise, both communities remained in place in a *reciprocal* manner.[74]

Thus, the Greeks of Istanbul (Rum), at least those who have lived there since 1918, have been granted the status of 'établis',[75] forming in some sense a material justification for the maintenance of the Patriarchate. Because of the insistence of Western powers, the Turkish delegation had only agreed to its maintenance on the condition that it remained a purely religious institution. To maintain a Patriarchate that deals with internal religious affairs in Turkey, without political or international pretensions, faithful followers and thus a substantial Orthodox community were needed.

Here is the situation following the Treaty of Lausanne: the Patriarchate was able to remain in Istanbul but was completely isolated. Isolated from the out-side world, the Orthodox world and even from other Greeks, the majority of whom were now outside the borders of Turkey. It has become, in a way, a local minority church dealing with the religious affairs of a minority of about one 100,000 members. This spatial isolation goes hand in hand with a substantial reduction in prerogatives. Indeed, as part of the standardisation of Turkish legislation, the new civil code became applicable to all Turkish citizens, includ-ing non-Muslim minorities, who in turn renounced paragraph 2 of Article 42 of the Treaty of Lausanne.

The Patriarchate and the New Republic of Turkey

What can be the place of a non-Muslim religious institution in the new configuration of the Republic of Turkey? First of all, it must be emphasised that
all religious institutions were considered by the Kemalist team as obstacles to
the painful transformation of Turkish society, whether they were Muslim or
not. In a country where an institution like the caliphate has been abolished,
how can a non-Muslim institution, maintained under constraint on Turkish
soil and accused of treason, retain some crumbs of its former influence? It
is obvious that the Greek 'oecumenical' Patriarchate in the early decades of
the Turkish Republic is only a shadow of its former self. Radical change in
the Patriarchate's prerogatives intervenes in this atmosphere: the legal unification of the Turkish population and the definitive disappearance of legal
enclaves amputated the Patriarchate of one of its main powers, that of prac-
tising the law, which had firmly attached the institution to the Orthodox
population for centuries. That the Patriarchate is affected by the metamor-
phosis of the Turkish legal system is natural. But this amputation, which is
normal in view of the Kemalist project, comes at a time when this institution
was obliged to reaffirm its legitimacy with the remaining Orthodox population of Turkey. In this sense, the loss of legal prerogatives is a blow to the
Patriarchate vis-à-vis the Greeks of Turkey. But one cannot help but think
that the severing of one of the ties with the minority will serve it later to
devote itself more to general problems of Orthodoxy and will prepare its
return to the international scene.

The first Turkish censuses confirm a relatively strong Greek presence in
Turkey at the beginning of the Republic. According to the 1927 census,[76]
there were 119,822 Greek speakers in Turkey, of whom 91,902 were in Istanbul (11.56 per cent of Istanbul's total population), and 109,905 Orthodox
Christians, of whom 100,214 were in Istanbul (12.61 per cent of the city's
total population).[77] Behind these cold numbers, there are individuals with a
strong sense of identity, who are more or less close to the Patriarchate. During the first few years when the Patriarchate kept some of its legal prerogatives, things did not completely change for the Greeks of Istanbul. However,
the new Turkish Republic had decided to abolish the legal enclaves seen as
the sources of the societal degeneracy. The unification of the state required the

unification of law. It was unthinkable for the Kemalists that certain groups be subject to a different legal framework. Continuing the tradition begun in the *Tanzimat* period (1839–76), the Kemalist team decided to adopt the Swiss Civil Code with slight modifications.[78] Subsequently, the three non-Muslim minorities, Jews, Armenians and Greeks were 'invited' to renounce their customary law. In each minority, a commission was established where civilians dominated the religious leaders.

This renunciation, a true revolution in the concept of citizenship among Turks, seems to have been relatively easy for the Jews, some of whose prominent leaders openly aspired to assimilation.[79] Things were more difficult for the 'non-assimilable' communities of Armenians and Greeks. Members of the minority commissions charged with discussing the renunciation of Article 42 with the government were chosen by the government itself. Despite this, although the process was relatively easy for the Armenian delegation,[80] this was not the case for the Greeks. This was the most resistant community to the pressures of the leaders, partly because of the presence of the Patriarchate as a tutelary institution. It is clear that the patriarchal authorities had no interest in the secularisation of the community, since many of the Patriarchate's prerogatives were disappearing. Following the resistance of the commission, Ankara mandated a sub-committee called the 'initiative committee', tasked with making a petition in favour of abandoning the rights arising from Article 42. Seeing the resistance of the entire minority, some members of this sub-committee were replaced by 'conciliatory' Greeks. On the day of the decision of the 'initiative committee', three delegates who were resolutely opposed were taken into police custody.[81] Finally, on 27 November 1925, six months after the Jewish minority approved it, 55 out of 75 members of the sub-commission approved the abandonment of the rights of Article 42.

Thus, after five centuries under Ottoman domination, the Patriarchate of Constantinople lost one of its most cherished powers. Throughout these centuries, the trend had been the opposite: the expansion of jurisdictional powers, both horizontally (more and more Orthodox community under its jurisdiction) and vertically (more and more prerogatives). However, it should be noted that the desire to abolish the legal enclaves of the state did not arise with the Republic. Already during the *Tanzimat* period, several European codes had been adopted, such as a secularised commercial code. On the other hand, for the civil code, the resistance of religious Muslim and non-Muslim circles had been too strong, and therefore the *Mecelle*, the Ottoman civil code, had been drafted taking into account religious considerations.[82] But if the opposition of Muslim ulema and non-Muslim religious dignitaries had been taken into account in 1870–7, sixty years later all references to religion had disappeared from the Turkish civil code, and one of the prerogatives of the Patriarchate as well.

During this period of shrinkage, the Patriarchate plunged into personal quarrels: since the foundation of the Republic of Turkey, patriarchal elections had always been problematic. In addition to the institution's own internal mechanisms, diplomatic considerations between Athens and Ankara also come into play, further complicating the situation. These quarrels also have an influence on the relations between the Patriarchate and the minority, which sees its supervisory element moving further and further away from it.

During the early years of the Republic, the Patriarchate entered a period of lethargy, confined to its role as the Church of the Greeks in Turkey. The first difficulties began with the new elections to the patriarchal seat, which had been vacant since the forced resignation of Meletios IV.[83] According to the new rules established by the government, not only the candidates and members of the Holy Synod had to be Turkish citizens, but they were also required to hold an effective position in Turkey on the date of the election.[84] Nevertheless, on 6 December 1923, the Metropolitan of Kadıköy was elected Patriarch under the name Grigorios VII. However, discussions about the Patriarchate were not over yet. The abolition of the Caliphate in Turkey in March 1924 brought the expulsion of the patriarchal institution back to the agenda, especially since there was fierce rivalry between The Greek Patriarchate and the Turkish Orthodox Patriarchate of Papa Eftim.[85] All these difficulties took a new turn with the death of Grigorios in November 1924, after only 11 months of patriarchy. From that date on, the institution entered a phase of instability that partly explains this lethargy.

First, the election of Konstantinos VI caused a crisis because he was considered 'exchangeable' by the Turkish authorities. With the support of the mixed commission for population exchange, Turkey expelled Konstantinos VI on 29 January 1925, sending him to Thessaloniki, which caused a serious Greek–Turkish crisis.[86] Greece described this act as 'more serious than the hanging of Grigorios V in 1821'.[87] This crisis was overcome thanks to a compromise, all the more welcome since both countries were facing difficult internal and external situations and did not need further external problems. Konstantinos V was forced to resign on 22 May 1925. Two names were presented for the vacant seat: the Metropolitan of Nicaea (Iznik) Vasilios and the Metropolitan of Chalcedon (Kadıköy) Ioakim. But the latter was very unpopular with the Turkish authorities because of his actions during the Greco-Turkish War. Thus, it was Vasilios who was elected Patriarch at the age of seventy-nine years. Due to his advanced age, his patriarchy was not very remarkable and ended four years later, in September 1929, with his death. After more than three months of procrastination and manoeuvring, Fotios II was elected Patriarch on 7 January 1930. The period of Fotios was flourishing due to the Greek–Turkish period of friendship established by Venizelos and Mustafa Kemal. In fact, it was Mustafa Kemal himself who, in a telegram of congratulations, somewhat legitimised the patriarch again by calling him 'the Orthodox Patriarch who is at the Phanar' instead of the usual '*Baş Papaz*' (chief priest). It was also during this period of normalisation of bilateral relations that we see the high representatives of the Greek state, including Venizelos in 1931, visiting the Patriarchate. At the death of Fotios in 1935, the Patriarchate had partly regained its prestige and emerged from its isolation. Several representatives of the Turkish state were present at the Patriarch's funeral, which had never happened before.

A few weeks after Fotios' death, on 18 January 1936, the Metropolitan of Iznik Veniamin was elected Patriarch, against the favourite, Metropolitan of Kadıköy Maximos, who was not wanted by the Turkish authorities. This succession of patriarchs from 1923 to 1936 should not obscure the delicate situation of the Patriarchate during these early years of the Republic, when the nationalisation (Turkification) of the entire country was underway. The true blossoming of the Patriarchate would come after the Second World War, with the election of Maksimos V in 1946 and the beginning of the Cold War.

Patriarchate during World War II

The institution welcomed the troubled period of the Second World War following the death of Mustafa Kemal because the regime had changed its orientation slightly, and a heavy suspicion had begun to weigh again on non-Muslims in the country. It is evident that this suspicion was exercised towards all non-Muslims, but the Patriarchate seems to occupy a particular place in the eyes of Turkish leaders as well as public opinion. Even in a phase of lethargy, the Patriarchate was considered a rooted and strong structure capable of betraying the Turkish nation, as it did in the past.

Mistrust is perhaps the word that best explains this general atmosphere. Nevertheless, it must be admitted that the Patriarchate was in such a situation of isolation that it could not even protect the Greek community of Turkey from discriminatory actions. One can say that the five years of this war, in which Turkey did not take part, were the most difficult for all non-Muslims and their institutions.

A first observation to be made about the situation of the Patriarchate during these years is that of its external isolation. Since 1923, when during the negotiations in Lausanne, the Turkish authorities only accepted the maintenance of the Patriarchate in Turkey on condition that it become a local church without ecumenical pretensions, the Patriarchate had remained apart from the Orthodox world. This isolation cannot be explained solely by the attitude of the Turkish governments. At least two other reasons that are equally valid can be proposed.

First, the personality of Patriarch Veniamin was quite unobtrusive, especially when compared to other patriarchs, such as Athenagoras or later Bartholomeos. He did not take many risks inside the country nor many initiatives outside. Veniamin was a compromising Patriarch. After the death of Patriarch Fotio II on 29 December 1935, Turkish authorities supported Iacob Papapaisou, Metropolitan of Imbros and Tenedos, for his pro-Turkish positions and his opposition to the Union of Churches movement, which could compromise its isolation wanted by Ankara. Greece, on the other hand, openly supported Metropolitan of Chalcedon, Maximos Vapozortis, who was considered too young by Ankara (in 1936 he was 38 years old) and too energetic! He was also very (too) popular among the Greeks in Istanbul. He gave the impression of wanting to update the institution's international network, which was not to the liking of Turkish leaders. The day before the election of the Holy Synod, his candidacy was invalidated on a technicality! Thus, on 19 January 1936, the Holy Synod reluctantly elected the elderly Metropolitan of Heraklion (Ereğli), Veniamin Christodoulou. Immediately after his election, a protest was staged by discontented Greeks in Turkey, and the Turkish police had to intervene.[88] Veniamin's short reign satisfied Turkish authorities. The little internationalisation initiated under his predecessor Photios II was abruptly stopped. The only action towards the outside world by Veniamin was not to hinder the independence movements of the Albanian (1937) and Bulgarian (1945) churches.[89]

But there was another reason for international isolation. It was the revival of the Patriarchate of Moscow, eternal rival of that of Constantinople. The Russian Patriarch Tikhon had died in 1925. He had left to the believers a spiritual testament telling them that while not compromising on matters of faith, they should be loyal to the Soviet government.[90] Apart from questionable ideological reasons, the Soviet authorities considered it difficult to find another patriarch as conciliatory. Tikhon's designated successors, such as Metropolitan Peter, Metropolitan Serge,[91] and Metropolitan Seraphim successively refused to submit to communist power,[92] leaving the patriarchal seat vacant. Thus, for more than 15 years, the Russian Orthodox Church withdrew from political life without disappearing. This Church did not seek to overthrow Soviet power and did not engage in politics, but it did not intend to serve the government or become a state institution. If the Church was forbidden from disapproving of the government's actions, it should not have the right to approve of them either, as that also amounts to meddling in politics. This radical separation of the Russian Church from politics is followed by an ideological period called the 'five-year atheistic period' (1932–7), during which churches and clergy were heavily taxed. Churches were closed, bells were removed and icons were burned. Repression and arrests of clergy intensified. Priests were often forced to hide, and itinerant priests appeared who travelled from village to village. It was during this time that the underground Church of the 'catacombs' emerged.

Throughout this period, the Patriarchate of Constantinople could have taken advantage of the situation to occupy a predominant place in the Orthodox world. However, being itself in a (passive) opposition situation to the central power, the Patriarchate of Constantinople found neither the energy nor the necessary conditions, and perhaps not even the will, to take the leadership in the Orthodox world. It was only from 1943 that the Soviets understood the importance of the Russian Church, especially for the domination of Eastern European countries that were engaged in the war. After 1943, the persecution of believers came to an end. Church life became more peaceful, religious services were restored, and some 200 churches and convents were reopened in 1943 and 1944. Priests who had kept their ecclesiastical activities secret returned to their pastoral work, and former monks were granted the opportunity to reintegrate into monasteries. From 1943, theology schools were reopened. The number of faithful continued to increase. A large number of believers who had joined the 'living church' or who had hidden their religious opinions for many years returned to the ranks of the traditional church.[93] But above all, in 1943, Sergei was elected Patriarch of Moscow and all Russia. Although his reign was very brief (he died in May 1944), it was indeed the revival of the Patriarchate of Moscow. In January 1945, the Council of the Russian Church elected Alexis, the former Metropolitan of Leningrad, as Patriarch of Moscow and all Russia. During the session of the Council in question, in addition to the two Patriarchs of the East (Alexandria and Antioch), representatives of the Patriarchate of Constantinople and dignitaries of other autocephalous Orthodox churches were present.

At the end of World War II, Moscow began to take an interest in the entire Orthodox world outside of Russia. The Balkans had a special place in this new policy, but the Orthodox of Syria, Lebanon and Palestine also attracted Moscow's attention, to the great deception of the Patriarchate of Constantinople. At the end of the War, the Patriarchate of Constantinople had truly become a small national church that could not claim any international role.

This situation of isolation on the international stage, both politically and spiritually, obviously had implications within Turkey. During this period of seclusion, the Patriarchate truly refocused its activities on the Greek minority of Turkey in accordance with the will of the Turkish authorities. The 1930s were the period when the Patriarchate and the Greek minority of Istanbul were closest. Despite this unprecedented closeness, and despite the concentration on internal religious affairs, the Patriarchate also showed signs of isolation internally. Above all, it no longer had the power, prestige or weight of the past with the Turkish officials to intervene in favour of the Greeks of Turkey. During World War II, the Patriarchate also lost its protective role for Orthodox people against the central government. Thus, not only did it no longer represent power vis-à-vis the Orthodox population, but it could no longer represent the minority vis-à-vis the government. This dual role, this intermediary function that made the Patriarchate an essential institution in the cohesion of the Ottoman population, has completely disappeared under the Republic, so much so that for the first time, the 'usefulness' of such an institution has become a subject of discussion, albeit timidly, within the minority. It is true that during World War II, the Greek minority of Turkey, to which the Patriarchate was organically attached, greatly needed a protective institution. Because with the outbreak of the War, minorities in suspicious Turkey were once again in a bad position.

With the outbreak of the war, it was the end of good times for everyone, certainly, but in Turkey, which remained steadfastly outside of the war, the situation of minorities became even more delicate. The country was hit hard by the economic, political, ideological and psychological impact of the war, caught between a difficult balancing policy and an exacerbated nationalism. Two facts will draw our attention, which concern more particularly the Greeks and other minorities: the military mobilisation of minorities in special groups in 1941 and the very infamous wealth tax in 1942.

It should be noted from the outset that the policy of the Turkish state towards non-Muslims in general and Greeks in particular has been very contradictory. While minorities were prohibited from attending military schools,[94] Turkey was aiding Greece under Italian and German rule[95]; while Jewish professors from Germany came to teach in Turkish universities,[96] a boat full of Jews, the Struma, was abandoned to its tragic fate,[97] and at the same time Turkish diplomats were working to save Jews from Western Europe.[98] Not everything is certainly black and not everything is white either. It is imperative not to view Turkey's minority policies during World War II as a uniform bloc. There were certainly Turanist and even racist circles in the political and military elites,[99] but those who had a humanistic approach were not lacking either. The facts and statements are so contradictory that the proponents of the two extreme visions, those who defend the thesis of Turkey's unquestionable tolerance and those who defend the idea of racism and ethnic discrimination find their account. It is by taking into account these paradoxes as well as the economic, political, but above all psychological position of Turkey, that the following lines should be read.

The Patriarchate's first weakness in protecting Greeks in Turkey was the military mobilisation of minorities in special battalions. It should be noted, however, that this kind of mobilisation was not new in Turkish history; during World War I, the labour battalions (*Amele Taburu*) were exclusively formed by non-Muslims. But in 1941, Turkey was not participating in the war, so this was a preventative action. Furthermore, military service was used as a punishment for all opponents of the regime and was perceived as such as long as it was carried out with minorities. After these warnings, attention can now be drawn to the disappointment of the Greeks in Turkey with the impotence of the Patriarchal authorities. While there were protests from the Patriarchate against this mobilisation, they were of no use.

There are few sources that clearly highlight the conditions under which this special mobilisation of minorities, commonly known in Turkey as 'Yirmi kura askerlik' ('Military service of twenty age classes'),[100] took place. According to testimonies, starting in 1941, non-Muslims aged 20 to 40 were mobilised into battalions specifically created for them, without the right to bear arms or wear standard military uniforms, and they used for public works such as road construction. We say 'according to testimonies' because there is no official text that clearly indicates such a situation. Moreover, it would be unthinkable in a country where the criterion of legal membership in the nation is citizenship to see official discriminatory provisions towards any particular component of the population. Thus, everything happens not in the texts but in the application of these same texts with a deliberate will of discrimination but also, and often, with unconscious attitudes.

The same question can be asked for the 'wealth tax' instituted in 1942, during a period of German victories. In any case, the wealth tax was the culmination of a policy of Turkification of the economy begun at the end of the Ottoman Empire.[101] The observer is struck by the concordance of the anti-minority climate created by the press and policies targeting these minorities. It is difficult to construct a chronology of the political agenda and the public agenda, and therefore it is difficult to know whether measures targeting non-Muslims are the result of pressure from public opinion or whether this public opinion is artificially created by decision-makers to prepare the ground for these measures. In both cases, it would be wrong to underestimate the role of popular and populist press.

It is symptomatic to see that the Patriarchate reacted to the implementation of this tax only when its own assets were targeted. In the memoirs of two

Greeks of Istanbul, Nikos Apostolidis[102] and Simos Bafeiadis,[103] we learn that the Greek community of Istanbul was very upset by this indifference; both protested to Turkish officials for a reduction in their tax but did not receive any discount. According to Bafeiadis, it was following the imposition of taxes on churches and institutions that the Patriarchate reacted (not in response to the individual imposition of taxes on Greeks of Istanbul). A committee was created under the chairmanship of the Metropolitan of Chalcedon (Kadıköy) to meet with Prime Minister Saraçoğlu, but this meeting was unsuccessful. However, Alexis Alexandris does not mention the creation of such a committee. He simply reports the opposition of the Patriarchal authorities to the exile of the Metropolitans of Chalcedon and Imbros to Bursa.[104]

This feeling of indifference is accentuated when we look at other small Orthodox communities, such as the 1,400 people in the Bulgarian Orthodox population who formed a separate community without recognising the supremacy of the Patriarchate. It should be noted that throughout the nineteenth and even twentieth centuries, Bulgarian Orthodox and Greek Orthodox populations were in competition. According to Halil İnalcık, there were attempts to 'Hellenise' the Bulgarians in the city, which the Bulgarians resisted.[105] The strong presence of this community in the 1940s is visible, and we can mention the restoration of the great Bulgarian Orthodox church of St. Stephen, on the shore of the Golden Horn, opposite the Patriarchate in 1946.[106] Therefore, the Bulgarian Orthodox population should not be considered part of the Greek Orthodox minority in Istanbul. The same goes for the Russian-speaking Orthodox population of Istanbul who, descended from the White Russians who arrived in the 1920s, form a separate community with their own social and religious networks, although there have apparently been mixed marriages between Russian Orthodox and Greek Orthodox communities.[107]

The case of the 7,000 people of the Arab-speaking Orthodox population is a bit more complicated. These is the Orthodox population of Antakya (Antioch) who, until the 1990s, were not part of the minority insofar as very few lived in Istanbul. However, minority Greek schools, minority religious foundations and other structures are located in Istanbul. Since the 1990s, they have been emigrating en masse to Istanbul, where they are integrating as best they can into the minority as we saw earlier while discussing the fate of Greek Schools in Istanbul.

As a result, the Patriarchate had not only been cut off from its traditional base, the Greek-speaking Orthodox population of Istanbul (not to mention those of Imbros and Tenedos), but it had also distanced itself from other Orthodox communities in the country, even though this could have been an opportune context for closer ties with these communities.

It is in these complex conditions that we can say the fate of the Greeks in Turkey diverges from that of other minorities. Starting from the 1950s, the Greeks separated themselves due to their primary role in Turkish foreign policy and in a broader sense than one may think. Not only were the Greeks in Istanbul an asset for Ankara in its dealings with Greece, but the Patriarchate, which had been very discreet during the war, became a major factor in Turkish–American, Turkish–Soviet and even Russo–American relations. After the 1950s, one can see the growing importance of the Patriarchate, which also transformed from a local actor to a bilateral and then international actor.

What can we take away from these early decades of the Republic regarding the Patriarchate of Istanbul? While 1923 (Treaty of Lausanne) was a rupture in Turkey's history, as well as for Anatolian Hellenism and Greco-Turkish relations, should it also be considered a rupture for the Patriarchate? It is evident that with the compulsory exchange, the Greek community in the city was amputated from a part of its members (those settled in Istanbul before 1918 or living outside the municipal limits), and it is also evident that with laws such as those on professions, names or civil rights, the status of the Greek minority changed. But can we say that in daily life, Greeks of Istanbul perceived this modification? Certainly, some of them, close to Ottoman power or hoping for the arrival of more Greeks from Greece were disappointed; this was different for the Greeks of Asia minor or Thrace who had their lives turned upside down. But this upheaval is valid for all Turkish citizens. We can see through testimonies that members of the minority continue to live in a more or less closed community, not to say closed in on itself. The opening to the majority, but paradoxically also a marginalisation, took place during World War II, when the Greeks of Turkey fully realised their fragile and even dangerous minority status. This same observation applied to the Patriarchate as well, whose situation is different from that of the minority. Despite this, we have the impression that precisely because of its isolation, the 1930s were the republican period when the Patriarchate was closest to the minority. These were the years when the Patriarchate truly functioned as a local church devoted to the religious affairs of the minority remaining in Istanbul. From the end of World War II, the destinies of the Patriarchate and the minority separated, the former becoming increasingly important and the latter becoming smaller and smaller.

The Istanbul Greeks in Greece

The presentation of the Istanbul Greek minority would be lacking without a mention of those who left. Indeed, a strong majority of them still have a Stanbuliot identity, or at least a memory of this identity, even for those born in Greece but with parents of Stanbuliot origin. Not unlike most 'exiled' communities, this one also entertains, and sometimes even amplifies, this identity. The memories of a painful past are deformed, and even the children born in Greece, such as the ones of those who left in the 1980s for economic reasons, talk about their 'unbearable experiences'.

According to an estimate, there are approximately 30,000 Turkish-native Greeks in Greece (excluding the exchanged population of 1923).[108] Even if the myth entertained in Turkey that Turkey's Greeks were never able to integrate is completely untrue, we must admit that, at least for Istanbul, Imbros and Tenedos Greeks, a geographical reunification and a community-like sense of solidarity occurred in Greece. This principally concerns the Athens suburbs, such as the Paleo Phaliron, Nea Smyrni and Kallithea neighbourhoods. There are more in big Greek cities such as Thessaloniki.

There are several associations founded by the community members living in Greece. The most important ones are: the Constantinopolitans Association; the New Circle of Constantinopolitans; the Association of Greeks Expatriated from Turkey; the Constantinopolitans Union of Northern Greece; the Thrace Association of Imbros, Constantinople, Tenedos and Western Thrace Citizens; and the Constantinopolitans Union. Their activities consist of mutual aid; publication of propaganda; lobbying to Greek authorities; and organisation of conferences, parties, dinners, concerts, and so on.

Among the Greeks from Turkey, those regularly travelling to Turkey are mostly Imbros Greeks. Indeed, in the summer months, a lot of elderly people go to the island, particularly on the occasion of the Imbros fair. Furthermore, several members of the minority go to Istanbul, notably to the Prince Islands, for a few months in the summer. The annulment of visa requirements for Greek nationals in the Özal era eased these sporadic travels. A few cases of definitive settlements were also observed.

Some of the Greeks from Turkey now living in Greece are still of Turkish nationality. We should specify that the double nationality, Turkish and Greek, is not allowed. Those of Turkish nationality are often people who followed their family of Greek nationality after 1964 and did not renounce their Turkish nationality for diverse reasons (inheritance, property in Turkey, and so on, but also, possibly, sentimental reasons). They live in Greece with residence permits delivered by the Greek authorities every year. It seems they have no difficulties obtaining such permits. When they travel abroad, they take their passport to the Turkish consulate in Athens and ask for a visa when the country asks for one of Turkish nationals. Those with Greek nationality are more diversified. Those expelled in 1964 were already of Greek nationality, but the children of Greeks of Turkish nationality usually chose the Greek nationality. Another case is that of the recent migrants, usually right out of high school, who lost their Turkish nationality because they did not carry out their military service. In order to obtain Greek nationality, one must first lose, or renounce, their Turkish nationality.

Conclusion: Is Survival Possible?

This quick analysis of the history and of the present of the Greek minority in Turkey relays several interrogations. First, it looked at the legitimacy of the studied subject. Are they rare birds, on the verge of extinction, that we should study before their last representatives disappear? First, I do not believe in the complete disappearance of the Greek community of Turkey. The tendency will, sooner or later, get reversed, and the younger members of the community will multiply (if the laws and demography permit it) without losing their identity. Moreover, the presence of the Patriarchate insures a more or less regular continuity. Second, the role of this minority is disproportionately important given its numbers, impacting Greco-Turkish relations as well as the internal coherence of the Turkish Republic. Even if the community is a small one, it remains important, both symbolically and historically. Furthermore, according to the theory of the minority sentiment, a member of a minority remains just that, no matter where they are. As we have seen, Istanbul Greeks living in Greece remain Istanbul Greeks, even if they do not have major integration issues.

Notes

1. For the specific identity of *Polites* see Örs, Romain Ilay, *Diaspora of the City: Stories of Cosmopolitanism from Istanbul and Athens*, London: Palgrave, 2018.

2. For a legal perspective on the concept of 'reciprocity' see Decaux, Emmanuel, *La réciprocité en droit international*, Paris: Librairie générale du droit et de juris-prudence, 1980. For the discussion on this concept in the Greek Turkish case see Akgönül, Samim (ed.), *Reciprocity: Greek and Turkish Minorities Law, Religion and Politics*, Istanbul: Bilgi University Press, 2008.

3. One should indicate that the exonym of 'Greek' is problematic not only for the Greek language but also for the Turkish language. In Greek, the distinction between Έλληνας and Ρωμιός is clear but also the term 'Polites' is used specifically for Greeks of Istanbul. In Turkish too, there is a strong distinction between *Yunan* (Greek from Greece, derived, paradoxically, from Ionia, Smyrna region) and Rum, Greeks of Anatolia.

4. Grigoriadis, Ioannis N. 'Between Citizenship and the *Millet*: The Greek Minority in Republican Turkey', *Middle Eastern Studies*, vol. 57, no. 5, 2021, pp. 741–57.

5. Here, I reproduce the texts of the convention and the treaty concerning Greeks and Turks, not for the purpose of filling pages but because for the general public these texts are public secrets (i.e., there is a political and historical *discourse* on these texts without ever referencing the original texts).

6. The translation of the Swiss Civil Code, the most recent at that time, was adopted on 17 February 1926, secularising *de jure* the familial and personal status. Temel, Ahmet, 'Between State Law and Religious Law: Islamic Family Law in Turkey', *Electronic Journal of Islamic and Middle Eastern Law*, vol. 8. no. 1, 2022, pp. 68–76. Two years later, on 10 April 1928, Islam as the official religion of the state was removed from the Constitution, Köker, Tolga, 'The Establishment of Kemalist Secularism in Turkey', *Middle East Law and Governance*, vol. 2, no. 1, 2010, pp. 17–42.

7. Alogoskoufis, George, *Historical Cycles of the Economy of Modern Greece from 1821 to the Present*, Department of Economics Athens University of Economics and Business, Working Paper no. 01-2021.

8. Kamouzis, Dimitris, *Greeks in Turkey: Elite Nationalism and Minority Politics in Late Ottoman and Early Republican Istanbul*, London: Routledge, 2021, pp. 230–4.

9. Kitsikis, Dimitri, 'Le Projet d'entente balkanique. 1930–1934', *Revue Historique*, no. 241, 1969, p. 118.

10. Barbera, Pablo, Casas, Andreu, Nagler, Jonathan, Egan, Patrick, Bonneau, Richard, Jost, John, Tucker, Joshua, 'Who Leads? Who Follows? Measuring Issue Attention

and Agenda Setting by Legislators and the Mass Public Using Social Media Data', *American Political Science Review,* vol. 113, no. 4, 2019, pp. 883–901. On the specific case of public opinion and foreign policy see Gries, Peter, Wang, Tao, 'Public Opinion and Foreign Policy: Beyond the Electoral Connection', Rudolph, Thomas, *Handbook on Politics and Public Opinion,* Cheltenham: Elgar, 2022, p. 430–45.

11. For example, Apostolidis, Nikos, *Αναμνήσεις από την Κωνσταντινούπολη,* Athènes: Troholia, 1996, pp. 214–18 or Bafeiadis, Simos, *Ενας Πολίτης Θυμάται,* Athènes: Ekdoseis Tsoukatou, 1998, pp. 83–6.

12. Baydar, Ertuğrul, *İkinci Dünya Savaşı İçinde Türk Bütçeleri,* Ankara: Maliye Bakanlığı Tetkik Kurulu, 1978, p. 78.

13. *Nüfus ve Demografi 1927-1990, Cumhuriyet Dönemi Istanbul istatistikleri,* Istanbul: Istanbul Büyükşehir Belediyesi, 1997, pp. 15–17.

14. Alexandris, Alexis, *The Greek Minority of Istanbul and Greek–Turkish Relations. 1918-1974,* Athens: Centre for Asia Minor Studies, 1992, pp. 225–33.

15. Leffler, Melvyn P., 'Strategy, Diplomacy, and the Cold War: The United States, Turkey, and NATO, 1945-1952', *The Journal of American History,* vol. 71, no. 4, March 1985, pp. 807–25.

16. Xydis, Stephen, 'Toward "Toil and Moil" in Cyprus', *Middle East Journal,* vol. 20, no. 1, 1966, pp. 1–19.

17. *Tercüman,* 2 July 1955.

18. *Trakya,* 29 September 1955. 'Batı Trakya'nın hiçbir tarafında, bilhassa gazetelerin körükleyici yazılarına rağmen, hiçbir hadise olmamıştır' ('Despite the provocative articles in the newspapers, there had been no incidents on any side of Western Thrace').

19. *Nüfus ve Demografi 1927-1990,* p. 15.

20. For the same period, the Armenian speakers change from 4.5 per cent to 2 per cent and the Judeo-Spanish speakers from 3 per cent to 0.9 per cent. Keep in mind that these are ratio decreases, not absolute numbers. In this decline, it is necessary to take into account the massive influx of internal migrants from the country to major cities, particularly Istanbul.

21. It should not be forgotten that if the name 'Yunanlı' is reserved for nationals of Greece, the term 'r-Rum' designates, still today, not only the Greeks of Turkey but also the Greeks of Cyprus. After the partition of the island in 1974, the Turks designated Southern Cyprus (The Cypriot Republic, the only internationally recognised one) as 'Kıbrıs Rum Kesimi', the 'Greek part of Cyprus' or 'Kıbrıs Rum Yönetimi', the Greek administration of Cyprus.

22. *Son Havadis,* 3 January 1964.

23. *Son Havadis*, 13 January 1964.
24. *Son Havadis*, 30 April 1964.
25. *Son Havadis*, 31 May 1964.
26. *Son Havadis*, 16 June 1964.
27. *Son Havadis*, 8 September 1964.
28. *Akşam*, 1 May 1964.
29. *Akşam*, 17 May 1964.
30. *Akşam*, 29 May 1964.
31. *Akşam*, 10 September 1964.
32. *Akşam*, 12 October 1964.
33. *Hürriyet*, 29 March 1964.
34. *Hürriyet*, 13 January 1964.
35. *Tercüman*, 18 April 1964.
36. *Ulus*, 15 April 1964.
37. *Milliyet*, 17 March 1964.
38. Demir, Hülya, Akar, Rıdvan, *Istanbul'un Son Sürgünleri*, Istanbul, İletişim, 1994, p. 71
39. 'Imroz ve Bozcaada' *Akşam*, 30–1 May 1964.
40. *Tercüman*, 21 May 1964.
41. Alexandris, Alexis, 'Tenedos, from the Treaty of Lausanne to nowadays', in *The Forgotten Island of Tenedos*, Athens: Anatoli, 1997, p. 32.
42. *Son Havadis*, 21 October 1964.
43. Erginsoy, Güliz, 'Tam ve Yarı zamanlı vatandaşlık, Gliki'den Bademli'ye Dört Kuşak', Akgönül, Samim (ed.), *Images et perceptions dans les relations gréco-turques*, Nancy: Genèse, 1999.
44. Alexandris, Alexis, *The Greek Minority*, p. 291.
45. Interviews with Dimitri Frangopoulos and Dimitri Karayani in Istanbul in 2005 and 2010.
46. *Trakya*, 19 November 1964. An article published in the *Athinaiki* newspaper of 4 November 1964 by Th. Draku includes the following passages, 'We must be very careful with the teaching body in Western Thrace . . . The young people want to modernize . . . Anti-Greek associations are formed'. In January 1965, the weekly *Komotini* sharply criticised law number 3065 of 1954, which allowed schools to call themselves 'Turkish', insisting that the Pomaks were in fact only Islamised Hellenes. The article attacks the concessions granted by Karamanlis, stating that these concessions continued with Papandreou.
47. *Trakya*, 26 August 1964.

48. *Trakya*, 1 December 1965, 'Azınlık maarifinde yeni engeller' ('New obstacles in the minority education').

49. *Trakya*, 25 October 1966, 'İstenmeyen Türk tebalı öğretmenler' ('Unwanted Turkish national teachers').

50. Akgönül, Samim, *Une communauté, deux États: la minorité turco-musulmane de Thrace occidentale*, Istanbul: Isis, 1999, p. 56.

51. Ibid. p. 63.

52. Yücel, Hakan (ed.), *Rum Olmak, Rum Kalmak*, Istanbul: Istos, 2018, p. 36.

53. Anastassiadou, Méropi, Dumont, Paul, *Les Grecs d'Istanbul et le patriarcat œcuménique au seuil du xxie siècle. Une communauté en quête d'avenir*, Paris: Les Éditions du Cerf, 2011, p. 17.

54. Interview with Fotini, A., in Istanbul, 12 December 2021.

55. De Tapia, Aude Aylin, 'The Rums of Greek-Orthodox in Turkey', Gültekin, Ahmet Kerim, Süvari, Çakır Ceyhan (eds), *The Ethno-Cultural Others in Turkey: Contemporary reflexions*, Yerevan: Russian-Armenian University Press, 2021, p. 180.

56. Interview with Takis, A., in Istanbul, 12 December 2021. Emphasis added.

57. Kaya, Nurcan, 'Teaching in and Studying Minority Languages in Turkey: A Brief Overview of Current Issues and Minority Schools', *European Yearbook of Minority Issues*, vol. *12, no. 1*, 2015, pp. 315–38.

58. Örs, Romain Ilay, *Diaspora of the City: Stories of Cosmopolitanism from Istanbul and Athens* London: Palgrave Studies in Urban Anthropology, 2018.

59. Kaymak, Özgür, Beylunioğlu, Anna Maria, 'İstanbul'da Yaşayan Antakyalı Ortodoksların Kendilerini Kimliklendirme Süreci ve İstanbul Rum Cemaatiyle İlişkisellikleri', Haris, Rigas (ed.), *Üç Milliyetçiliğin Gölgesinde Kadim Bir Cemaat: Arapdilli Doğu Ortodoksları*, Istanbul: Istos, 2018.

60. Kalafat, Oguz, *Türkiye'de Özel Okullar Tarihi*, Istanbul: Akademisyen, 2021.

61. Kotam, Aleksia, 'Greeks Settling into Turkey is Like a Shot in the Arm for Greek Community in Turkey', Agos, 7 January 2016, https://www.agos.com.tr/en/article/15819/greeks-settling-into-turkey-is-like-a-shot-in-the-arm-for-greek-community-in-turkey.

62. Afet ve Acil Durum Yönetimi Başkanlığı, *Türkiye'deki Suriyelilerin Demografik Görünümü, Yaşam Koşulları ve Gelecek Beklentilerine Yönelik Saha Araştırması*, 2017, https://www.afad.gov.tr/kurumlar/afad.gov.tr/25337/xfiles/17a-Turkiye_deki_Suriyelilerin_Demografik_Gorunumu_Yasam_Kosullari_ve_Gelecek_Beklentilerine_Yonelik_Saha_Arastirmasi_2017.pdf.

63. Kuneralp, Sinan, 'Les Grecs en Stambouline: diplomates Ottomans d'origine Grecque' in Vaner Semih, *Le différend gréco-turc*, Paris: L'Harmattan, 1988, pp. 41–6.

64. Gautier, Théophile, *Constantinople en 1852*, Istanbul: Isis, 1990.

65. *Balat ve Fener semtlerinin Rehabilitasyonu (Istanbul Tarihi Yarımadası)*, Istanbul: Fatih Municipality, European Union, UNESCO, IFEA, 1998, p. 6.

66. Benlisoy, Yorgo, Macar, Elçin, *Fener Patrikhanesi*, Istanbul: Ayraç, 1997, p. 63.

67. Especially for political and financial reasons. It should be noted that churches in certain regions of Greece are still attached to the Patriarchate and not to the Church of Greece. Additionally, according to oral sources, the Patriarchate is demanding from Greece the assets that belonged to it during the Ottoman era but were transferred to the Church of Greece following the successive expansions of the country.

68. Sofuoğlu, Adnan, *Fener Patrikhanesi ve Siyasi Faaliyetleri*, Istanbul: Turan, 1996, p. 207.

69. See for example Güler, Ali, *Pontus meselesi ve Rum-Yunan Terör örgütleri*, Ankara: Rizeliler Derneği, 1984.

70. See for example Helmreich, Paul, *From Paris to Sèvres: The Partition of the Ottoman Empire at the Peace Conference of 1919–1920*, Columbus, OH: Ohio State University Press, 1974.

71. Dumont, Paul, *Mustafa Kemal*, Paris: Complexe, 1997, pp. 136–7.

72. Inönü, Ismet, *Hatıralar*, Ankara: Bilgi, 1987, Volume 2, pp. 130–2.

73. Arı, Kemal, *Büyük Mübadele. Türkiye'ye Zorunlu Göç*, Istanbul: Tarih Vakfı Yurt Yayınları, 1995, p. 17

74. Akgönül, Samim, *Une communauté, deux États: la minorité turco-musulmane de Thrace occidentale*, Istanbul: Isis, 1999, pp. 25–6.

75. The qualification of 'établis' posed major problems for Turkish and Greek officials during and after the conference, taking on a political meaning. According to Turkish members of the joint commission created to oversee the exchange, individuals settled in Istanbul before 30 October 1918 can claim established status under Turkish laws. However, Greek delegates drew attention to the fact that the internal laws of Greece or Turkey were not mentioned in the convention, so the meaning of the term 'according to the spirit of the conference' had to be interpreted without reference to internal laws. The commission could not find a compromise on the issue, so at the initiative of the League of Nations, they sought advice from the Permanent International Court of Justice in The Hague. The Hague provided a sterile interpretation of the question, and the controversy worsened, becoming a bilateral political tension. The conflict could only be resolved amicably in 1926, three years after the signing of the Exchange Convention, in Athens. The main objective was to keep as many Greeks as possible in Turkey

from the Greek perspective, and vice versa from the Turkish perspective. In addition, a controversy over the status of the new patriarch exacerbated the issue. Arı, Kemal, *Büyük Mübadele. Türkiye'ye Zorunlu Göç*, p. 18; Gönlübol, Mehmet, Sar, Cem, *Olaylarla Türk Dış Politikası*, Ankara: Ankara üniversitesi Siyasal Bilimler Fakültesi Yayınları, 1982, pp. 56–7; Erim, Nihat, 'Milletlerarası Daimi Adalet Divani ve Türkiye, Etabli Meselesi', *Ankara üniversitesi Hukuk Fakültesi Dergisi*, vol. 2, no.1, 1944, pp. 62–73.

76. Dündar, Fuat, *Türkiye Nüfus Sayımlarında Azınlıklar*, Istanbul: Doz, 1999, pp. 37–8.

77. Regarding a discussion on the reliability of data concerning Greeks contained in Turkish censuses, see Akgönül, Samim, 'Les Grecs d'Istanbul pendant les premières décennies de la République turque', *Deltio*, December 2002, p. 11 *et passim*. The difference between Orthodox and Greek-speaking individuals comes from the presence of Muslim exchanges from Greece who declare themselves as Greek-speaking.

78. Bozkurt, Gülnihal, *Batı Hukukunun Türkiye'de Benimsenmesi. Osmanlı Devleti'nden Türkiye Cumhuriyeti'ne Resepsiyon Süreci (1839–1939)*, Ankara: Türk Tarih Kurumu, 1996.

79. Bali, Rıfat, *Cumhuriyet Yıllarında Türkiye Yahudileri. Bir Türkleştirme Serüveni (1923–1945)*, Istanbul: İletişim, 1999, p. 84.

80. Few sources mention the conditions under which the Armenian declaration was made. It must be admitted that both Turkish and Armenian historiography as well as Western historiography favour the situation of the Armenians at the end of the Ottoman Empire rather than during the Republic for obvious reasons. Despite this, the renunciation of the Armenian community to Article 42 is briefly mentioned in Şahin Recep's 'Türk Devletlerinin Ermeni Politikaları', *Türk Tarihinde Ermeniler*, Izmir: Dokuz Eylül Üniversitesi, 1983, pp. 99–114, in the impressive work of Uras, Esat, *The Armenians in History and the Armenian Question*, Istanbul: Documentary Publications, 1988 (the fact is mentioned in a few words, p. 1001); see also Moser, Pierre, *Arméniens, où est la réalité ?*, Saint-Aquilin-de-Pacy: Mallier, 1980, p. 107.

81. Aktar, Ayhan, *Varlık vergisi ve Türkleştirme Politikaları*, Istanbul: İletişim, 2000, p. 113.

82. Dumont, Paul, 'La période des Tanzimat', Mantran, Robert (dir.), *Histoire de l'Empire Ottoman*, Paris: Fayard, 1989, p. 476 *et passim*.

83. Meletios IV resigned partly under pressure from Athens and was subsequently elected Patriarch of Alexandria, a position he held until his death in 1935.

84. Vasilios, Stavridis, *Η Οικουμενικη Πατριαρχη 1860-Σιμερον*, Athènes: Eteria Makedonikon Spudon, 1977, quoted by Macar, Elçin, Benlisoy, Yorgo, *Fener Patrikhanesi*, p. 50.

85. For the attempted coup by Papa Eftim see Cihangir, Erol, *Papa Eftim'in Muhtıraları ve Bağımsız Türk Ortodoks Patrikhanesi*, Istanbul: Turan, 1996, pp. 132–44.

86. Psomiades, Harry J., 'The Ecumenical Patriarchate under the Turkish Republic: The First Ten Years', *Balkan Studies*, no. 2, 1961, pp. 47–70.

87. Alexandris, Alexis, 'The Expulsion of Constantine VI: The Ecumenical Patriarchate and Greek–Turkish Relations, 1924–5', *Balkan Studies*, no. 22, 1981, pp. 333–63.

88. Alexandris, A., *The Greek Minority*, p. 204.

89. Mavropoulos Dimitros, Πατριαρχικές Σελίδες., *Τό Οίκουμενικόν Πατριαρχείον 1878-1949*, Thessaloniki: n.e., 1960, pp. 245–6.

90. Curtiss, John Shelton, *The Russian Church and the Soviet State 1917–1950*, Gloucester: P. Smith, 1965, p. 39.

91. Serge's attitude is somewhat more complex as he was suspected of being in collusion with the Soviet authorities upon his return from exile.

92. Struve, Nikita, *Les Chrétiens en URSS*, Paris: Seuil, 1962, p. 290.

93. Kolarz, Walter, *Religion in the Soviet Union*, London: Macmillan, 1961, p. 111.

94. Levi, Avner, *Türkiye Cumhuriyet'inde Yahudiler*, Istanbul: İletişim, 1992, p. 140. In 1941 and 1942, a circular from the Ministry of Defence stated that being of 'Turkish race' was a condition for admission to military schools.

95. Macar, Elçin, *İşte geliyor Kurtuluş* – Türkiye'nin 2. Dünya Savaşı'nda Yunanistan'a Yardımları, İzmir: İzmir Ticaret Odası, 2017.

96. Galanti, Avram, *Türkler ve Yahudiler – Tarihi, Siyasi, İçtimai Tetkik*, Istanbul, 1947, p. 136.

97. Gökay, Bülent, 'Belgelerle Struma Faciası', *Tarih ve Toplum*, no. 116, 1993, pp. 42–5.

98. For example, Faruk Sayar who helped 176 Jews escape from France, Topuz, Hıfzı, *Eski Dostlar*, Istanbul: Remzi, 2000, pp. 16–17, Necdet Kent, the Consul General of Marseille at the time, who saved 80 Jews, *Şalom*, 27 September 2000, or Selahattin Ülkümen who helped the Jews of Rhodes, Ülkümen, Selahattin, *Bilinmeyen Yönleriyle Bir Dönemin Dışişleri*, Istanbul: Gözlem, 1993, pp. 153–4 and *Şalom*, 27 June 1990 to 11 July 1990. To avoid falling into the trap of oversimplification, it should be noted that even during this difficult period for Jews in Turkey, Jewish Zionist activities continued to exist, finding a fertile ground in the country; on this subject, see Benbassa, Esther, 'The Clandestine', *CEMOTI*, no. 28, 1999, pp. 54–5.

99. Mumcu, Uğur, *40'ların Cadı Kazanı*, Ankara: umag, 1990.

100. The Jews of Turkey refer to this event as 'Las vente Klasas' in Ladino (Judeo-Spanish), for the Armenians of Turkey it is 'Kisan Tasagark and the Greeks have named it 'Ικοσι Πληκεις'.

101. Bali, Rıfat, *Cumhuriyet yıllarında*, p. 424.

102. Apostolidis, Nikos, *Αναμνήσεις από την Κωνσταντινούπολη*, Athènes: Troholia, 1996, pp. 214–18

103. Bafeiadis, Simos, *Ενας Πολίτης Θυμάται*, Athènes: Ekdoseis Tsoukatou, 1998, pp. 83–6.

104. Alexandris, *The Greek Minority*, p. 230.

105. İnalcık, Halil, *Tanzimat ve Bulgar Meselesi*, Ankara: n.e., 1943, p. 18.

106. Hasan, Kuruyazıcı, Mete, Tapan, *Sveti Stefan Bulgar Kilisesi. Bir Yapı Monografisi*, Istanbul: Yapı Kredi Yayınları, 1998, p. 56.

107. Deleon, Jak, *Beyoğlunda Beyaz Ruslar*, Istanbul: Remzi, 1996, p. 133. It must be said that all the authors who have been interested in Istanbul during the 1930s and 1940s seem fascinated by the presence of these White Russians who, for a significant part, worked in the 'night sector', such as bars, restaurants, cabarets, etc. In addition to Jak Deleon's work, one can consult Birsel, Salâh's *Ah Beyoğlu vah Beyoğlu*, Ankara: Yonca, 1983, p. 187 and elsewhere where there is a 'literary' description of the Petrograd pastry-tea salon, while others like Tutel, Eser (*Beyoğlu Beyoğlu İken*, Istanbul: Oğlak, 1998) dwell more on the Rejans.

108. Hirschon, Renée, *Heirs of the Greek Catastrophe*, New York: Oxford University Press, 1989; Örs, Romain Ilay, *Diaspora of the City: Stories of Cosmopolitanism from Istanbul and Athens*, London: Palgrave, 2018.

5

A SPECIFIC BRANCH OF TURKISH DIASPORA AND TRANSNATIONALITY: GREECE'S MUSLIMS

Introduction: Muslims or Turks?

When Greece gained independence in 1830, Muslims made up a very small proportion of the population and had no special institutional protections. However, with the annexation of Thessaly in 1881, the Treaty of Constantinople granted protection to Muslim communities as a minority within Greece, preserving the Ottoman millet system. By the end of the Balkan Wars in 1913, this status was extended to over 500,000 Muslims who chose to become Greek citizens, including those in the newly annexed territories.

However, after the Greek–Turkish war of 1919–22, a population exchange occurred under the Lausanne Convention of 1923, with 450,000 Muslims leaving Greece for Turkey. A smaller number of Muslims with Greek citizenship, including Turkish-speakers and Bulgarian-speakers (also known as Pomaks) in Thrace and Albanian-speakers in Epirus, remained in Greece. The Muslim Albanians were later forced to flee to Albania in 1945 due to the German occupation. In 1947, the annexation of the Dodecanese Islands resulted in approximately 12,000 Muslims becoming Greek citizens.

During the 1960s and 1970s, a wave of Muslims emigrated from Thrace to Turkey and Germany for political and economic reasons, with an estimated 120,000 living abroad today. Muslims of Greek citizenship primarily speak Turkish and identify with Turkish nationalism, with around 20,000 speaking Pomak (a Bulgarian dialect) and expressing an ethnic Pomak identity, often alongside a Turkish identity. About 5,000 Muslims speak Roma, but most of the Muslim Roma are monolingual Turkish speakers. However, as religion and mother tongue are no longer included in national censuses since 1951, these figures are rough estimates. Since 1990, Muslim migrants from African and Asian countries, as well as Albania, have been present in Greece as part of the general flow of migration. The 2011 census recorded 911,929 non-Greek citizens, with an estimated 250,000 Muslims (not including Albanians who may not identify with Islam) based on nationalities and figures provided by Muslim organisations, although there are no official figures on the number of Muslims in Greece.[1]

The rapid growth of transportation and communication in the second half of the twentieth century reinforced diasporas through the facilitating of inter-polarity and relations with the country of origin, while mitigating the old-world partition based on introverted nation-states. The acceleration of the globalisa-tion process is rather favourable to the maintenance, and even the expansion, of diasporas.[2] A diaspora is characterised by an idealised memory of a mythi-cal homeland. Indeed, for the Turkish people, Turkey exerts a gravitational force in terms of identity and politics, underscored by the paternalistic gover-nance of the Turkish state. Spheres of interaction in the diaspora are built on a three-pronged social communication network between the motherland, the majority society and other communities possessing the same diasporic identity throughout the world. In the case of the 'Turkish diaspora', segmented origins play a key role in building social and identity-based networks. The diaspora is intersected by three, virtually insurmountable divides between Turks and Kurds, Sunnis and Alevis and conservative and secular communities. In the case of Muslims in Greece, the community is strongly connected to Turkey and Germany through migration to both countries since 1960 but also divided between Turks, Pomaks (Muslims speaking a dialect of Bulgarian) and Roma, most of them being assimilated into Turkish identity.

In the twenty-first century, a new notion appeared, that of 'transnational community'.[3] If 'old minorities', such as the groups that remained in post-Ottoman territories were part of the 'old Turkish/Muslim diaspora', new seg-ments have been added. Countries that were on the periphery of the Northern industrialised world, often ex-colonies or ex-developing countries, including Greece and Turkey, have started to send an increasing number of migrants looking for work and income transferable to their original community, with which they maintain a strong connection. Historical minorities were, for decades, more or less cut off from the nation surrounding them as well as their 'original' nation, leading to the development of micro-societies. Modern communication means allowed them to renew strong ties to the imagined or real original nation, as well as with other minorities from the same group, spread around the world, but also with the nation they live in, although this type of relation has grown increasingly contentious. The 'awakening of nations' at the end of the twentieth century must be studied through the lens of evolving means of communication, which led to the birth of transnational communities.

These minorities are related to a nation-state, having lived in these states for varying amounts of time. The facilitation of communication and transportation has made it possible for them to regularly go there and invest a part of their income in that very nation-state. These minority members usually share several identities. Their regional identity is first, which is, in their eyes, an intermediary territory that does not belong, on a sentimental level, to the original nation-state, nor to the sovereign state of that region. Second, they share the identity of their original nation-state, to whom they have an allegiance and with which they maintain political, ideological, linguistic and religious connections. Finally, they belong to a vaster entity, such as the 'Hispanics', Latinos in the United States or the Turks in Europe. Similarly, Greeks in Germany or Turks in France maintain a very strong bond with the nation-state from whence they came, through satellite TV and the presence of teachers paid by the Turkish government to integrate the children into that national identity.[4] In Latino American, Caribbean or Philippine examples, the members of one family can pursue (simultaneously or successively) political careers in both host and original countries. The members of a transnational community belong to two nation-states, that of origin, which is 'deterritorialised', because of the relative proximity of the place of installation and because of the ongoing traffic between them and the place of origin. They also seek to acquire the citizenship of both of these geographically close countries. This dual membership is not only a facility, it is also a way of life; the transnational community exists on the condition that the concerned countries are not at war and that the borders are easily crossed, even if it is done in illegal and sometimes clandestine conditions. There is no desire to come back permanently, since the 'transmigrant' has, in reality, never fully left their place of origin, with whom they maintain family and community connections, which are made easy by the growth, regularity and safety of communication means.

The term 'transnationality' hides a lot because of the vague concept of 'nation' that it encompasses, the meaning of which varies according to the point of view, the history or the political context. In a world that grows increasingly small through communication means, every nation is transnational in its broad definition, in the sense that identity, community and even national cohesion no longer depend on a defined and limited territorial existence. Migrations, frequent border evolutions and population displacements that marked this century, *de facto* and sometimes *de jure*, create nations shattered across several sovereign states, but sometimes nurturing their common identity as a nation. In a broad sense, the Turkish case is symptomatic, first because of the ambiguous nature of Turkishness, and secondly because of historical twists and turns. That is how the experience of citizenship of Greece's Turks, a small part of this Turkish nation, can serve as an example to other groups present in Europe.

This experience is complex, but it is not unique. The solutions that were developed because of identity, citizenship, legal, ethnic belonging, linguistic, religious and psychological issues must be carefully studied, in order to find clues to better understand the global mechanisms of transnational societies.

Greek Muslims: The Foundations

The Turkish Muslim minority in Greece is a community born of the events that occurred in the south-east of Europe at the beginning of the twentieth century. According to protocol signed following the Greek–Turkish war of 1920–2, all of Greece's Muslims were exchanged with all of Turkey's Greek Orthodox population, with the exception of two communities, Istanbul's Greeks and Western Thrace's Muslims. Western Thrace is a region situated in the north-east of Greece, at the Greek–Bulgarian and Greek–Turkish borders. This territory situation led to privileged relationships with Bulgaria (in the case of Pomak Muslims)[5] and Turkey (in the case of Turkish Muslims) for the Muslim minority. A total of 10 per cent of the 120,000 Muslims of Greece[6] are also Muslim Roma, usually assimilated into Turkishness, especially since they were removed from the Alexandropoulis area, mainly to Xanthi and Komotini.[7]

The community obtained minority rights during the Lausanne Treaty, through Articles 39 to 44. Negative rights, guaranteeing the equality of all Greek citizens, and positive rights, that is to say rights which were granted, additionally, to Muslims, especially in the domains of religion and education, as well as personal and family jurisdiction. There is no need to specify that all members of Greece's Muslim minority are Greek citizens in their own right.

A certain number of issues related to this double membership have preoccupied the community since the beginning. Mainly, they are issues stemming from the reciprocity concept applied between this minority and the Greek minority in Turkey. Among these issues, we can quote that of education (textbooks, teachers, schools), as well as the legal and religious organisation (*muftis* and *vakıfs* issues).

Religious Belonging and Transnationality

Among all these issues, that of muftis is certainly the most telling. Given the ethno-religious nature of the Ottoman millet system until the *Tanzimat* period but also the social structure of the Ottoman society at the end of nineteenth century, the importance of muftis within the minority group goes beyond their spiritual and legal role.

Apart from its religious tasks, the mufti possesses the role of judge in family affairs, and more particularly in issues of marriage, divorce, alimony, custody, guardianship, wills under Islamic law and inheritances in the absence of a will. The Mufti's decisions are, depending on the case, certified by the competent civil state office.

The Greek law number 1920 (4 February 1991), provides that the mufti's decisions should not be executed, and do not serve as definitive judgement as long as the competent court has not declared them binding. The court examination's purpose is only to judge whether the mufti, in rendering his decision, acted in the limits of his prerogative. The competence of the court does not extend to the interpretation of Islamic sacred law, nor to the evaluation of the case examined.

In both the existence of such a position and in the designation mode in place, we can see Greece's strong Ottoman inheritance. We must first specify that the texts provide for a *mufti as leader*, similarly to a Cheik-ül Islam from the Ottoman period. The position of head mufti, supposed to balance out that of the patriarch, was never occupied by anyone. However, two out of three designated mufti positions were filled, those of Komotini (Gümülcine) and Xanthi (İskeçe). In Alexandroupolis, there never was a mufti.

Several remarks can be made about the notion of mufti election that created so much polemic. The first one concerns the existence of a head mufti, envisioned by the Athens treaty in 1913, which was never applied, fearing it would upset the Turkish Republic, who had abolished the Cheik-ül-Islamat. It is clear that the choice of this head mufti could be traced from the choice of the Istanbul Orthodox Patriarch.

A second remark on this method concerns the election of the muftis by the Muslim voters of each constituency according to the 1913 treaty and law 2345/1920. According to this law, the Minister of Worship was allowed to bar the name of undesirables from the candidacy list. A problem remained, that of neither the treaty nor the law specifying the election mode. It felt like it should have been a legislative election, where voters could post their ballots. Neither the treaty nor the law concerning the mufti election were ever applied. The muftis have always been nominated, even those who were considered symbols of the minority.

In the context of reciprocity, when the Xanthi mufti died in 1985, the minority's elite started to demand elections, pointing to the example of the patriarch. However, in 1990, two muftis were elected by show of hands in mosques, and the minority elite continues to challenge the legitimacy of the two muftis named by the centralised power. We should mention here that these types of elections for religious dignitaries have previously existed in the Ottoman Empire; therefore we see, to the exception of the patriarchate, a continuity of Ottoman habits in the religious organisation of the Muslim minority of Western Thrace.

Currently both systems remain in place with their representatives. Two muftis elected on show of hands and two muftis named by the prefect of 'distinguished Muslims' face each other. Because of the public prerogative of the muftis, the situation presents a serious issue, that is to say that of legal decisions (on marriages, divorces, inheritance, etc) pronounced by the elected muftis but not recognised by Greek law. In this case, those suffering from this chaotic situation are the uneducated peasants who are only pawns in the elite's personal ambitions.

Diasporic Phenomenon

Because of all these political problems and economic and social ones, the community has experienced a rather strong emigration, especially since the 1950s. Thus, the community, which counted approximately 120,000 people in 1923 still counts at around 140,000, despite a 2.5 per cent growth.[8] We are facing a mini-diasporic phenomenon, given the sociological aspect of this situation: absence of territoriality, strong identity cohesion, strong marital bounds, economic relations with the country of origin and, more importantly, a complex multiple citizenship.[9]

Indeed, Western Thrace Turks offer several scenarios through their legal relation with the different states. Because of this emigration, there are members of this community, excluding the 140,000 people in Thrace, in the following places.

- Turkey, with 200,000 people, principally in Bursa and Istanbul.
- Europe, principally in Germany, estimated at 30,000 people.
- Other Greek territories, notably in Thessaloniki and Athens, where they are a few thousand.
- And, finally, in other faraway destinations, such as Australia, towards which there was an economic migration, but also Libya, Egypt and Saudi Arabia where mostly 'students' live.

The complex territorial situation gives way to another complex situation, the legal one. Three situations can be observed.

Greek citizens

The members of the minority living in Greece are Greek citizens, but a strong majority of the minority live in two main cities, Komotini and Xanthi, commuting between Greece and Turkey. Most have either economic interest in the 'motherland' (property, business associations, etc) or close family members, including children in secondary and higher education. In this case, these Greek citizens enter Turkey with tourist visas, and so get out of the country every three months or they have long-term stay permits and remain, especially for retired people, half the year in Greece and the other half in Turkey. We must note that Turkey no longer requires visas for Greek citizens since 1989. Indeed, during the Greco-Turkish reconciliation of the late 1980s, Turgut Özal, the Turkish president at the time, unilaterally decided to end this obligation. Of course, members of the minority benefited most from this measure, as they literally live between two sovereign and sometimes rival, states.[10]

For students, the situation is clearer. We must specify that minority education in Greece is extremely weak and that access to university is decided by an entrance exam. Furthermore, in Turkey, there is a quota for foreign citizens. A lot of young people from the minority take advantage of this quota to do a couple of years of study and then transfer to a Greek university. Of course, they keep their Greek citizenship. In either case, the Greek citizens belonging to the Turkish 'nation' fully use the double legal and psychosocial belonging card.[11]

Also in the case of Turkish–Greek citizens, we must mention those in Western Europe. There are two sorts of emigration to Western Europe, particularly for Germany. The first one, temporary, primarily concerns the Pomaks of the Rhodope mountains, who commute between Greece and Germany. The second is more definitive and concerns other Turks living in Germany who are of Turkish origin. In both cases, Greece's Turks have a considerable advantage compared with the other Turkish migrants in Germany, that of a European citizenship. Thrace's Turks in Germany are very active in the minority affairs, certainly much more than Greek migrants and as much as Turkish migrants. They are grouped into 29 associations, which form a Federation, the 'Federation of Associations of Western Thrace Turks in Germany'.[12] It seriously works for the minority's well-being, notably through demonstrations and through actions led alongside international organisations. From 1983 to 2021, we were able to count 24 delegations sent to the Council of Europe.[13] The action of Greece's Turks in Germany in favour of the minority (and therefore against the way Greek authorities treat the minority) was not in vain. Through these interventions, not only a favourable European public opinion emerged, but the awareness from the European authorities on these difficulties experienced by the minority also grew. This was translated into a political pressure put on the Greek government in order to settle certain legal issues, such as Article 19 of the nationality code.

Turkish citizens

The second most frequent scenario is that of Turkish citizens. We are not talking about the Balkan Turks who came to Turkey in the nineteenth and early twentieth century and who obtained, *de facto*, Turkish nationality in 1923, but about the true members of the Greek minority from Greece who, since the 1950s, have been massively emigrating to Turkey and have obtained Turkish citizenship in a number of ways.

Turkey's attitude towards this immigration has been rather volatile. During the Greco-Turkish reconciliation period of the 1930s, both countries signed the treaty of 'residency, commerce and maritime traffic'. According to its first article, the citizens of both countries had the possibility of 'freely settling in the opposite country under the condition of respecting this country's laws; to freely circulate and leave the country'. In the context of this treaty, in 1958, Turkey offered Greece's Muslims the right to 'free immigration' (*serbest göç*). The departures towards Turkey were thus accelerated in the late 1950s, especially given the rumour of a possible second exchange with Istanbul Greeks, though the Greek minority representative Alexandros Hacopoulos formally denied it.[14] The agreement of free emigration came to an end in 1964, with the deterioration of Greco-Turkish relations. In these 33 years, the Muslim minority has lost its richest and most enterprising elements.

The emigration to Turkey was accompanied by a change in the socio-professional situation. Thus, the places where they settled were, in general, big cities, two in particular. Istanbul, of course, and Bursa. Surprisingly enough, we cannot observe a strong concentration of Thrace Muslims in the important city of Edirne. Logically, there should have been such a concentration, because of its geographical situation. The absence of Thrace immigrants from Edirne or in other Eastern Thrace cities is rather revealing of the prevailing state of mind. In the minds of most *Rumelili* (that is how they are called in Turkey), settling in the 'motherland' is definitive, and they wish to maintain no relations with the original region. On the other hand, Istanbul and Bursa exert such an attraction that it is hard to settle elsewhere. The importance of Istanbul is a dual. Of course, this city is an attraction pole in itself for Balkan and Central Anatolia emigrants. However, in addition, there is in Istanbul a very old welcoming structure for Thrace migrants. With the acceleration of emigration in 1941, due to the Germano–Bulgarian invasion of the region, the issue of the treatment of Western Thrace refugees emerged in Turkey. During these years, most fugitives were placed in a *muhacirhane*, a sort of refugee camp installed at the edge of the Golden Horn, in the Sirkeci neighbourhood.[15] Among the refugees, those who found work left this 'shelter' to integrate into Istanbul society and life. When the second emigration wave of 1945, which lasted until 1951, started, because of the civil war in Greece, those from the preceeding wave who were able to integrate into Turkish life decided to help their 'countrymen', who were in the same situation as they had been a few years prior. In this context, an association was founded in Istanbul in 1946, under the name *Batı Trakya Göçmenleri Yardım Cemiyeti* (Western Thrace Refugees Help Society). In 1975, the name of the association became *Batı Trakya Türkleri Dayanışma Derneği* (Western Thrace Turks Mutual Help Association), which still operates as a Turkish ultra-nationalist organisation.[16] Today, it is a very active organisation, with media outlets, propaganda publications and with the support of wealthy Thrace Turks settled across the country. Its presidents are always chosen among businessmen who, alongside lobbying and propaganda work, are tasked with overlooking the installation of those who continue to arrive. Most of them are Turkish citizens.

Bursa answers to similar criteria. It is a big, industrial city, very close to Istanbul. Moreover, it is also a traditional place for Balkan immigrants to settle. Since the Balkan wars, several groups of Bulgarian and Greek Turks have settled there.[17] The presence, in Bursa, of businessmen and politicians who have been very active in helping other members of this community is another argument for settling there. One last reason for explaining the attraction for Western Thrace Muslims towards this city is the presence of a prestigious university, still very accessible compared with Istanbul universities.

Though both cities are the favourite destination for Turks of Greece in Turkey, other cities have also been a place for them to settle, sometimes forcibly. Here, we are talking about 'forced residency'. Though the settlement in both these cities of Western Turkey concerned Thrace Muslims of Greek nationality, this 'forced residency' concerns those asking for asylum in Turkey. For a very long time, in order to ask for asylum, they had to first lose their Greek nationality. Those who voluntarily renounced their nationality in order to obtain Turkish citizenship were constrained by the Turkish state to reside in an eastern city or one in Central Anatolia. This process complicated everything for 'refugees' who had invested in property in a western city of the country. For example, in June 1988, six families, twenty-two people in total, crossed the river Evros, marking the Greco-Turkish border, and went to the Edirne police station. After waiting for eighteen days, they were sent to Bursa, which was the city where they wished to settle and where they had already bought property through their parents. But in the police station, they were told that their residency permits were given for the city of Adıyaman, in the south-east of Anatolia, 1,150 km away from Bursa. Upon learning the news, the twenty-two Turks coming from Western Thrace sought refuge on the premises of the Western Thrace Turks Mutual Help Association and asked for its president at the time, Mustafa Rumelili, to intervene. After he did, the refugees were able to obtain a staying permit in Bursa. This event, which was featured in the media, in fact hides several similar scenarios. The forced residency as a limitation of asylum demands is applied in contradiction with the policy of the central Turkish power, which encourages the money transfer from Thrace to Turkey, knowing that the investors will sooner or later follow their investments.

The Stateless

The third and last scenario is that of the stateless – a very interesting situation from a sociological point of view but very embarrassing on a human dimension. The *heimatlos* situation is exclusively due to Article 19 of the code of Greek nationality.

Ex Article 19 of the Greek Nationality Code (GNC, Legislative Decree (Law) 3370/1955) was a provision applied from 1955 until 199 in the following terms:

> A citizen who is not from Greek race may be deprived of citizenship in case he/she leaves the country without the intention to come back. Deprivation of citizenship may be applied to the ones that are not from the Greek race, born abroad and still live out of the borders of Greece. The underage children whose parents or the alive parent have been deprived of citizenship may be denaturalised as well. Ministry of Interior Affairs decides with the ratification of Citizenship Council of Greece.

It was the instrument that was used to exile the 'foreign' communities that were mostly the Macedonians in Northern Greece and the 'communists' during the

Greek Civil War. The end result of ex Article 19 of the GNC was the denation-alisation from 1955 to 1998 of 60,004 Greeks 'of different descent' ('*allogenis*'). During the tensions between the two countries between 1981 and 1998, using the pretext of travels of these Greeks citizens to Turkey, 7,182 Muslims of Western Thrace lost their citizenship.[18]

Basically, according to this article, if the Ministry of Interior felt that a person no longer wished to come back, their nationality could be taken from them. That was a discriminatory article, founded upon a racial and ethnic criterion, a direct violation of the Greek constitution of 1975 itself.

Article 19 of the nationality code was all the more dangerous for the respect of human rights since no specification was given on the criteria upon which the Ministry could decide that the person who had left the country wished to come back. It would seem that after the departure of an individual, the state civil servants came to interrogate the neighbours and received from the municipality's mayor a document which attested to the definitive departure of the individual. Then, in accordance with the national Council, the Ministry of Interior decided to remove that person's nationality, without bothering to inform the concerned people of this decision. In most cases, the Muslims learnt that they were now *heimatlos* upon their return, at the Greco-Turkish border. On the international scene, Article 19 was denounced for the first time in 1990 by the report on human rights of the US State Department (chapter D, section 2). According to that report, in 1988, at least 122 Muslims had lost their nationality that way, and 60 had in 1990. In October 1990, a list of hundreds of Muslims who had had their nationality taken away was published in the local Turkish newspaper: the youngest had been born in 1987! In the first months of 1991, 544 more people lost their nationality. Following the protests by international organisms, such as the US State Department or the Helsinki Watch, more flexibility was implemented. Furthermore, Greece's European partners started to look more closely at this 'only discriminatory law of Europe'. In 1993, the EU parliament condemned this article in its annual report.[19]

We must, however, add that certain members of the minority had, for a long time, been trying on purpose to lose their Greek nationality in order to ask for a Turkish one. Ever since Turkey stopped requiring the loss of the Greek nationality and since Greece became an EU member, these cases started to diminish, although some still occurred. Article 19 continued to be strongly criticised in 1994 and the previous king, Constantine, himself was a victim of it. In 1995, the new president of the Western Thrace Turks Mutual Help Association put the subject back on the agenda during the conference on racism and antisemitism of the Council of Europe.[20]

In July 1998, Greek authorities finally decided to abolish this law, without, however, retroactive effects. Thus, the situation of the stateless is still precarious, because of the fact that they cannot enjoy civic rights in either country, nor can they travel abroad. In 1981, the military Turkish government had decided to grant Turkish nationality to the 3,000 Western Thrace *heimatlos* living in Turkey. Since the number of stateless migrants from Greece living in Turkey in 2020 is estimated between 1,000 and 2,000. In mid-1999, a campaign for 'reintroduction to Greek citizenship' (*politografisi*) was started through the actions of the then Minister of Foreign Affairs, Georgios Papandreou. We must specify that a big majority of the stateless live in Turkey and obtained Turkish nationality.

Case Study: Sadık Ahmet, a Nationalist Leader

All groups have constructed their history and historical figures, in other words their mythology. This mythology necessarily contains real facts, distorted facts, imaginary facts, rumours, oral tradition, a bit of Manichaeism, a bit of romanticism, a dose of literature, another of demagogy, and finally, actors, founders and other heroes. The Turco-Muslims of Greece are no exception to this rule. It is especially in the last ten years, with the awakening of Balkan nationalism and the resurgence of minority issues, that the Turks of Greece have also created a mythology that follows all the rules of the genre. The place of Sadık Ahmet is particular in this mythology. A complex character, a hero for some, an opportunist for others, an undisputed leader for some, manipulated for others, he does not leave one indifferent. And sometimes chance gives a boost to the creation of a hero. His death in admittedly trivial circumstances (car accident), but at a time when he was at the height of his popularity, contributed to the strengthening of a myth. Because of this mythification, the analysis of the trajectory and personality of this public figure is obscured. We will simply try to outline the broad lines of his action to glimpse the significance of this character who was more than a politician for the minority; he was a social phenomenon.

The Typical Path of a Turk of Greece

Sadık Ahmet was born in 1947 in the village of Küçük Sirkeli near Komotini. After primary studies in his village and secondary studies at the Celal Bayar high school in Komotini,[21] he left for Turkey in 1966, like most young people from the minority, for his first year of medicine at Ankara University. At that time, when secondary minority education was embryonic and very weak in Western Thrace, it was almost impossible for a young minority person to pass the entrance exam to Greek universities. So, the few young people who wanted to continue their higher education (the Turkish society in Greece being mostly agricultural; even secondary education was rare in the 1960s), had no choice but to compete in Turkey as foreign nationals and then transfer their registration to a Greek university. This is also what Sadık Ahmet did – in 1967 he transferred his registration to the Faculty of Medicine in Thessaloniki, where he graduated as a general practitioner in 1974. After thirty-four months of military service in the Greek army, he fulfilled his obligation to practise for one year in central Greece (as in Turkey, doctors in Greece must practise for one year where the state assigns them). It is worth noting the period in which he began his adult life. His nearly three-year military service was carried out at a time when Greek–Turkish relations had reached their climax due to the Cyprus conflict. It should not be forgotten that Turkish nationalists in Thrace often compare their situation to that of the Turks in Cyprus, and Greek nationalists gladly cite the Cypriot example to denounce Turkish ambitions in Thrace. It is more than likely that it was in this atmosphere of extreme tension between the two nations (populist and nationalist propaganda was rampant in both countries to denounce the enemy) that Sadık Ahmet became aware of his difficult identity without engaging in a demanding process.

It was only in the early 1980s that his commitment became clear. Indeed, not only was the situation favourable due to a revival of minority conscious-ness among the Turks of Thrace, but he also encountered difficulties in his personal life. In 1978, he returned to Thrace and specialised as a surgeon. At the end of his specialisation in 1984, he applied for a position at the hospital in Thessaloniki, but his application was rejected. It is from this date that his political commitment began. His detractors often criticised him for getting involved in minority affairs only at this point and therefore out of desperation because he had nothing else to do, and they doubt his sincerity.

An Opportunistic Political Commitment

In any case, starting from 1985, following the refusal of the hospital in Thessaloniki to grant him a vacant position even though he was the only candidate, Sadık Ahmet began to become known within the narrow circle of leaders and politicians of the minority. The first public action that brought him into the spotlight of controversy was the petitions affair. In retrospect, it can be said that this action was the starting point for concrete demands of the minority but also the beginning of the internationalisation of the problem.

Since the beginning of the 1980s, the Turks of Greece who had emigrated to Germany, like other Turks and Greeks, had begun to become active once they had achieved a relative economic ease.[22] In 1985, the associations of the Turks of Western Thrace in Germany intensified their activities. Among these activities, which aimed to make themselves heard by the European public, was the idea of a petition under a text listing the problems of the minority. According to the officials of these associations operating in a Western environment, the only way to obtain concessions from Athens was to use European pressure within the framework of the European harmonisation process. Greece had only been part of Europe for a few years and Turkey was not only far away but also barely out of a period of military dictatorship. In July 1985, the association in Düsseldorf was tasked with leading this operation, which in turn informed the leaders of the minority about this campaign. After the publication of the appeal by the minority newspaper *Trakya'nın Sesi*,[23] the 'supreme council of the minority'[24] met and decided to start the petition,[25] but the subject did not come back on the agenda, and the text under which signatures were to be collected was not drafted. The reason for this change of attitude was the opposition of Hasan Hatipoğlu, owner of the newspaper *Akın* and prominent member of the minority elite. According to him, this action could harm Greece and therefore the minority.[26] In September 1985, Sadık Ahmet, who had just been rejected by the hospital in Thessaloniki and who held the position of secretary of the Association of University Graduates of the Minority of Western Thrace,[27] had already begun to gather signatures on a blank sheet in the villages where he went to perform circumcisions.[28] The period coincided with the bold campaign against the appointment of Cemali Meço as interim mufti in Komotini.[29] Sadık Ahmet's opponents accused him of using this division within the minority to serve his own ambitions.[30] He was accused of telling villages that were favourable to Cemali Meço that he was gathering signatures for him, and in opposing villages, saying that it was against him. Nevertheless, Sadık accelerated the petition after a short stay in Germany at the beginning of 1986. This visit proves the unfounded nature of the accusations against his intentions, but he still operates individually.[31] In the course of 1986, he decides to prepare a text to be included at the top of the signatures, but the text was not approved by the University Graduates Association, being deemed too severe.[32]

Sadık Ahmet was arrested for a routine check on 9 August 1986 on the way back from Alexandropolis, where he had performed a circumcision. During the search of his car, the gendarmes found a text entitled 'The Complaints and Requests of the Turkish-Muslim Minority Living Within the Borders of the Republic of Greece' with 1,300 signatures below it.[33] The Evros prefecture filed a complaint against dissemination of false news and the use of false signatures. After his deposition, he was released and his trial was postponed to an unspecified date. Following this arrest, Sadık Ahmet, seeing that the board of the University Graduates Association did not support him, resigned from his position as secretary.[34] From that moment on, supported by İsmail Rodoplu's newspaper *Gerçek*, he began creating slogans to 'make the pressures of Greece known to the world'.[35] These slogans would serve him throughout his political career. In this context, still on his own, he went to Thessaloniki to distribute the English translation of his text ('Grievances and Requests of Turkish-Muslim Minority Living in Western Thrace') to the Council of Europe's Conference on Human Rights and Democracy. He was expelled from the room by law enforcement. Following this event, the Evros prosecutor decided on 28 January 1988 as the date of Sadık Ahmet's trial but later postponed it to 21 April 1988.

Meanwhile, the events of 29 January 1988 sadden and divide the minority. This date marks a significant protest march by the Turks of Greece and has now become part of the nationalist mythology of the minority. On 2 October 1987, the Greek Court of Cassation confirmed the 1984 decision to dissolve associations with the name 'Turkish'. The Supreme Court then ratified the previous decisions on 4 January 1988. This decision came at a time when the 'Spirit of Davos' was launched between Greece and Turkey, under the impetus of Turgut Özal and Andreas Papandreou, and Özal did not want the Turks of Thrace to sabotage the process. Ankara's lack of interest played a catalytic role, and the leaders of the minority (including Sadık Ahmet, but in a discreet role) took a series of measures, ranging from boycotting schools to threatening to bring the matter before the European Court of Human Rights. It was also on this occasion that a large demonstration was organised in the streets of western Thrace. The march of 29 January was the first true mass movement of the minority.

Due to the tension caused by these events, Sadık Ahmet's trial was first transferred to Thessaloniki, then postponed to 27 May 1988 and 22 June 1988. At the end of this trial, on 24 June, Sadık Ahmet was sentenced to thirty months in prison and received a fine of 100,000 drachmas, for spreading false news and using false signatures; at the same trial, Vacip Kanarya accused of aiding him, was sentenced to fifteen months in prison and a fine of 50,000 drachmas. Both defendants appealed the decision and were released.[36] The appeal trial was set for 20 December.

Sadık Ahmet Embodies the Turkish Minority of Greece

These trials were launched at the beginning of the case as the trials of the minority. Gradually, Sadık Ahmet was presented, especially by *Gerçek*, as the national hero. The support of Turkey was also undeniable. In Özal's new nationalism, leaders who exalted the Turkishness of the minority were welcomed. Moreover, the rapprochement was visible during the visits to Athens by the Minister of Foreign Affairs Mesut Yılmaz and the Prime Minister Turgut Özal himself, during which Turkish officials met with Rodoplu, Aga and Hatipoğlu, who were the creators of the Sadık Ahmet phenomenon.

On the eve of the appeal trial, these nationalist propaganda efforts accelerated. On November 23rd, 'the Supreme Council of the minority' held an extraordinary session and decided that 'the entire minority will be present at Sadık Ahmet's trial'.[37] Turkey, which was increasingly interested in the Sadık Ahmet case, participated in the general enthusiasm. In the Turkish National Assembly, the issue was put on the agenda and the deputies decided to send a delegation to the appeal trial.[38] In the meantime, Akın launched the trial as follows:

> Fellow Turks! The trial that will take place on December 20th is not the trial
> of Dr. Sadık Ahmet! It is the trial of our rights that have already been violated

in previous trials, despite being protected by laws, the constitution, and international treaties, and it is the trial of human rights. In short, the condemnation of the Turkishness of the Muslims of Western Thrace will be analysed on December 20th. The Supreme Council of our minority sees it this way. Each of our villages must send its delegation to Thessaloniki on December 20th. Our motto is: 'One for all, all for one, we strongly support each other'.

Such a call had a great effect on the minority. The acceptance of this trial as the 'trial of the minority'[39] by the Supreme Council had the same effect. In addition to the delegation of Turkish parliamentarians, TRT (Turkish national television) and 800 members of the minority came to attend the trial. But once again, the trial was postponed, this time to 29 November 1989.

Meanwhile, Sadık Ahmet, who already symbolised the nationalist trend, entered politics as a candidate in the elections of 18 June 1989. In the spring of 1989, a new attempt was made to form an independent list.[40] The idea had already been tried in the 1985 elections but had failed. According to some notables of the minority, including Sadık Ahmet, minority elected officials belonging to Greek political parties cannot serve the interests of the minority because they are drowned out in these larger formations. In May 1989, a list called Güven (trust) was established in Komotini. According to this list, İsmail Rodoplu, Sabahattin Emin[41] and Sadık Ahmet were independent candidates in the 18 June elections. The list was launched by Rodoplu in his journal Gerçek in these terms[42]:

> Oh! Turkish voter of Western Thrace. Trust the candidates of the Güven list, who have emerged from within you. There may be people outside of Güven who threaten you or deceive you with shiny promises. But you have seen many threats, listen to your conscience and vote for Güven, who you can trust. No one can deprive you of this right.

Everyone seemed to support the idea of independent candidates, except perhaps Abdülhalim Dede from Trakya'nın Sesi.[43] With the formation of an independent list called İkbal (happiness) in Xanthi as well, the Council of the Minority had completed its work. It is true that on the eve of the elections, Athens was embarrassed. Not only would it be difficult to control independent deputies, but they also risked taking votes away from the major parties and thus changing the configuration of the Vouli. Thus, several dubious measures were taken to prevent Turks from Western Thrace living in Turkey from coming to vote in favour of the independents.[44] Despite these measures, the votes obtained by the independent lists were spectacular.[45] Nevertheless, it should be noted that it was not the candidates or the lists that mobilised the people, but Sadık Ahmet himself. His propaganda before the elections, the trials launched as 'judgments of the minority' and finally his professional activity[46] all combined to unite the approximately 22,000 votes, which are a record in Western Thrace. Apart from the particular case of Sadık Ahmet, we can say that the attempt at having independent lists rather resulted in failure. In Komotini, only one deputy was elected (Sadık Ahmet) and in Xanthi, the minority was deprived of a representative in the Assembly.

On the eve of the 5 November elections, Athens took the same precautions, including closing the border due to strikes.[47] But the main event was the cancellation of Sadık Ahmet's candidacy due to a technicality. He had forgotten to specify in his request that he was not running for another region in Greece within another party.[48] Despite the appeal of the decision and numerous protests, he could not run as a candidate. Under these conditions, Sadık Ahmet called on the minority to vote for the only candidate of Güven, namely İsmail Rodoplu. After these elections, İsmail Rodoplu was elected as an independent deputy in Komotini. Once again, the Muslims of Xanthi were deprived of a deputy.

The year 1990 began with great turmoil in Western Thrace. Following the conviction of Sadık Ahmet, the 'Supreme Council of the Minority' decided on protest measures, including a commemorative march on 29 January 1990, the second anniversary of the 1988 demonstration. On the eve of the march, local radio stations broadcast provocative news and amplified the tense atmosphere in the region. Thus, on January 29, incidents erupted where violence and looting of Turkish shops occurred in the evening. The minority press covered the subject in a passionate way. Just before that, Sadık Ahmet and the other convicted person İbrahim Şerif were arrested. The accusation came from the use of the word 'Turk' during the election campaign. Two accusations combined: on the one hand, that of spreading false information by declaring that Nea Democratia,[49] Panhellenio Socialistiko Kinema[50] and Sinaspismos[51] were creating an atmosphere of anarchy and terror, and on the other hand, that of inciting people to violence and creating divisions in society by using the word 'Turk' during the election campaign. The trial on 25 January was still launched as a judgement on Turkishness by *Gerçek*.[52] At the end of the trial, Sadık Ahmet and İbrahim Şerif were sentenced to eighteen months in prison and three years of deprivation of their civil rights. This judgement and the course of the trial were certainly one of the causes of the events of 29 January 1990.

In any case, as they prepared for the early elections of 8 April 1990 (as is evident, Greece itself was going through a crisis of political instability, and these successive elections were decisive in the political birth of Sadık Ahmet), the minority was deprived of its 'natural leader'. It was essential to get Sadık Ahmet out of prison at all costs. Turkey decided to use strong means; in addition to the Turkish parliamentary delegation, a delegation of German Greens came to attend the appeal trial on 30 March 1990 in Patras. Before the trial, the March 5 initiative by Andreas Politakis, the president of the Abdi İpekçi Prize, which was addressed to the Prime Minister Zolotas, was decisive.[53] At the end of the trial, the sentences were reduced to fifteen months for Sadık Ahmet and ten months for İbrahim Şerif; moreover, since the sentences were suspended, they were released.[54] Thus, a week before the elections, Sadık Ahmet was free. The two independent lists were established. The arrival of foreign observers for the 8 April elections[55] certainly prevented the Greek authorities from taking the same measures as in the previous elections.

To advance his own career, İsmail Rodoplu had to support Sadık Ahmet from outside. In Xanthi, the two figures vying for the title of leader, Mehmet Emin Aga and Ahmet Faikoğlu, were satisfied: the former became the mufti and the latter became a deputy. Now, the two Turkish and independent deputies in the Greek Assembly could play 'the key role'.[56] Especially since, at the national level, Nea Democratia had been able to obtain 151 out of 300 seats to form the government.

By the end of 1990, Sadık Ahmet's team was complete. Sadık was the independent deputy of Komotini, as was Ahmet Faikoğlu for Xanthi. Mehmet Emin Aga was elected mufti of Xanthi, and finally, İbrahim Şerif, Sadık Ahmet's prison companion, was elected for Komotini. The only sour note was the new election law number 163 proposed on 24 October 1990, which required obtaining at least 3 per cent of the votes at the national level, even for independent candidates. That is, to be represented in the assembly, at least 200,000 votes were needed nationwide. While small parties were thus excluded, independent candidates from the minority also lost any chance of being elected.

Here, we need to open a parenthesis regarding the size of the Turkish Muslim minority in Western Thrace. It should be noted that there is no consensus on the exact number of the minority. According to Turkish sources and the minority press, the figures vary between 120,000 and 150,000.[57] In fact, the figures vary depending on the position one wants to defend. When one wants to prove that Greece exerts pressure and forces members of the minority to emigrate, authors use figures around 120,000. Conversely, when it is necessary to demonstrate that this is an important minority that should be represented in the Vouli by three deputies and that it should intervene in local administration, estimates oscillate between 150,000 and 200,000. Conversely, the Greek authorities also use several estimates depending on the idea being defended. When it is necessary to prove that there is no pressure and that the minority is happy, especially compared with the spectacular drop in the number of the Greek minority in Turkey,[58] the figures are around 150,000. When it is necessary to minimise the importance of the minority, the figure of 110,000 is used,[59] and the minority is subdivided into several sub-groups such as Turks, Pomaks and Gypsies.[60] In any case, whether one takes into account the high or low estimate, the number of voters was far from ensuring the election of independent candidates with this new electoral law.

The bill was accepted in November 1990. Despite opposition from all parties, the 151 votes of the Nea Democratia were enough. With the announcement of the new law, independent deputies, the notables who had supported them and even Turkey, which had been hostile to other candidates, were very embarrassed. Indeed, during the election campaign, Muslim candidates from political parties had been called 'traitors' and 'sellouts'. Now that the only way to be represented was to join political parties, the situation was very delicate.[61]

To get out of this predicament, the charisma of Sadık Ahmet had to be used again. At his initiative and with the support of the Mutual Aid Association of Western Thrace Turks in Istanbul, and therefore of Turkey, the foundation of a minority political party was decided.[62] It is the foundation of this party that separates the paths of Ahmet Faikoğlu and Sadık Ahmet. Ahmet Faikoğlu had already been a deputy and several times a candidate of the

Panhellenio Socialistiko Kinema, and he knew that the founding of a party would not only deprive the minority of MPs in the Assembly, but above all would block his career path. On the contrary, Sadık Ahmet had started in politics as an independent candidate, and his goal was to become the undisputed leader of the minority on an international scale.

Ambiguous Relations with Turkey

A duel was launched between the two deputies, especially since, in Turkey, Anavatan Partisi (ANAP) had lost the elections, and the new cohabitation between the DYP (Doğru Yol Partisi – the party of the right path – of Süleyman Demirel, centre-right) and the SHP (Sosyalist Halkçı Parti – the popular socialist party – of Erdal İnönü, centre-left) was less interested in the affairs of the minority than Turgut Özal, now President of the Republic. In the fight between the two deputies, anything was allowed. Sadık Ahmet accused Ahmet Faikoğlu of being a spy for the KIP (Greek intelligence).[63] He even went so far as to call him a traitor by referring to his Roma origins.[64]

For his part, Ahmet Faikoğlu, who had secured the support of İsmail Rodoplu and *Gerçek*, accused Sadık Ahmet of 'collaborating with the Greeks'.[65] The opposition of the two elected deputies began to irritate Ankara, and the Turkish press widely reported on it.[66] In this opposition, Sadık Ahmet gradually lost the support of Turkey. His habit of acting alone, which dated back to the petition affair, distanced him from his supporters.

Those who had opposed the independent deputies were delighted with this division. *Trakya'nın Sesi* did not miss an opportunity to criticise, especially Sadık Ahmet. Ahmet, in order to justify his election, tended to declare that there were improvements. When he said this to the Committee of Ministers of the Council of Europe, he was called a traitor by his opponents.[67]

The DEB: Greece's First Ethnic Political Party

At the same time, the founding work of the minority party was accelerating. The founders of the party chose the name *Dostluk, Eşitlik ve Barış Partisi* (The Party of Friendship, Equality and Peace) or DEB. The first meeting of the party was held at the premises of the Young Turks Association in Komotini. Sadık Ahmet had excluded all those who could overshadow him among the founders of the party.

The foundation of the DEB party, the rivalry between the two deputies and the loss of Turkey's support are the three factors that put Sadık Ahmet in trouble when the early elections were announced for 10 October 1993. In 1993, Antonis Samaras resigned from Nea Democratia under Konstantinos Mitsotakis, the government party, criticising its foreign policy in particular. He founded his own party, 'Political Spring',[68] and called on majority MPs to resign to allow for new elections. Following the resignation of four deputies who listened to this call, Mitsotakis, who lost the majority in the Assembly, asked the President of the Republic to announce early elections. This was done for 10 October. The unexpected announcement of the elections forced the divided leaders of the minority to act quickly. The DEB founders met on 11 September and made the following decisions[69]:

1. The DEB will participate in the elections on October 10th.
2. The DEB is open to all political parties that want to collaborate with us.
3. If a political party proposes collaboration before October 10th: a) Human rights will be prioritised and no concessions will be granted. b) In case of an agreement, Sadık Ahmet will be the candidate in Rhodopes, and a person will be chosen by the DEB in Xanthi.
4. In the absence of a proposal from a political party or in the absence of an agreement, our people will participate in the October 10th, 1993 elections through independent candidates.
5. The deadline for declaring candidacies is set for September 20th. In light of developments up to this date, the party presidency will convene its General Council, which will declare the final decision.

No party made a proposal to the DEB. The situation was becoming more and more difficult. Participating in the elections with independent candidates was simply equivalent to not having representatives in the Assembly. Despite opposition from several newspapers, two independent lists were still established. Those who insulted each other two weeks ago were once again united, at least on the pages of the newspapers. The slogan of the free candidates claimed to be elected not as simple deputies but as leaders on the international level.[70] Those who ran for office under the colours of a party were still treated as traitors. The two major parties, the Nea Democratia and Panhellenio Socialistiko Kinema, took advantage of the situation. In Xanthi, Nea Democratia did not allow its candidate Orhan Hacıibram to use the word 'Turkish' on the posters during his campaign, while the same party itself used this word during previous elections. Orhan Hacıibram was forced to remove his posters and lost points in the eyes of minority members. The same provocation was made by Panhellenio Socialistiko Kinema in Komotini against its candidate Ahmet Mehmet, who preferred to resign.[71] Thus, the two major parties had guaranteed the absence of Muslim deputies in the Assembly for the first time since the junta period.

Sadık Ahmet: A Troublesome Politician

Independent candidates, without supporting each other, sought the votes of the minority to elect the 'world leader', while party candidates countered by stating that these were elections to elect deputies and that if they wanted, later elections could be held for a world leader! But the election results once again showed Sadık Ahmet's influence on the people: his charisma was still working. But in the end, for the first time in its history, the minority of Western Thrace was not represented in the Vouli. The attempt by independent deputies had exceeded expectations, and the minority had fallen into this trap.

In the April 1990 election, the number of votes given to Muslim candidates reached 50,000. Since the total number of Muslim voters in Western Thrace was estimated to be 60,000, this can be considered a great success, especially since in the 1981 elections, before the appearance of independent candidates, Muslim candidates were only able to obtain 36,590 votes,[72] and even in the November 1989 election, where Sadık Ahmet was not a candidate, this number was exceeded. Thus, we can conclude that the attempt by independent candidates was generally beneficial to minority candidates but paradoxically did not achieve the main objective, which was to send Muslim deputies to the Assembly.

The 'success' of the 10 October 1993 elections did not prevent the hardening of relations between Sadık Ahmet and other notables of the minority. Sadık Ahmet was becoming increasingly violent and aggressive. He was distancing himself from Ahmet Faikoğlu and İsmail Rodoplu. His relations with Turkey were also rapidly deteriorating. But it should be noted that there was an acceleration of the internationalisation of the problem of Western Thrace under his impetus, assisted in this by the Turks of Western Thrace in Germany. In fact, since the end of communist regimes in the Balkans, Westerners were increasingly interested in the fate of minorities in this region. Taking advantage of this situation, we very often see Sadık Ahmet in Strasbourg and Brussels denouncing real or supposed violations of the rights of Greeks of Turkish origin.

The situation and behaviour of Sadık Ahmet had reached this point when, on 24 July 1995, death found him in a car accident.[73] Despite several statements from minority leaders insisting on the accidental nature of his death, doubts were entertained for a while. Insinuations about the circumstances of the accident, including the personality of the tractor driver who had collided with Sadık's car, filled the pages of *Batı Trakya'nın Sesi*[74] magazine. A prize called the 'Sadık Ahmet Prize for Peace and Democracy' was created.[75] Attempts to prolong the DEB experience with his wife Işık Ahmet were quickly abandoned. Nevertheless, the issue of this magazine, which features Sadık Ahmet's death on the cover, was more devoted to the imprisonment of Mehmet Emin Aga than to Sadık's death. Moreover, Sadık Ahmet had not been invited to the activities of the Mutual Aid Association of Western Thrace Turks for some time, while İsmail Rodoplu, İbrahim Şerif and Mehmet Emin Aga (the two elected muftis of the minority) were still present.[76]

Today, apart from certain ultra-nationalist circles, discussions about his death have ended. But from this unexpected death, the mystification of Sadık Ahmet has accelerated. He is now compared with Rauf Denktaş or even sometimes to Mustafa Kemal. His journey and personality have been rewritten for political recovery purposes. A street and a hospital in Istanbul now bear his name. From all sides, from Islamists to nationalists, his name is mentioned as that of a national hero. We can say that from now on, as an imaginary personality, he is part of the history of the minority in his own right.

Conclusion: Transnational and Ethnic Multi-belonging

Hence, the Turkish population residing in Western Thrace, whether situated within the borders of Greece, Turkey, or even other countries, presents a nuanced and multifaceted interplay of relationships with two distinct nation-states, namely Greece and Turkey. This intricate dynamic has given rise to an ongoing evolution of novel and diverse expressions of national identity, which, while inherently intertwined with the governance of their respective states, is not devoid of a concurrent sense of affiliation with the status of a minority group.

Indeed, this phenomenon stands as a paramount factor regardless of the geographical context – be it within the territorial confines of Greece, the expanse of Turkey or even the realm of Germany. Irrespective of the geographical coordinates or geopolitical affiliations, whether they identify as Greek nationals, Turkish citizens, Europeans by virtue of geographic proximity or even individuals bereft of a defined national anchor, the common thread that endures is an unwavering identification as integral constituents of Greece's Turkish minority.

It is this shared thread of minority status that invariably shapes their perceptions, influencing their perspectives and casting an indelible filter through which they interpret the world around them. Regardless of their specific circumstances or locations, this lens of minority membership remains an indomitable facet of their self-perception and understanding of their place in the broader global panorama.

Notes

1. http://www.statistics.gr/2011-census-pop-hous, accessed 9 December 2020.
2. The term 'diaspora' is used here on purpose. If the Turkish case does not fall within the framework of classic definitions of diasporas, such as that of William Safran or Robin Cohen, more contemporary conceptualisations such as that of Kim Butler are perfectly suited to the Turkish case. Butler, Kim, 'Defining Diaspora, Refining a Discourse', *Diaspora, A Journal of Transnational Studies*, vol. 10, no. 2, 2001, pp. 189–219.
3. Nadje, Al-Ali, Koser, Khalid, *New Approaches to Migration? Transnational Communities and the Transformation of Home*, London: Routledge, 2002, pp. 7–9.
4. Akgönül, Samim, 'The Turkish Diaspora–A Channel of Influence', *Yearbook of Muslims in Europe*, no. 14, 2021, pp. 5–14.
5. Tsvetana, Georgieva, 'Pomaks: Muslim Bulgarians', *Islam and Christian–Muslim Relations*, vol. 12, no. 3, 2001, pp. 303–16.
6. Nowadays, it is estimated that some 90,000 Muslim Turkish speakers live in Thrace, predominantly Turkish, as well as Pomak and Roma. Furthermore, more than 10,000 Thracian Muslim Turkish speakers live elsewhere in Greece (mostly in Athens), Tsitselikis, Konstantinos, Mavrommatis, Giorgios, *Turkish: The Turkish Language in Education in Greece*, Mercator European Research Centre on Multilingualism and Language Learning, 2019, p. 5.

7. Katsikas, Stefanos, *Islam and Nationalism in Modern Greece*, Oxford: Oxford University Press, 2021, p. 173.

8. According to information available on the website of the Hellenic Statistical Authority (www.statistics.gr), based on the results of the latest census (2011), the resident population of Greece is 10,816,286, of whom 9,904,286 have Greek citizenship. A total of 199,121 residents are citizens of other EU countries, 708,054 are citizens of non-EU countries and 4,825 are without citizenship or have no specified citizenship. As regards religion, Greece is a Christian state. An estimated 96 per cent of the population belongs to the Eastern Greek Orthodox Church. There is a small community of Roman Catholics (0.5 per cent) and an even smaller one of Protestants (0.2 per cent). There is also a small number (2,325) of Uniates (Greek (Byzantine) Catholics). In the north-eastern part of the country (Thrace), there is a small minority population of Muslims (1.24 per cent, about 140,000 people); the Muslims of Western Thrace are not homogeneous either ethnically (50 per cent are of Turkish origin, 35 per cent are Pomaks and 15 per cent are Roma) or religiously (nearly 90 per cent are Sunnis, whereas the rest are Sufi, and more particularly Bektashi). There also exists a small Jewish population (0.05 per cent). Koumpli, Vassiliki, 'Managing Religious Law in a Secular State: The Case of the Muslims of Western Thrace' Yassari, Nadjima, Foblets, Marie-Claire (eds) *Normativity and Diversity in Family Law. Ius Comparatum, Global Studies in Comparative Law*, vol. 57, 2022, pp. 327–49.

9. Alioğlu Cakmak, Gizem, Hüseyinoğlu, Ali, 'Muslim Turks of Western Thrace and Greek–Turkish Relations: The Troadic relational Nexus', Yürür, Pınar, Özkan, Arda (eds), *Conflict Areas in the Balkans*, London: Lexington Books, 2020, pp. 3–24.

10. Interview with Ahmet Mehmet, in Istanbul, 30 June 2020.

11. Duman, Gökhan, 'Devletlerarası İkili İlişkilerde Azınlık Kimliği Etkisi: Batı Trakya Örneği', *Sivas Cumhuriyet Üniversitesi İktisadi ve İdari Bilimler Dergisi*, vol. 22, no. 1, 2021, pp. 379–94.

12. https://www.abttf.org/main.php.

13. The last one being on 11–12 October 2021, during which the delegation led by Melek Kırmacı Arık met several executives of the CoE, including Zoë Bryanston-Cross from the Secretary General's office. The purpose was to underline the support of the Federation in several cases at the ECHR, such as the Turkish Union of Xanthi vs Greece.

14. Akgönül, Samim, *Minorités en Turquie, Turcs en minorité*, Istanbul: Isis, 2010, p. 89.

15. Tekir, Süleyman, 'The Issue of Civilian and Military Refugees in Turkey in World War II Years', *Kafkas University Journal of the Institute of Social Sciences*, no. 23, Spring 2019, pp. 227–56.

16. http://www.bttdd.org.tr/.
17. Nichols, Theo, Sugur, Nadir, Sugur, Serap, 'Muhacir Bulgarian Workers in Turkey: Their Relation to Management and Fellow Workers in the Formal Employment Sector', *Middle Eastern Studies*, vol. 39, no. 2, 2003, pp. 37–54.
18. Sitaropoulos, Nicholas, 'Freedom of Movement and the Right to a Nationality v. Ethnic Minorities: The Case of ex Article 19 of the Greek Nationality Code', *European Journal of Migration and Law*, no. 6, 2004, pp. 205–23.
19 *Eleventh annual report to the European Parliament on Commission monitoring the application of Community law* 1993. COM (94) 500 final, 29 March 1994, http://aei.pitt.edu/34956/.
20. Grigoriadis, Ioannis, 'On the Europeanization of Minority Rights Protection: Comparing the Cases of Greece and Turkey', *Mediterranean Politics*, Vol. 13, No. 1, March 2008, p. 26.
21. The minority has two high schools, one in Xanthi founded in 1965 by a private individual named Muzaffer Salih, and the other in Komotini inaugurated in 1952 on the occasion of the visit of Turkish President Celal Bayar as part of the Greek-Turkish rapprochement of the 1950s. Throughout the 1960s, it was the flagship institution of the minority. From 1967, the school fell into disuse for obvious reasons related with the colonels' junta.
22. Akgönül, Samim, 'Les musulmans de Thrace en émigration', *Mésogeios*, no. 3, 1999, pp. 31–49.
23. *Trakya'nın Sesi*, 22 August 1985.
24. This council, founded in the early 1980s, includes, in addition to the two muftis, the deputies and former deputies of the minority, the officials of the associations, the former officials of the associations, a part of the journalists, the Muslim mayors of the villages, the members of the municipal councils, as well as other notable figures.
25. *Gerçek*, 21 September 1985.
26. *Akın*, 31 December 1985, 'İmza mı toplanıyor? Dikkatli olalım' (A petition is being made? Let's be careful).
27. This association, founded in 1982, tries to bring together the scholars of the minority to prepare advocacy actions. It is very politically engaged, and the personalities that dominate it have all had political careers like Sadik Ahmet and also Ismail Rodoplu.
28. Oran, Baskın, *Türk Yunan İlişkilerinde Batı Trakya Sorunu*, Istanbul: Bilgi, 1991, p. 197.
29. There was a controversy between the Greek authorities and the minority elites regarding the issue of the appointment/election of muftis. Cemali Meço is accused by the minority notables of being at the service of Athens. For more details on

this matter, see Akgönül, Samim, 'Religious Institutions of the Muslim Minority of Greece', Shadid, A Wasif, van Koningsveld, P.S. (eds), *Religious Freedom and the Neutrality of the State: The position of Islam in the European Union*, Leuven: Peeters, 2002, p. 145–57.

30. Ömeroğlu, Aydın, *Batı Trakya Türkleri ve Gerçek*, Istanbul: Avcı Ofset, 1994, p. 144.
31. *Gerçek*, 19 March 1987.
32. *Gerçek*, 25 August 1986.
33. *Gerçek*, 18 August 1986.
34. *Akın*, 14 November 1987.
35. *Gerçek*, 7 April 1987.
36. *Gerçek*, 30 June 1988.
37. *Akın*, 12 December 1988.
38. It appears that the policy of retaliation also played a role in sending a delegation to Sadık Ahmet's trial. A Greek delegation from left-wing organisations had come to Ankara to attend the trial of members of an illegal organisation (DEV-SOL). During the trial, there were provocations and the Greeks were arrested. They were released following the intervention of the Mayor of Athens, Miltiadis Evert. In the same spirit, the Motherland Party (Anavatan Partisi/ANAP), which was in power, decided to send this delegation to Sadık Ahmet's trial. Ömeroğlu, *Batı Trakya Türkleri ve Gerçek*, p. 176.
39. Ömeroğlu, *Batı Trakya Türkleri ve Gerçek*, pp. 172–3.
40. *İleri*, 28 April 1989.
41. Lawyer, comrade of Hasan Hatipoğlu from *Akın*, but he quickly abandoned the movement.
42. *Gerçek*, 23 May 1989.
43. *Trakya'nın Sesi*, 4 May 1989.
44. For the details of these measures, see Akgönül, Samim, *Une communauté, deux États: la minorité turco-musulmane de Thrace occidentale*, Istanbul: Isis, 1999, p. 111.
45. Ömeroğlu, *Batı Trakya Türkleri ve Gerçek*, pp. 182–3.
46. Since 1985, his main occupation has been circumcision. This occupation, which may seem amusing, is of crucial importance in understanding the phenomenon of Sadık Ahmet. Circumcision for the Turkish people is an act of great significance. Not only does it symbolise the passage from childhood to adolescence, but it is also a great occasion for organising festivals in villages. Thus, Sadık Ahmet travelled from village to village, making contacts with the notables of rural areas. Moreover, this occupation allowed him to make a living while continuing to serve his political ambitions.

47. Oran, Baskın, *Türk Yunan İlişkilerinde*, pp. 205–6.
48. *Trakya'nın Sesi*, 26 October 1989.
49. New Democracy – right wing.
50. Panhellenic Socialist Movement.
51. Coalition of Communist reformers.
52. *Gerçek*, 20 January 1990, '25 Ocak'ta Bağımsız *Güven* Listesinin Davası Görüşülüyor. Türklüğümüz Bir Kez Daha Dava Konusu Yapılıyor' (on January 25, the trial of Güven's list is examined, and our Turkishness is still subject to judgement).
53. *İleri*, 16 March 1990.
54. According to one of Sadık Ahmet's fierce opponents, Aydın Ömeroğlu, they were released after 'confessing' that they were of Turkish origin and not Turkish. Ömeroğlu, *Batı Trakya Türkleri ve Gerçek*, p. 179. The same accusation was made by *Trakya'nın Sesi*, 2 April 1990.
55. Including Eric Siesby from the Helsinki Watch Committee of Denmark and Yvo Peeters from the same committee in Belgium, *Batı Trakya'nın Sesi*, March–April 1990.
56. *Hürriyet*, 6 September 1990.
57. In the weekly magazine *Akın*, between December 1990 and September 1992, the number of the minority increased from 120,000 to 170,000. In *Gerçek*, for the year 1991, in the space of five months, one can see the figures of 130,000, then 120,000 and finally 170,000. In electoral brochures, these numbers can go up to 250,000.
58. On the decrease of the number of Greeks in Turkey, see Akgönül, Samim, 'The Greeks of Istanbul', *Mésogeios*, no. 6, 1999, pp. 64–106.
59. *To Vima*, 14 January 1993.
60. *Kathimerini*, 14 March 1994.
61. *Trakya'nın Sesi*, 1 November 1990. 'What will happen now? Will those who run in the party lists in the upcoming elections be collaborators, sell-outs, traitors, or not? . . . Will we vote for these party candidates to elect deputies? . . . If the current deputies run again under the colours of a political party, will they also be collaborators, sell-outs, traitors?'
62. *Batı Trakya'nın Sesi*, April 1991, p. 3.
63. *Trakya'nın Sesi*, 23 July 1992.
64. Ömeroğlu, *Batı Trakya Türkleri ve Gerçek*, p. 180.
65. *Türkiye*, 24 September 1992.
66. *Hürriyet*, 10 September 1992.
67. *Trakya'nın Sesi*, 8 October 1992.

68. *Politiki Anoixi* (right wing).

69. *Batı Trakya'nın Sesi*, September 1993, p. 10.

70. Sadık Ahmet, in his propaganda journal *Balkan*, on 21 September 1993, declared the following: 'At these elections, we will not have a deputy but our only loss will be the deputy's salary . . .'

71. Ömeroğlu, *Batı Trakya Türkleri ve Gerçek*, p. 192.

72. *Trakya'nın Sesi*, 26 October 1981.

73. *Trakya'nın Sesi*, 9 August 1995

74. 'Dr. Sadık Ahmet'in Ölümü ile İlgili Soru İşaretleri Ortadan Kalkmalı' ('The Question Marks Regarding the Death of Sadık Ahmet Must Disappear'). *Batı Trakya'nın Sesi*, June–August 1995, p. 6.

75. *Batı Trakya'nın Sesi*, September–December 1995, pp. 2–4.

76. *Batı Trakya'nın Sesi*, March–April 1995.

6

ONE HUNDRED YEARS OF GREEK–TURKISH RELATIONS: BREAKING POINTS, EVOLUTIONS AND CONTINUITY

Introduction: Human Dimension in General Perspective

In this last chapter, it's time to have a general look at Greek–Turkish relations, which present structural patterns on the one hand, but also unexpected shifts on the other.

The term 'Greco-Turkish relations' can be understood in different ways. The most common meaning to it is the bilateral relations between both states, and it is widely used for the purpose of their analysis in both academic study and in everyday language. However, new dimensions should absolutely be added to this evaluation grid, given the internationalisation of bilateral conflicts, the development of Greek and Turkish democracies and the spectacular expansion of the means of communication. Indeed, during the last three decades, since the end of the Cold War until today, traditional bilateral disputes have almost disappeared from the international scene, at least in the Western world. Consequently, other angles of analysis, which are the relations between the two nations, between individuals and between their different forms of civil societies, should be taken into consideration as well, although conventional state relations still prevail in these studies. Society approaches are non-state centric, and some forms of systems approach are now the most favoured unit of analysis, with stress on the importance of processes and interactions.[1]

The increase in conflicts and the complexification of their components should also be added to the multiplication of analysis prisms and of actors.

Certainly, as Greek–Turkish disputes progressively stalled, new territories of competition appeared. In a traditional approach, in the 2020s, we can list the components of this dispute as follows:

1. Cyprus.
2. Aegean Sea:
   - Continental shelf;
   - Territorial waters;
   - Flight Information Region;
   - Demilitarisation/militarisation of the Aegean Islands;
   - 'Grey areas'.
3. Minorities:
   - The Muslim minority in Western Thrace (an issue of identity-based recognition, of muftis and of academic education);
   - The Greek Orthodox minority in Turkey (related to the Patriarchate, to the Halki theological School, to the religious foundations, to the ageing of the population and to minority schools).
4. The Kurdish question in Turkey.
5. Turkish–European relations.

Over the past century and especially after the collapse of the bipolar world, the above-mentioned points of friction and tension have had varying fates. Ruptures, through radical changes in these situations and slow but significant evolutions, as well as continuity, have been observed. Of course, approaching these disputes in a completely independent manner is impossible, as they are so intertwined. Thus, for more clarity in the reading that follows, I will first focus on the breaking points which caused both states' attitude to change in regards to human issues, before analysing the domains in which significant evolution, related to these ruptures, occurred. Finally, I will mention a few stagnation points, which are mainly linked to the attitude of nationalist circles that gained power in both states after the 2010s. It is also difficult to take into account Greek policies in regards to Turkey or Turkish policies in regards to Greece as a whole. In both countries, as players acting on bilateral relations are increasingly diverse, state policies are no longer the only determining ones.

Breaking Points

The New World Order: The Redistribution of Regional Maps

Greek–Turkish relations evolve in an open circuit. The 1990s turmoil of the geopolitical world map, caused by the collapse of the authoritarian regimes of the USSR and Eastern Europe, is one of the most important sources of ruptures in the bilateral policies at the time. Greece's and Turkey's place in the new world order was undefined, in a macro-political sense. During this decade, Turkish leaders feared losing the strategic place they held for the United States, the only hyperpower remaining at the end of the Cold War. Meanwhile, Greek leaders had to deal with the old demon of nationalism in order to become a Western European (liberal) democracy. The Turks were quickly reassured: their country's importance as a geopolitical actor in the strategic Middle Eastern region was rendered clear during the first Gulf War, led by their American allies and protectors. As for the Greeks, they succeeded in positioning their nation in Europe, both economically and politically, in the second half of the 1990s, before discovering the torments of unregulated capitalism. These were the changing circumstances within which bilateral relations should be analysed.

The changes following the fall of the so-called communist regimes are not limited to the international conjuncture. Indeed, on a regional level, radical modifications have pushed Turkish and Greek leaders to change their position on a number of matters. As soon as the early 1990s, Turkey reconnected with Balkan countries, establishing warm, sometimes close, relationships with Bulgaria, Bosnia, Kosovo and Macedonia. This unprecedented situation increased the Greek public opinion's feeling of being dangerously surrounded. However, in the first months following the collapse of the Eastern bloc, a wind of optimism blew over Greece. With the end of the Cold War, Turkey's strategic importance could decrease, and finally, a Greek–Turkish equilibrium could be established in the eyes of Washington. However, the Gulf war, the issues in Balkan nations (mainly in Albania and Macedonia) and the Yugoslavian war, during which Greece was isolated because of its religious solidarity with Serbs, have led to this wave of optimism suddenly transforming into an identity setback and a nationalistic aggravation. Certainly, danger was coming from the East, no longer from the North, but the North was now associated with the

East! Furthermore, the end of the Cold War as a breaking point in Greek–Turkish relations was paralleled by a new competition between both states in their shared objective of becoming a regional power. Thus, a new theme of rivalry appeared in the axis of Turkey, the Balkans and Central Asia versus Greece, the Balkans and Europe. Curiously, this interconnected opposition is still operative thirty years later. Turkish involvement in the Balkans, mainly through Muslim populations, became structural.[2] Turkey's increasing involvement and activism in the Western Balkan countries, mostly between 2002 and 2018, under the rule of the Justice and Development party, was successful. Ankara sought post-Ottoman domination in the Balkans in the context of the broader shift in Turkish domestic and foreign policy under the AKP from a realist-secular orientation to a more religious and active one within its new state identity. Relations with Central Asia evolved towards more realistic and equal partnerships without completely avoiding identity rhetoric.[3] Greece, on the other hand, tightened its links to Europe after the financial crisis of 2007–8 because it became obvious that Greece's economy and diplomacy outside of Europe was not viable.[4] In addition, the settlement of the Macedonian question with the recognition of the Republic of North Macedonia in 2019 and the relatively successful integration of Albanians in Greek society made Greece a stable actor of the Balkans, mainly as European and Orthodox.[5]

This global breaking point was followed by others, regional, bilateral or contextual. On one of the most technical aspects of the Greek–Turkish dispute, that of the Aegean Sea, the breaking point occurred in January 1996. On 25 December 1995, a Turkish cargo ship crashed off a group of rocks, near a small seaside Turkish town, called Turgutreis. These rocks were immediately doubly baptised: Kardak in Turkish and Imia in Greek. The Greek authorities that came to the aid of this cargo ship were accused by Turkish authorities of violating Turkish territorial waters. After an exchange of varyingly violent diplomatic messages, the populist and nationalist forces of both countries came into play, and a flag race began. On January 26th, the mayor of Kalymnos Island came to the rocks to plant the Greek flag. Immediately afterwards, two 'journalists' of the populist Turkish daily newspaper *Hürriyet* came to the islet in a helicopter and planted a Turkish flag. The Greek navy intervened to remove the flag and replace it with a Greek one, in order to reaffirm Greek sovereignty over these rocks. In return, the Turkish army sent a commando onto another nearby rock. The press of both countries outrageously exploited these events, talking about a possible 'Falkland war' between Greece and Turkey. As it happens, Turkey was simultaneously in the middle of a political crisis during which Tansu Çiller, its very nationalist Prime Minister at the time, was being confronted with the issues of forming a new government. Provokingly, she used this incident, creating a wave of nationalistic exasperation, encouraged by the media. Greece was also in the midst of an unstable political period. Following Andréas Papandreou's retirement, internal struggles had occurred and the moderate branch of Panhellenio Socialistiko Kinema had taken over the party's power and was forming its first government under the guidance of Costas Simitis. When the Imia/Kardak crisis occurred, the Simitis government found itself prisoner to the usual Panhellenio Socialistiko Kinema nationalist attitude before even obtaining the Vouli's vote of confidence, as the party's more extreme wing was represented in the Ministry of Foreign Affairs, with Theodoros Pangalos. US President Bill Clinton's intervention on 31 January put an end to the dispute's escalation. It was clear that both countries had avoided a very threatening situation, and this world event revealed the fragility of the status quo. While Greco-Turkish bilateral relations entered a new era of '*détente*' (similarly, to some extent, to the US–USSR *détente* that followed the Cuban crisis)[6] after this point of rupture, a new element of conflict appeared, that of the 'grey areas'. Indeed, since 1996, Turkish authorities support the idea that certain areas of the Aegean Sea do not have a clear status and wish to include this issue in the larger one that is the Aegean Sea dispute. In the Greek leaders' eyes, there is but one Aegean conflict, that of the continental shelf, that should be settled by the Hague tribunal. Some more general issues occurred after 2015 with the concept of 'Blue Homeland', which pushed Turkey to claim the majority of the Aegean Sea and Eastern Mediterranean and, concretely, to provoke tensions by sending oil and gas explorations to territorial waters of Cyprus and Greece.[7]

The Öcalan Affair: The Enemy of My Enemy Is My Friend

The Imia/Kardak crisis constitutes a veritable breaking point in the improvement of bilateral relations. Public opinion in both countries realised that an armed confrontation was a realistic threat. However, it was not until the Öcalan affair of 1999 that overall relations spectacularly improved. It should be noted, however, that Abdullah Öcalan, and the Kurdish issue in general, represented one of the taboo subjects in Turkey up until the mid-2000s. Turkey has been accusing Greece of taking advantage of its weaknesses by supporting the PKK and its leader since the 1980s, notably by entertaining rumours about the actual function of the Lavrion refugee camp. In the same way that Greece fears Turkish–Balkan alliances, Turkey fears Greek–Iranian and Greek–Syrian alliances (until Turkish–Syrian relations improved up until the start of the Syrian war in 2011). The Öcalan affair confirmed Turkey's worries, as it indeed proved that some Greek nationalist circles supported the PKK's armed struggle and its leader. In October 1998, following diplomatic tensions between Syria and Turkey, during which the latter threatened to invade the former, Damas was forced to extradite Abdullah Öcalan. After being turned away by Greece, the Kurdish leader arrived in Moscow, before being arrested in Rome on 12 November. On 16 January 1999, Abdullah Öcalan left the Italian territory after a wrestling match between Turkish and Italian authorities (and a boycott of Italian products organised by the Turkish press). He first returned to Russia, then Greece, before attempting and failing to enter the Netherlands. This is the point where nationalistic and military Greek circles came into play. Indeed, Costas Simitis, fearing a deterioration of Greek image, protested, which led to the transfer of Öcalan to Nairobi, Kenya. There, he refused the offer to stay with a Greek businessman, and took refuge in the city's Greek embassy. Forced to leave the embassy, he was then picked up by a commando to be brought to Turkey.[8]

Öcalan's arrest represents one of the most important events in Turkey in this decade, and Greece's role in the affair has given much cause for Ankara to accuse Athens of supporting terrorism. Turkish president Süleyman Demirel accused Greece of terrorism, and kept his army in a state of mobilisation, using the same intimidation technique as he had against Syria.

Öcalan's arrest led to a new '*détente*' era, contrary to the unprecedented tensions and possible armed confrontation one could have imagined would arise from the crisis. Costas Simitis' attitude played an important part in this. Indeed, in the days following the situation, Simitis declared not to have been informed of the events and fired his Ministers of Foreign Affairs, Pangolos, Interior Affairs, Papadopoulos, and Public Order, Petsalnikos. We cannot ignore that, thanks to the Öcalan crisis, Simitis was able to rid himself of the

Panhellenio Socialistiko Kinema's old guard, which enabled him to adopt a more conciliatory attitude towards Turkey. One of the main consequences of this breaking point was the arrival of Georgios Papandreou, son of Andreas Papandreou (yet always opposed to his father's nationalistic and populist politics) in the Ministry of Foreign Affairs. The duo he formed with the Turkish Minister of Foreign Affairs, Ismail Cem, was undoubtedly a major contribution to the improvement of bilateral relations. March 1999 marked a radical change in Greek policy towards Turkey. This new *détente* would reach its zenith during the European Helsinki summit of 1999 where, for the first time, Greece did not oppose the Turkish process of integration to the EU. Since 2009 and the start of the 'Kurdish opening' of the AKP government in Turkey, at least until 2015,[9] the 'Kurdish issue' ceased to be one of the major stumbling blocks between Greece and Turkey.

Earthquake Effect on Turco-Greek Relations

These political changes would not suffice in the absence of breaking points at the level of civil society. On 17 August 1999, at 3:07 am, Turkey was hit with one of the most violent earthquakes in its history. The whole world was moved by the images transmitted on television just hours after this unprecedented event started, the catastrophic numbers killed as reported by journalists and the relative powerlessness of Turkish authorities. The Greek population was no exception and expressed an unrivalled flow of solidarity as early as the first day. Turkish public opinion was strongly moved by the arrival of Greek first responders, aid campaigns launched by different Greece-based organisations and a blood drive of unimaginable proportions. Turkish newspapers which had, thus far, been treating every Greek-related topic with prejudices and stereotypes, suddenly changed their tone. Several of them published thankful messages in Greek, television channels started their broadcasting with messages of friendship in the same language. Despite a few voices protesting the acceptance of Greek (and Armenian) help, the whole of the Turkish political class, media and various civil society organisations expressed their gratitude to the Greek people and their leaders.

The bonds which formed after the Turkish earthquake were reinforced following the earthquake that struck Athens's suburbs on 7 September. Though it was less violent, it provided an opportunity for Greeks and Turks to feel their shared destiny, born of the partition of a territory *de facto* shared, an immutable parameter of Greco-Turkish relations.[10] Since these two events, bilateral initiatives of cooperation, of aid for victims and, more generally, of peace, were multiplied. In a sense, public opinion has outpaced public institutions in the quest for better neighbourly relations. It would be rather simple to come to the usual conclusion, that of people aspiring to peace and governments artificially maintaining tensions. In reality, it was not only the political breaking points mentioned earlier that were paramount to these civilian breaking points occurring, but it was a veritable political will that drove the slower positive evolution that developed in the 2010s. Though Greek civilian society had already spontaneously mobilised in favour of the Turkish people, political initiatives have created, since the Öcalan affair, significant improvement, notably thanks to the Minister of Foreign Affairs of the time, Georgios Papandreou.

Evolutions

Greece's Turks are Doing (Relatively) Better

A rather curious observation could be made that, in every *détente* era, minority issues are at the root of improvements, proving that finding solutions to these problems is not as costly as it would seem. At least, it appears, in this light, 'easier' for leaders to address. In this domain, Greece took the first steps. Indeed, in June 1989, the popular vote put an end to a decade of Panhellenio Socialistiko Kinema leadership, tarnished by financial scandals, such as the Kosotas one. In April 1990, after a year of political instability and three consecutive elections, Nea Demokratia was finally able to constitute a government, under the leadership of Constantine Mitotakis, bearing the *katarsis* (clean-up) motto. Given recent geopolitical turmoil, foreign policy was one of the main challenges faced by the new government. Turkey's 'Balkans comeback' obliged Athens to resume the Greco-Turkish dialogue. At first, when both Prime Ministers met in London during the NATO summit on 6 July 1990, they agreed on continuing the bilateral dialogue, avoiding points of tension, such as Cyprus, the Aegean Sea and the minority issues in Western Thrace, where a protest movement was starting. For Greece, in the early 1990s, the Macedonian issue had replaced the Turkish one in the role of the main external threat. Despite the Greek willingness to pursue the dialogue,

Turco-Greek relations re-entered a phase of traditional tensions in 1991, when the Özal era came to an end in Turkey. Unilaterally, Greece brought improvements to the situation of Western Thrace Muslims, following a principle of 'equal citizenship' (*isonomia isopolitea*). The 1990s witnessed an unprecedented minority nationalistic awakening in the Balkans. Muslims in Greece (claiming the appellation of 'Turks') became increasingly demanding. They were, for the first time, represented by a nationalist and opportunistic leader, Sadık Ahmet. Despite rather serious issues remaining, several aspects of their everyday life significantly improved, although they did not occur until the second half of the decade, when a more 'European' government came to power in Greece. Refusing to recognise this government's, especially Georgios Papandreou's, merit concerning Western Thrace would be unfair.

The first improvement came at the end of communist regimes in Eastern Europe, which caused the abolition of the 'prohibited zone' covering the mountainous Rhodopes region, at the Greco-Bulgarian border. This region in the North of Western Thrace called 'the Balkan branch' is the home of most Muslim Pomaks, who are an important part of this Muslim minority in Greece.

The establishment of this restrictive zone dates back to a 1953 decision based on a 1936 law. Originally, the aim of such measures was to prevent possible communist infiltrations coming from Bulgaria. This zone starts on the 8 kilometres of the Greek–Turkish border, spreads over 50 km towards the east, with an approximate width of 30 km, stopping North of Komotini and Xanthi. Within its borders are 150 villages and a bigger municipality, Echinos. All in all, the region's population is estimated at 40,000 people, most of whom are Muslim and Pomak. Such a zone was not necessary within the Greek–Turkish border, as Muslims were not present in this region following the evacuation of Romanophone Muslims from the Alexandroupolis region. For those living in the zone, entering and exiting was possible only with a special certificate, and for non-residents, an authorisation from the police station was required. From midnight to eight am, these entries and exits were forbidden, and foreign observers had a hard time accessing the zone during the Cold War.

Minority members complained about this archaic implementation, and rightly so. According to these complaints, this restriction was not about filtering Bulgarian communism, but aimed at dividing the Muslim minority, hindering contact between Turks from the two bigger cities in the region and Pomaks from the villages in the mountains. Moreover, the fall of the Bulgarian communist regime made it no longer possible to justify this zone. Additionally, this measure in a European country was frowned upon by its regional allies. Ultimately, the zone was abolished in 1995, following a protest led by the Echinos population.

The most important measure taken, which changed the everyday life of Greece's Muslims, was the suppression of the Article 19 of 1955 from the Greek Nationality Code in 1998. This article was discriminatory, based on ethno-racial criteria, and its very existence violated the Greek Constitution of 1975 itself. It was all the more dangerous as no details were given as to the criteria on which the Ministry based its assessment that a person had left the country with no intention of coming back. On the international scene, Article 19 was first denounced in 1990, when citizenship loss became common for Turks travelling to Turkey, and it was highlighted in a report on human rights written by the US State Department. Other international entities followed, such as the European Parliament, in 1993. Before this international pressure, Greek authorities, under the guidance of Giorgios Papandreou, deleted this article without, however, making this suppression retroactive. However, *de facto*, since the Greco-Turkish reconciliation of 1999, Greek courts have agreed to the individual requests of *heimatlos* people for the return of their citizenship, and most of these requests have been granted. Though the suppression of Article 19 predates the Greco-Turkish *détente*, this *détente* is what led to the flexible attitude of the courts.

Still in the second half of the 1990s, other positive evolutions concerning the minority's everyday life occurred, in particular, the disappearance of administrative hassles, which often burdened Turks in Greece in the 1980s and early 1990s. Acquisition of property, obtaining various permits and licences, obtaining driver's licences and other administrative steps that mark the life of an individual were strewn with pitfalls. The improvements on this front were due not only to the Greco-Turkish reconciliation (as both minorities always were hostages of these bilateral relations), but also to the Europeanisation of the Greek state, making the respect of minorities and equality of its citizens a new objective.

Starting in the 2010s, Greece's Turkish Muslims entered a period of legitimation, mainly due to the Europeanisation of Greek political attitudes but also the arrival of more Muslims, mainly from the Middle East but also Afghanistan and Pakistan. Thus, the appeasement of the Albanian immigrants was eclipsed by these new arrivals, especially those from Syria during the refugee crisis of 2016–19.[11] Indeed, the Turkish–Greek border, both in the sea and on land, during this crisis became a very important tension line, not only between the two countries but also between democrats and the far-right in two countries.[12]

Tensions Decreasing around the Question of the Patriarchate

A parallel evolution can be observed in Turkey, though it was less significant in the 1990s. These *relative* improvements progressed in the 2000s, particularly around the question of the Ecumenical Patriarchate and the property of religious organisations. Some of the problems of the Turks in Greece have partially evolved, with significant advances around the Patriarchate and association of faith, or at least their institutions have (their link to the minority involved is decreasingly obvious because of their increasing demographic weakness).

In October 1991, while Turks in Greece were in the middle of a crisis about muftis, Patriarch Dimitrios I died and was replaced by Bartholomeos I. His election in the Holy Synod was the first, since the foundation of the Turkish Republic, which unfolded without the Turkish authorities intervening through the Istanbul Prefecture. The then President, Turgut Özal, did not want this election to cause him any trouble. Since 1991, Patriarch Bartholomeos has revived the Patriarchate, with the implicit approbation of Turkish authorities. He internationalised an institution that had become obsolete. On the international level, the new Patriarch's task was not an easy one. The collapse of the Soviet regimes had not only changed the Eastern–Western political equilibrium but had disrupted the Orthodox world as well. In Russia, a nationalist awakening paralleled a religious awakening as Orthodoxy became, once again, an integral part of Russian identity. Furthermore, the Orthodox populations of the Soviet bloc wished to be emancipated from Russian authority at any cost, including in the religious domain, and some sought Phanar's support in this quest. Finally, the new patriarch increased the institution's relations with the ecumenical movement and the Vatican, resuming relations that had been paused since Athenagoras.

This internationalisation naturally led to the issue of the Patricarchate's ecumenical nature. It should be noted that Bartholomeos I, in his international activities, had found allies in Turkey, who saw an opportunity to increase Turkish prestige through a strong Patriarchate, as well as the possibility to influence its scope of action. The Patriarchate also enjoyed a good standing on the external front, notably in the United States and in the European Union. Though in different Turkish circles conspiracy theories were, as usual, rampant, accusing Phanar of pursuing a separatist agenda, the patriarchal situation was generally more favourable for development than it was a decade earlier. After 2010, on the contrary, Bartholomeos became a reliable partner for the AKP government that saw as him a guarantee of non-provocation and stability. Thus, several activities of the patriarchate have since been encouraged, at have at least not been blocked, including external diplomatic activities. Nevertheless, the main issue, the reopening of the Halki theological schools, was not resolvable, especially because of the negative interpretation of the reciprocity concept.[13]

Another matter that has significantly evolved is that of religious foundations. Since 1974, *vakıfs*, a pillar of minority institutions, were under threat. Immediately following the Turkish intervention in Cyprus, the General Bureau of Religious Foundations (*Vakıflar Genel Müdürlüğü*), in keeping with the Prime Ministry's services, decided to compel non-Muslim religious foundations to return to their beneficiary's goods acquired by any means since 1936 (inheritance, donation, purchase). On this date, in compliance with law 2762, the Turkish state demanded from all non-Muslim religious foundations an exhaustive declaration of their real estate property. This list, now known as the '*36 Beyannamesi*' (1936 declaration), was established and communicated to the authorities before being put aside and forgotten for almost forty years. It was only in 1974, following the Turkish intervention in Cyprus, that it appeared again on the agenda. Under the pretext of foundations not having declared, in 1936, that they could, in the future, accept donations or purchase new property, any acquisition of goods between 1936 and 1974 was declared null and void. At the time, this decision was not much heard of, going unnoticed amidst the general euphoria about the Turkish intervention in Cyprus. Even minority newspapers did not relay the decision. Only afterwards did it gain visibility, when the foundations in question started to progressively lose their real estate to the supposed or true heirs before their donation or purchase, to the Public Treasury (*Hazine*) or to the Bureau of National Real Estate Property (*Milli Emlak*) in the case where heirs could not be found. Both organisations are, in passing, rivals. Directors of religious foundations realised the situation's seriousness a couple years after it started, as trials multiplied. The issue of religious foundations' goods became the main problem of Turkish Greeks, Armenian and Jewish people until 2003. Indeed, on 8 August 2003, in the midst of a series of reforms carried out within the framework of European integration, three crucial decisions were made. First, the abolition of the death penalty; second, the authorisation of the teaching of minority languages; and third, the authorisation for minority religious foundations to acquire new goods under specific conditions. This new law implicitly recognised that, beforehand, such acquisition was not possible. Turkish Greeks, along with other minorities, celebrated this significant step forward, although the decree implementing them caused controversy. In the 2010s and even more in 2020s, the Greek minority of Istanbul entered into a legitimation process with not only the arrival of the Arabic-speaking Orthodox population in the city, who have been after two decades now accepted,[14] but also after the economic crisis in Greece that has witnessed a small but significant settlement of Greeks from Greece in Istanbul. Thus, both the Patriarchate and the minority seem to be more confident in 2020s than in 1990s, but they are still objects of suspicion and hate speech from nationalist circles.

Civil Society: Initiatives and Attitudes

One only needs to consider these evolutions to recognise the influence of Greece's Europeanisation and that of Turkish European integration perspectives. It is within this framework that the construction of a mosque in Athens,[15] supported by Bartholomeos I, and the authorisation of a Turkish Muslim TV station in Greece, were made possible. However, such changes were not only caused by governmental decisions and policies. Indeed, the emergence in both countries of a civilian society relatively independent from the political institutions also played an important part in them. A network of associations, non-governmental associations and various lobbies developed, seeming sometimes more advanced than both peoples in the quest for normalised relations between the two states. These groupings worked in two ways. On the one hand, they allowed for a slow but steady transformation of public opinions through activities addressing them directly. On the other hand, they joined forces in the context of cultural, economic and academic activities, thus laying a foundation for political initiatives.

For example, academic projects born of students' initiatives from both countries, resulted in surprising outcomes. For example, the official decisions taken in the two nations on school books should be mentioned. While in Turkey an ongoing reform aims at erasing anti-Greek 'hate speech' in history books, Athens University is currently working on a European project of special school books for minority elementary schools in Thrace. To this list of initiatives, one should add the private actions led by men and women on both sides of the Aegean Sea, notably in hosting online forums. For instance, I personally counted over thirty websites that are platforms for reconciliation projects. Since the 1999 earthquakes, the number of similar websites has exponentially increased.

Shared concerts held by Greek and Turkish musicians, such as Sezen Aksu and Haris Alexiou, following in the footsteps of Mikis Theodorakis and Zülfü Livaneli, or simply shared activities, such as cultural and commercial events, give colour to the more serious cooperation initiatives between businessmen, financiers, travel agents, journalists and diplomats. One should not forget that, from time to time, even during times of intense crises, friendship and reconciliation efforts are carried out by these types of groups. These initiatives have considerably increased and are more and more visible in the media, which had previously taken a bellicose approach. Thus, the normalisation of relations has become realistic, desirable and, more importantly, trivial.

One may say that during the 2010s, the 'elite' reconciliation was completed insofar as not only approximately 3,000 Greeks came to settle in Turkey after the Economic crisis of 2004 but in addition Greece became one of the main holiday destinations for the Turkish middle class. Moreover, after the 2016 coup d'état attempt, when the Turkish AKP regime started to become more and more oppressive towards not only Gülen movement but all left and liberal opponents, Greece was one of the asylum countries for the Turkish intelligentsia. Walking in the streets of, let's say, Leros island during the summer or Kolonaki during the winter allows you to come across top figures of this liberal/leftist intelligentsia who cannot go to Turkey anymore because of trials but who smell Istanbul's atmosphere in exile more than those in Berlin or Paris.

Continuity

Cyprus

This chapter's first two sections undoubtedly paint an optimistic picture for the last thirty years. However, although this relative positive situation is real, it is not definitive. Indeed, it is now crucial to nuance this analysis. Though there are domains in which continuity withstands breaking points, it is not entirely impermeable to evolutions. A certain number of bilateral issues remain unresolved and continue to poison future Greek–Turkish relations by generating tension. Of course, the first of these unresolved 'problems' is the Cyprus issue, which is not only the catalyst for other disputes but also remains the central cause for the entirety of the Greek–Turkish conflict. Though I do not agree with this analysis, the peaceful resolution of this issue would undeniably have a very beneficial impact on this bilateral relationship's other domain, notably through the impact it would have on public opinion.

I will not go into a detailed description of this complex question over the course of the 1990s here, but I simply make a few observations. Any breaking points mentioned above have, of course, a link to the Cyprus issue as well. However, in regard to specific disputes, more factors come into play, the first of which is the Europeanisation of the conflict. Indeed, we must first take note of the Greek policy's success in transferring bilateral issues onto a more favourable terrain, Europe's. It is in this context that, since the early 1990s, Cyprus has become one of the most important variables in Turkish–European relations. In July 1990, the Cypriot Republic first applied to the European Union, supported by Greece and shocking Turkey in doing so. This candidacy was not only the source of inflammatory comments made by Turkish authorities but also led to the links between them and the 'Turkish Republic of Northern Cyprus' (TRNC) tightening. According to Turkish authorities and Rauf Denktaş, the Cypriot Turkish president at the time, Cyprus' candidacy to the EU was impossible, both politically and legally. Politically, because the Greek administration of the country did not represent its Turkish population, a constitutionally united community since 1960. Therefore, the administration could not apply for the Cyprus Republic's membership, because of the federal issues dividing the island. In case of EU membership, Greek Cypriots would have their voice doubled, making the implementation of community rules impossible. Turkish leaders also denounced its legal impossibility. Indeed, the 1960 Cyprus Constitution forbade the island from unifying with another country or from becoming a member of an organisation that Greece and Turkey are not part of.

Despite Turkish protests (from both Ankara and Nicosia), the Cyprus candidacy was indeed accepted by the European Union. This application had, of course, several consequences. Beyond the rapprochement between Turkey and the Northern part of the island, it has been one of the main paths for UN conflict resolution efforts. These efforts were rooted in Boutros Galli's 'chain of ideas', which grew to unprecedented heights through Kofi Annan's initiatives that led to a new UN plan. However, in the meantime, the Cyprus issue's sclerosis manifested in a complex, multi-faceted crisis that is the S-300 crisis. In January 1993, the Russian missiles bought by the Greek Cypriot administration were not installed on the island because of the pressure and threats exerted by Turkey against this installation. This crisis highlighted that Cyprus was a potential trigger for armed conflict, and that finding a solution to this dispute was more than necessary.

In the same period of time, a new issue of international law came into play. In July 1998, the European Court of Human Rights in Strasbourg condemned Turkey to pay allowances to Tartina Loizidou, a Greek Cypriot accusing the Turkish government of preventing her from going to her home. This binding ruling embarrassed Turkey because complying with it would amount to recognising its occupation of North Cyprus. Moreover, hundreds of similar cases were pending, awaiting a judgement. Beyond the legal implication, this event demonstrated to what extent Turkish policies on Cyprus were at an impasse and how the *status quo* provided no solution.

It is surprising to observe that, despite the fragile agreement to inter-community negotiations in 1997 and these worrisome developments, the situation, in reality, did not evolve much. It is true that South Cyprus had found a significant ally in the context of its perspectives of European membership, but the EU also preferred, by far, welcoming a united Cyprus, however that might be achieved. Nonetheless, Europe's sudden role as a determining factor in the Cyprus dispute constituted a new parameter. While this situation depended on Greco-Turkish relations until the 1990s (and vice-versa, to a certain extent), from the second half of this decade, it also depended on Turco-European relations (and vice versa). Thus, though discourses on both sides of the conflict

(European institutions and Turkish authorities) clearly distinguish the Cyprus reunification process and the Turkish integration development, the two processes are undeniably profoundly related.

The European prospect, in addition to an economic and social crisis, as well as a diseased state structure, caused new actors to emerge in North Cyprus. The consolidation of civil society paralleled the rise of anti-Denktaş' forces, creating a climate of discontentment in the TRNC. This atmosphere was well understood by Turkey's new government, that of the AKP, dissident Islamists formerly of the Prosperity Party. Indeed, this new power's first speeches forecast a radical change in Turkey's attitude towards the Cypriot issue. This change was however related to contextual circumstances, and in the late 2010s, this very government shifted back to the usual adamant, nationalistic rhetoric (it adopted this nationalist rhetoric after 2010). Admittedly, this discourse was diluted under the pressure of the army and of the nationalistic circles, as well as Denktaş', and it is in that context that one may designate these shifts as continuous. However, the intensifying of public pressure in Northern Cyprus following the Cypriot EU membership in 2004 had unexpected consequences, notably strategic manoeuvres led by the Island's Turkish and Greek administrations, such as the decision for 'free movement' on the island.

Nonetheless, despite UN efforts, the evolutions mentioned above and even an appreciable change in Turkey's and Greece's attitudes, Cyprus remains divided. Ankara's use of this issue in the process of its own EU candidacy led to rising concerns about the possibility of a turnaround in the conflict, although the desire of Turkish Cypriots to join Europe limits such risks.

The results of the Annan Plan referendum play a part in this continuity. Its final version planned for the creation of the United Cypriot Republic, which would span the entire island, except for the two territories under the United Kingdom's rule. This new country would regroup the (Greek) Cyprus Republic and the Turkish Republic of Northern Cyprus in the form of a flexible federal government.[16]

The plan envisioned a revision of the 1960 Constitution in favour of new federal organisms, including the following.

- A presidential council composed of six voting and three non-voting members, representing both communities proportionally.

- A president and vice-president, chosen by the presidential council amongst its members, one from each community, shifting their functions every twenty months for a five-year mandate.
- A bicameral system, with a senate of forty-eight members, from both communities, and a house of representatives with the same number of members, proportionally representing the two groups.
- Finally, a supreme court with an equal number of Greek and Turkish judges and three foreign 'neutral' judges, all appointed by the presidential council.

The plan also envisioned a new federal constitution, as well as the maintaining each state's constitution, a series of federal and constitutional laws and a national flag and anthem. It also conceived a reconciliation commission for the island's communities, in order to settle unresolved disputes.

Prior to Cyprus' EU membership, this plan was submitted to both groups in a referendum on 24 April 2004. The very high participation rate of both concerned parties proved how important the question was to all Cypriots. However, although 65 per cent of Turkish Cypriots voted 'yes', over 75 per cent of the Greek electorate voted against this plan.

Community	Yes	No	Participation
Greek Cypriot	24.17% (99,976 voters)	75.83% (313,704 voters)	88%
Turkish Cypriot	64.90% (50,500 voters)	35.09% (14,700 voters)	87%

The Greek refusal of the Annan plan, although this plan had been negotiated amongst the parties, can be explained by the Greek Cypriot politicians claiming it was an imbalanced agreement that did not present the project of the return of all Greek Cypriot refugees in the northern part of the country – it applied to only half of them (92,000 instead of 200,000). Furthermore, they denounced that it did not plan for the complete expulsion of the Turkish settlers: out of the 140,000 living on the island, some 14,000 longstanding settlers would be able to stay; the island would not entirely be demilitarised as both Greece and Turkey would be allowed to keep a symbolic contingency after 2018.

Furthermore, the new political system established a power partition between the Greek and Turkish communities, which was considered too advantageous for Turkish Cypriots by Greek Cypriots. In the context of a political equilibrium between the executive, legislative and legal branches of power, this system would have permitted the Turkish party to veto Greek decisions and vice versa. The plan's over-representation of the Turkish Cypriot population compared with its actual demography was also a reason for Greek Cypriots to denounce and reject it.

Finally, and most importantly, Greek Cypriots were not motivated to vote in favour of these concessions, given that its EU membership, under the Greek administration's authority, was already guaranteed, whatever the result of the referendum might be. Despite their reluctance, European leaders finally accepted this adhesion, notably because of Greece's insistence on threatening to block the nine other EU candidacies of 2004 (Estonia, Hungry, Latvia, Lithuania, Malta, Poland, the Czech Republic, Slovakia and Slovenia) if Cyprus could not join the Union with them.[17] We may say that in the 2020s, despite the change of policy of the AKP government towards progressive currents in Turkish Cyprus, preferring nationalist policies again in the island, things are better. Almost 100 per cent of Turks of Cyprus obtained Cyprus citizenship and doors are open. Niyazi Kılızyürek, from AKEL (the Progressive Party of Working People), is one of the representatives of Cyprus in the European Parliament and a federative solution is closer than ever.

Aegean Problems

Apart from the Cyprus issue, multiple disputes have taken place in the Aegean Sea and have remained mostly unchanged for years. The only developments that occurred in the 2000s are two additions made to an already long list of conflicts. The first addition is the issue of 'grey-areas', and the second is the appearance of a new actor in the possible resolution of these disputes, Europe. Similarly to the Cyprus conflict, the Turkish EU candidacy has led the Union to study the Aegean disputes. The December 1999 Helsinki declaration proclaimed that if both protagonists could not agree on these issues by 2004, the International Court of The Hague would take over to decide on this matter. Evidently, this solution – which was never accepted by Turkey – presented Ankara with a *fait accompli*. Thus, the resolution of the Aegean litigation became one of its mid-term objectives. In reality, this solution was not a satis-fying one for Greece either, which considered its only Aegean issue to be that of the continental shelf. Obviously, this decision was not implemented when the deadline passed in 2004, though the Aegean problems were not settled.

Meanwhile, the usual frictions nourished complaints on both sides of air-space violation, although this specific issue became less frequent in the second half of the 2000s. Every quarrel jeopardised the reconciliation climate, espe-cially given the ongoing stereotypical discourses and attitudes. In May 2003, the Turkish press were still relating Simitis's and Giorgios Papandreou's state-ments on the continuity of the Greek policy on Aegean issues, to which Turk-ish leaders responded with similar remarks. The technical dimension of the dispute hinders any improvement because the policies and discourses around this issue have remained, for far too long, frozen, unchanged, to the point where leaders are prisoners of both their own past statements and of possible future public opinion. This precise aspect of the bilateral conflict has not been able to take advantage of either the real policy openings that occurred thanks to mutual concessions or of the 'Kokoretsi' diplomacy, tinged with populism.[18]

The Aegean disputes are not imagined, they are part of a traditional con-flict of borders, almost archaic. It is the most technical, almost dehumanised, Greek–Turkish conflict, since it does not revolve around any human groups and only affects a few fishermen who would gain a lot from a fair resolution. After 2010, and then after 2016 and the military coup d'état attempt in Tur-key, one of the main targets of the nationalist discourse of the AKP diplomacy became, again, Aegean waters and islands, in the framework of the broader 'Blue homeland' discourse.[19]

Minorities

With regards to the topic of minorities, falsely called 'reciprocal', there are two domains that remain stuck, despite the aforementioned evolutions: the reli-gious domain for Muslim Greeks and the educational one for Turkey's Greeks. Obviously, the mufti issue in Western Thrace goes beyond the simple issue of freedom of worship. Let us recall the facts.

According to the Lausanne Treaty of 1923, Western Thrace Muslims have religious family rights upon marriage, inheritance, divorce and so on. In this context, Komotini and Xanthi muftis both have legal prerogative in addition to their religious role. These two muftis have always been appointed by Greek authorities, which agreed with the minorities up until the 1980s. They both died during this time of nationalist awakening, an awakening notably led by Sadık Ahmet. On 2 June 1985, Komotini's mufti, Hüseyin Mustafa, died of a heart attack at 73 years old. The minority's elite went into a complete panic. Indeed, no plans had been drawn up for the mufti's succession. Because of the usual cronyism and prevailing family ties that governed over these institutions, the late mufti's son in law envisioned following in his steps even before his father-in-law had died. However, the situation became more complex as a preacher was appointed temporary mufti by the city's prefect. Haçan Paçaman, the son in law, and his supporters, immediately opposed this decision, accusing the man, who had studied in Egypt, of being close to Arab nations and to Greek power. Under popular pressure, a seven-month gap followed the decision of the acting mufti. During this time, part of the minority dignitaries agreed on electing a mufti on the basis of a 1920 law, which the Greek authorities deemed obsolete and null. At that time, another imam, Cemali Meço, seen as close to Arab nations as well, was named interim mufti. While part of the minority's intelligentsia actively supported him, those closer to Turkey thoroughly opposed this nomination. A raging press campaign was launched against Meço, and his designation took a new turn in the 1990s. On 3 November 1988, the Greek government presented a bill to the Vouli. This bill proposed that interim muftis would automatically become named muftis and that the Muslims' two muftis would become civil servants attached to their region's prefects. In February 1990, as the tensions were running high, Xanthi's mufti died. In order to avoid the same fate as Kotomini had a few years earlier, the minority leaders gathered immediately after his funeral – which was held in Istanbul with 10,000 people in attendance – and let the government know that their people would not accept a new mufti nomination from Greek leaders. Thus, on 17 August 1990, in 52 Xanthi mosques, clandestine elections were held and Mehmet Emin Aga, the late mufti's son, was elected. On 15 December 1990, the preaching committee decided to organise a similar election in Kotomini, which was held on December 28th. In this election, İbrahim Şerif prevailed against Cemali Meço, the mufti previously nominated. The Greek government did not respond until 22 August 1991, when it named Mehmet Emin Şinikoğlu as Xanti's mufti. In both cities, there are still two muftis to this day. The defenders of elected muftis still refuse to recognise the nominated mufti's authority, and vice versa, despite the European Court of Human Rights condemnation of the Greek government on this matter. After the arrival of Syriza in power in Greece in 2015, the leftist (and atheist) prime minister Alexis Tsipras declared that Muslims of Western Thrace should be able to elect their own muftis;[20] this reform could not be realised before Syriza lost power in 2019. In September 2022, an election was again organised to replace Ahmet Mete, elected Mufti of Xanthi since 2007 who died in July 2022. A total of 7,320 people participated in the voting held after the Friday prayer in 83 mosques, and 2,570 of them preferred Mustafa Kamo, and 4,750 people voted for Mustafa Trampa who became the new 'elected mufti of Xanthi'.[21] In Komotini, Ibrahim Serif has been the 'elected mufti' since 1990, and until recently he was always under judicial harassment of the Greek authorities accusing him of 'usurping authority'.[22] On the other hand, Bilal Karahalil was the recognised Mufti of Xanthi, named by central Greek authorities, until march 2022 when a new acting Mufti, Necdet Hemşeri,[23] was named. Halil Jihad is the acting recognised mufti of Komitini and, a new development in the twenty-first century, Osman Hamza is named as acting mufti of Didymoteicho. The conflict of muftis is not only symbolic because muftis have not only jurisdiction over civil code but they also control important financial resources through religious foundations. In addition, they have a political agenda in favour of Greece or Turkey. For example, after the spectacular transformation of Hagia Sophia Museum as a Mosque by the Turkish Regime, the Mufti of Komotini, Halil Jihad, declared that this was a Christian church.[24]

Evidently, Greece's Muslims have other untouched issues, the problem of schools and the question of religious foundations, amongst others. However, the mufti issue remains the most emblematic one. Nonetheless, for Greeks in Turkey, educational issues prevail over other matters and are the subject of more complaints. Generally speaking, Greek minority schools in Turkey suffer from a lack of students and from constant suspicion from Turkish authorities. I would like to mention the ancillary but symptomatic issue that is the case of the Halki Theological School. In its role as the school for religious personnel, it is one of the most important institutions for the Patriarchate, indispensable to its survival. This school, founded in 1844, aimed, notably, at providing a unifying theological education against nationalist movements rising throughout the

Orthodox world. After several status changes, in 1951 a four-year high school education was dispensed there, followed by a three-year theology teaching. The school was under the direct management of the Patriarchate, and its director was chosen among the Metropolites. Throughout its existence, the school has welcomed students from Turkey but also from foreign churches, such as the English or Ethiopian ones.

In the context of the 1971 ban of private universities and academies, the Halki Theological School closed following the constitutional Court's decision on 'the annulment of certain clauses of law number 625 on private educational institutions'.[25] Here we should underline the mistake made by most observers on this shutdown, whether they are Greek or Turkish. Indeed, it constituted more of a decision on ceasing the school's activities (and not an administrative shutdown) under the control of the Turkish Ministry of National Education, a decision that was taken by the Patriarchal bodies. For the 127 years during which the school operated, 930 theologians and religious dignitaries studied there, and 343 of these graduates became archbishops and twelve of them became Patriarch. These numbers demonstrate the importance of this institution, on an administrative level as well as on a religious and psychological one. Admittedly, a theological academy currently exists in Boston, but it is far from fulfilling the Patriarchate's needs and requirements. As for Turkish governments, although they give signs of a possible reopening, they also ask for a *quid pro quo* in Western Thrace in exchange, as if it were not Turkish citizens in Heybeliada. Any activity for or against the minority there is judged on 'national interest' criteria, and the school's reopening depends on this judgement.

Recently, the Halki Theological School came back on the agenda, notably because of the increasing pressure exerted by the American administration on its reopening. Indeed, due to the rise in importance of the Patriarchate in the 1990s, the attention of Washington was drawn to the problem, and several high-ranking American officials pushed for a 'gesture' from Ankara to reopen the school. Several of them expressed repeatedly that they wished it so, from Madeleine Albright, ex-Secretary of State, to Bill Clinton, ex-US president. It is surprising to see how much Greece supports this reopening, given the rivalry between the Greek church and the Patriarchate. Already in February 1992, the Greek Prime Minister directly addressed his Turkish counterpart, asking for the reopening. After the 1999 Greco-Turkish rapprochement, this demand became one of the gestures Athens expected from Ankara in exchange for Greece supporting Turkey in its process of European integration. At first glance, Athens insisting on this reopening seems surprising, but a deeper analysis helps us understand. Indeed, from 1950, the Turkish government had permitted foreign students to join the school, and from 1950 to 1969 (when the last foreign student left the school), the Halki Theological School welcomed 225 foreign students, thirty-eight of whom were Greek, with Turkish citizenship, and amongst the 187 foreign nationals, 162 were Greek citizens. During this period of time, Turkey's Greeks were numerous, which they no longer are. Thus, given that the reopening of the school is now insured, and given the number and age of Greek Turkish citizens, a lot of Greek citizens will naturally attend. This aspect, amidst others, provokes strong reactions in Turkey. Among those defending the reopening of the school, there is the Gülen movement, a branch of the Turkish brotherhood *Nurcu*, advocating for interreligious dialogue, as well as some intellectuals who reckon that this school's graduates would help rehabilitate the country's image, to the point where the term 'religious dignitaries exports' was even used. Opposing them are two main groups: the Turkish nationalists who view this school as a nest for spies harmful to the Turkish state, and the ultra-secular Kemalists who regard such reopening as an encouragement for other communities, notably Muslim ones, to ask for the opening of autonomous Islamic theological institutions, which clearly explains Fethullah Gülen's support in favour of this reopening. A middle-ground proposal seems to have been made by the Turkish government. It proposes the Halki theological school's reopening under the condition of it existing as part of the of the 'High Section of Culture and Religion', itself part of the Muslim Theology Department of the Istanbul University. However, the patriarch is bothered by the implied dependency to the YÖK (*Yüksek Öğrenim Kurumu*, Institution of Higher Education, which oversees all Turkish universities and colleges). Thus, for now, the matter remains frozen, mainly due to the inconsistent attitude of the AKP government that still uses this issue as a political tool of 'reciprocity'.

On 30 October 1998, the Turkish government unilaterally revoked the secular members of the administration council of the religious foundation upon which the Halki theological school depends. This decision provoked the

Patriarchate's and Greek government's anger. Bartholomeos, usually discreet *vis à vis* the Turkish government, denounced this decision as an infringement of minority rights. He declared to the Church's followers during a mass in the Arnavutköy church: 'Your rights are being violated'.[26] As for the Greek government, they used this decision to show their Western allies that Ankara was mistreating Turkey's Greeks. The Turkish government justified this action during a press conference with the Minister of Foreign Affairs, explaining that the council members violated the laws on religious foundations, since 'they were using the school's buildings and terrain for extra-scholar activities'.[27] Some have interpreted this decision as a precursor to the definitive and administrative shutdown of the school, while others, on the contrary, thought Ankara to be in the process of placing its own pawns in the council before the reopening of the school. In any case, through my numerous visits to the Halki theological school in the 1990s and 2000s, I was able to observe for myself the spotless state of the equipment and buildings, as if students could be welcomed in the school the next day. This demonstrates how they are not only expecting this reopening, they are preparing for it.

Conclusion: Crises and Constants

The breaking points, evolutions and continuity mentioned in this chapter are natural. Even the problems that seem completely frozen evolve. Some problems find more or less durable solutions while new issues appear. However, it is undeniable that, since the 1990s, the context has been suitable for positive changes, in every aspect of Greco-Turkish dispute. Nonetheless, one should not forget that it is not the first time that such *détente* eras have occurred. Sometimes they were even more explicit, but all ended with the rise of serious tensions. The warm relations period started with the Ankara Treaty of 1930 and was degraded during the second World War. The new reconciliation initiated after the war thanks to American policies led in the region ended abruptly in 1955 when the Cyprus problem started. The 'Davos Spirit' that began in 1988 slowly faded away in the following years. Thus, it would be misleading to consider these last few years as a definitive step towards a global resolution to the Greco-Turkish conflict. Indeed, this dispute's causes run deep, linked to the two nations' collective memories. However, the ongoing *détente* is special, on three levels. The end of the Cold War and the European perspective create a context favourable to the development of bilateral and multilateral relations on a macro-political level. On a local level, Greece has been getting rid of its nationalist vestiges, which came to their height during the Colonels' junta, in order to fully become a European state, while remaining a victim of wild capitalism.

However, its social and identity problems remain. Finally, the collective trauma we talked about in this chapter seems to no longer prevent Greek and Turkish public opinion from opening up to each other. Thus, maybe a way exists for the ongoing good relations era to last and to produce positive evolutions.

In light of several bilateral crises between 2018 (Eastern Mediterranean crisis) and 2022 (Aegean islands crisis), one can easily notice that the tension between Turkey and Greece is useful, in Carl Schmitt's understanding. Especially in Turkey, but also from time to time in Greece, regimes that are in difficulty internally may orient public anger to the outside. In such artificial hatred periods, Greece and Turkey remain the best targets because they are close enough, yet estranged.

On the matter of bilateral relations, an overview of these last few years paints a relatively positive picture. Between 2002 and 2022 (so during the AKP government in Turkey, with Greece being more 'unstable'), twenty-seven bilateral agreements of different types were signed. Among them, those concerning economic cooperation seem most important. For instance, investments of up to 600 million dollars were made to prevent double taxing. The volume of exchanges of goods was 2 billion dollars in 2002 and became 5.2 billion dollars in 2022. Technical and economic cooperation, especially in the context of the unprecedented economic crisis of Greece in 2004 and similar economic turmoil in Turkey in 2022, gives hope for a renewal in solidarity from Turkish citizens to their Greek neighbours, if they can overcome the traumas of the twentieth century, especially that of the forced exchange of population.

Notes

1. Groom, A.J., Barrinha, Andre, Olson, William C., *International Relations Then and Now: Origins and Trends in Interpretation*, London: Routledge, 2019, p. 131.
2. Öztürk, Ahmet Erdi, Akgönül, Samim, 'Turkey: Forced Marriage or Marriage of Convenience with the Western Balkans?', Bieber, Florian, Tzifakis, Nikolaos

(eds), *The Western Balkans in the World. Linkages and Relations with Non-Western Countries*, London: Routledge, 2019, pp. 269–88.

3. Aydın, Mustafa, 'Between Euphoria and Realpolitik: Turkish Policy toward Central Asia and the Caucasus', Aydın, Mustafa, Ismael, Tareq Y. (eds), *Turkey's Foreign Policy in the 21st Century*, London: Routledge, 2019, pp. 211–28.

4. Lisi, Marco, Llamazares, Iván, Tsakatika, Myrto, 'Economic Crisis and The Variety of Populist Response: Evidence from Greece, Portugal and Spain', *West European Politics*, vol. 42, no. 6, 2019, pp. 1284–309.

5. Tziampiris, Aristotle, 'Greek foreign Polity and the Macedonian Name Dispute: From Confrontation to Europanization?', Anatasakis, Othon, Bechev, Dimitar, Vrousalis, Nicholas, *Greece in the Balkans: Memory, Conflict and Exchange*, Newcastle: Cambridge Scholars Publishing, 2019, pp. 138–56.

6. Bahcheli, Tozun, 'Cycles of Tension and Rapprochement: Prospects for Turkey's Relations with Greece', Aydın, Mustafa, Ismael, Tareq Y. (eds), *Turkey's Foreign Policy in the 21st Century*, London: Routledge, 2019, pp. 229–36.

7. Dalay, Galip, 'Turkey, Europe, and the Eastern Mediterranean: Charting a way out of the Current Deadlock', *Brookings*, 28 January 2021, https://www.brookings. edu/research/turkey-europe-and-the-eastern-mediterranean-charting-a-way-out-of-the-current-deadlock/.

8. Varouhakis, Viron, 'Greek Intelligence and the Capture of PKK Leader Abdullah Ocalan in 1999', *Studies in Intelligence*, vol. 53, no. 1, 2009, pp. 1–8.

9. Christofis, Nikos, 'The State of the Kurds in Erdoğan's 'New' Turkey', *Journal of Balkan and Near Eastern Studies*, vol. 21, no.3, 2019, pp. 251–9.

10. Çarkoğlu, Ali, Rubin, Barry (eds), *Greek–Turkish Relations in an Era of Détente*, New York: Routledge, 2005.

11. Hüseyinoğlu, Ali, 'Rethinking Limits of Anti-Muslim Hatred and Discrimination in Contemporary Greece', *Stratejik ve Sosyal Araştırmalar Dergisi*, no. 5, 2021, pp. 1–20.

12. Hüseyinoğlu, Ali, Utku, Deniz Eroğlu, 'Turkish–Greek Relations and Irregular Migration at the Southeasternmost Borders of the EU: The 2020 Pazarkule Case', *Migration Letters*, vol. 18, no. 6, November 2021, pp. 659–74.

13. Macar, Elçin, 'The Ecumenical Patriarchate under Patriarch Bartholomew and Greek–Turkish relations', Heraclides, Alexis, Alioğlu Çakmak, Gizem (eds), *Greece and Turkey in Conflict and Cooperation: From Europeanization to De-Europeanization*, London: Routledge, 2019, pp. 129–44.

14. Kaymak, Özgür, Beylunioğlu, Anna Maria, 'İstanbul'da Yaşayan Antakyalı Ortodoksların Kendilerini Kimliklendirme Süreci ve İstanbul Rum Cemaatiyle

İlişkisellikleri', Haris, Rigas (ed.), *Üç Milliyetçiliğin Gölgesinde Kadim Bir Cemaat: Arapdilli Doğu Ortodoksları*, Istanbul: Istos, 2018, pp. 71–142.

15. Votanikos, Mosque, Τζαμί Βοτανικού, in Athens, the first since the Ottoman times, was opened in 3 November 2020. The mosque construction was financed entirely by the Greek Government. Koutrolikou, Penny, 'Reading Perceptions of the "Other" Through the Debates and Public Discourses about Islamic Religious Practices and the Presence of Mosques in Athens', Micha, Irini, Vaiou, Dina (eds), *Alternative Takes to the City*, Volume 5, New York: Wiley, pp. 125–50.

16. Hoffmeister, Frank, *The legal aspects of the Cyprus Problem: Annan Plan and EU accession*, Leiden: Martinus Nijhoff Publishers, 2006, pp. 130–54.

17. Murphy, Alexander B., 'The May 2004 Enlargement of the European Union: View from Two Years Out', *Eurasian Geography and Economics,* vol. 47, no. 6, 2006, pp. 635–46.

18. Kalaycıoğlu, Sema, 'Türk Yunan dostluğuna gastronomik bir yaklaşım, Kokoreç diplomasisi', *Finansal Forum*, 27 January 2000.

19. According to Marshall, Tim, *The Power of Geography: Ten Maps That Reveal the Future of Our World*, London: Elliott & Thompson, 2021, the Aegean dispute is one of the current and future conflicts in the World's geopolitics.

20. 'Government to Introduce Bill Making Mufti Islamic Jurists Optional for Muslims', *Greek Reporter*, 22 November 2017, https://greekreporter.com/2017/11/22/government-to-introduce-bill-making-mufti-islamic-jurists-optional-for-muslims/.

21. 'İskeçe'nin yeni seçilmiş müftüsü Mustafa Trampa oldu', *Azınlıkça*, 9 November 2022, https://azinlikca1.net/yunanistan-bati-trakya-haber/item/61687-iskecenin-yeni-secilmis-muftusu-mustafa-trampa-oldu.

22. 'Greece Sues "elected" Mufti of Komotini for "Usurping Authority"', 11 march 2018, https://www.keeptalkinggreece.com/2018/03/11/mufti-komotini-sued/.

23. 'Atanmış müftü naibinin yerine yeni müftü naibi atandı', *Gündem*, 4 March 2022, https://gundemgazetesi.com/detayh.php?id=12936.

24. 'Greek Islamic Leader: It Is Clear from the Name That Hagia Sophia Is a Church', *Greek City Times*, 11 July 2020, https://greekcitytimes.com/2020/07/11/greek-islamic-leader-it-is-clear-from-the-name-that-hagia-sophia-is-a-church/.

25. *Düstur*, 5. Tertip, t. 10, 12 January 1971, pp. 1176–229.

26. *Apoyevmatini*, 8 November 1998.

27. Ibid.

CONCLUSION: TURKEY, GREECE AND COMPLEX INTERDEPENDENCE

This book is based on a postulate: there is a role, even a need, for the Other in the process of nation-making in Greece and Turkey. I do not want to say that without the Turks the Greek do not exist, nor that without the Greek the Turks would not exist, but the building of the two nations drew largely from this opposition to the Other. This is the one face of Janus, of the human dimension. In the twentieth century, this opposition appeared on three occasions: the Greek–Turkish war of 1920, the compulsory exchange of populations between 1923 and 1930 and the attitude towards the minorities weakly defined by the treaty of Lausanne.

In these three historically important phases of the national construction of these two states, the characteristics allotted to the Others were used as bench marks to identify the characteristics which define Us. In Greek and Turkish nationalist discourses, the population of the other side of the Aegean Sea presented as a threat for the existence of the nation, but this population was furthermore used as a justification for radical positions, and hence became the argument showing the need for a 'national unity'.

In light of the several chapters of this book, focused on the human dimension of Greek–Turkish relations, one may now measure how the Other functions as part of the construction of Greek and Turk nations through three distinct parts. Initially, these chapters allow us to theorise the concept of the constitutive enmity on the basis of the Turkish and Greek case. In addition, one can comprehend the criteria of belonging to Turkishness and Greekness that was established for the compulsory exchange decided in 1923. One can scrutinise the non-exchanged groups, in other words, the minorities that remained within both nations-states.

The analysis of the identification of Turkishness and the identification of Greekness cannot obviously be done without placing them in a more general context: the birth of nations and consequently of nation-states. Given the debate on durability of the nations or their construction, we must start by announcing that this book is not neutral: it defends, not alone, the idea that the national construction is an analysable and datable process. There are no nations in the nature.

It should be specified that this nation-building process is not a commonly accepted concept by the academic world. Researchers such as Greetz,[1] Van Den Berghe,[2] Connor[3] or Armstrong[4] defend the idea of a quasi-eternal nation, independent of the concept of nationalism and the creation of nation-states, without even distinguishing between ethnic groups and nations. In this perspective, the nation is not a historical object, and it is independent of a political construction.

The thesis of the modernity of the concept of nation is well known, and Deutsch,[5] Gellner,[6] Hobsbawm[7] and Schnapper[8] propose the concomitance of national construction and creation of political organisations. In both cases, one can easily speak about the nineteenth century as a century of nations.

> A nation is a spirit . . . a great unity created by a feeling for the sacrifices one has already made and for those one is prepared to make in the future. It implies a past but expresses itself in the present by an obvious fact-the consent of the people and their clearly expressed desire to continue life in common.

Is this elegant and romantic definition of a nation by Renan[9] at the same time the definition of a minority? In other words, for those who live in the heart of a nation, while belonging to another, and who consequently 'would perhaps not be laid out to make sacrifices' for the other citizens. It is tempting to use the same definition. Moreover, aren't the concepts of nation and consequently of minority, fruits of the same process, born from the French revolution, which reached its maturity in the current of the nineteenth century?[10] I mean here the birth of the concept, and not of the minorities themselves, whose presence dates back probably to the first human communities. But whereas until the nineteenth century we see deprivations of rights for those who did not belong to the dominating group, from the nineteenth century one sees, on the contrary, the claim of substantive rights. The concept of protection of minorities is born in this context. Not only the existence of the minorities is recognised but moreover one accepts that they have to be protected. Consequently, in law there are rights known as negative rights, guaranteeing the equality of the individuals belonging to the dominating group and of the individuals belonging to the minorities, as well as rights known as positive, granted specifically to the minorities.

But let us return a few moments to our first definition. The question of the definition of a nation brings forth the definition of a minority. Who are the individuals living surrounded by a nation and forming a distinct group? If, according to Emile Giraud, we consider that in order to form a nation it is necessary for the individuals to 'have the same origin, to speak the same language, to have received the same moral and intellectual heritage, to have lived under the same laws and to have known the same joys and the same pains',[11] what will we do about the individuals who do not share one or more of these criteria? We have to consider them as belonging to the 'minorities'. Thus, all the attempts to define this concept start from a negative definition (i.e., finding a definition of the nation, taking those who do not tally there, and putting them in the category of minority). The minority is then inseparable from the nation. Where there is no nation, there is no minority. Given that, in empires, *a fortiori* in the Ottoman Empire, one cannot speak about a nation, to consider that there were minorities is nonsense.

The 'problem' of minorities was born in the nineteenth century with the emergence of the concept of nation-state.[12] In international law, the first case of attribution of the title of 'nation' to a distinct group within a nation-state took place with the Congress of Vienna in 1815, which recognised the right of the Polish to have national representation and the right to establish 'national' institutions.[13] But it was necessary to wait another century to see the appearance of the term of 'minority' when the United Kingdom addressed, in 1914, a note to Greece about the protection of the Muslim minorities on its territory. Indeed, happy were the countries where the state and the nation had emerged in a spontaneous and synchronic way.[14] If the state was preceded by the emergence of the nation, wars of independence took place and were often seen as rebellions by the dominating power.

Within the territories of the created state, distinct groups have always remained; the founders of the state, as well as both the nation corresponding to this state and the individuals belonging to these minority groups themselves, also considered them as distinct. Therefore, we encounter at the same time a matter of perception and of self-perception. If the state was established before the nation, then this nation had to be built, in other words it was necessary for the already founded state to correspond to a 'pure' nation as far as possible. Again, the main ideology of this construction was nationalism. Then, what to do with those who do not correspond? Eliminate them physically by the means of exterminations, expulsion, exile or exchange of population? Try to divide the group in order to create sub-groups, as a possible antagonist for better control? Try to melt the group into the nation by imposing a dominant language, a dominant religion and/or a dominant culture? Or accept the minority as it is and encourage it with a series of rights in order to attach it definitively to the state. The latter choice will cause a series of agreements, treaties, legislations, fiddling, all composing the base of the 'regime of minorities' in international law. Because, after all, even if one takes the point of view of nationalism, at least in its Latin perception, a few subjective elements can suffice for a state to legitimately incarnate all of its citizens. The first of these elements are solidarity and the will to live together.

After these theoretical thoughts, we can concentrate more specifically on the case of relationship between Turks and Greeks in their human dimension. This relationship begins within the political and legal framework of an empire but not a colonial one in the sense of the Western European empires, where the colonial possessions are remote and have more or less preserved their cultural and ethnic characteristics. In the eighteenth and even the nineteenth century, the centre of gravity of the Ottoman Empire was around the Aegean Sea. On the three borders and in the middle of this sea, the population was religiously mixed, but its way of life, let's say its culture, was unified in a sort of *convivenza*.

Thus, all movements of independence in the Ottoman Empire were perceived as revolts. If it is subdued, a revolt remains a revolt and enters the history books as such. It is only if it succeeds that it becomes an independence war. This is the case for the 'Greek revolt' as well as for the 'kemalist revolt'. These wars have two functions. They are certainly used to release a territory and a population considered under occupation. But they are also used to begin a heroic myth, necessary to the national construction.

Nations are constructed as much on victories as on defeats, on the 'catastrophes', traumatisms that form one of the pillars of the common membership. The pains are magnified as much as the joys; they are common points as much as the heroic acts of the founders of myths.

Admittedly, the Other of the Greek is not only the Turk: and the Turkish nation was not exclusively built in opposition to the Greekness either, but these two nationalisms drew from their mutual opposition to continue or reaffirm themselves. The nation being identified, one of the principal problems relating to the area was the 'purification' of the population, which was done in two manners: by including those considered as belonging to the nation and by excluding those regarded as foreigners. The compulsory exchange of populations between Greece and Turkey tried to achieve this purification and to reach, with a relative success I'm afraid, this objective of living 'between us'.

The compulsory exchange of populations between Greece and Turkey decided in January 1923, six months before the signature of the Treaty of Lausanne, is exceptional in its 'compulsory' nature. Other examples of exchange exist in the history of decolonisation, but this compulsory character is exceptional.[15] The convention of exchange has legitimated a *de facto* situation since 1920: the mass escape of the Greek Orthodox populations from Western Asia Minor. But by including groups such as the Turkish-speaking Christians of Cappadocia or the Greek-speaking Muslims of Crete in this exchange, the two countries clearly showed their understanding of 'unmixing of populations'.[16]

Throughout the Ottoman Empire, the principal criterion of identification was religious belonging, and although other criteria of identity had appeared at the beginning of the twentieth century (such as the common past or the feeling of having a common destiny), the compulsory exchange, as an important stage of Greek and Turkish national construction, exclusively took into account the religion of individuals. Thus, the ideologists of the two nations implicitly placed religious membership as the most important criterion of belonging, capable of overwhelming other common identity criteria, such as sharing the same geographic area, the same way of life or even the same language.

Identity constructions of the end of the nineteenth and the beginning of the twentieth century are based mainly on two supports: language and religion. After the exchange of 1923, one can say that one of these two supports, the language, was weak. It was weak mainly because the *millets* system is a religious categorisation system. It is surprising to note the force of the national paradigm: it was able, in two generations, to erase the linguistic distinction and to create descendants of Pericles with Turkish-speaking Anatolians and descendants of Atilla from Greek speaking Cretans! The refugees on both sides suffered so much of the 'natives' regarding them as aliens, that they not only did not transmit their language to their own children, but moreover developed a certain number of identity markers to prove their Turkishness or Greekness. This is how the Karamanlides refugees came to feel the need to declare 'my language is Turkish but my heart is Greek'.[17] Thus, we have to note that the 'unmixing of population', absurd as it is, succeeded at the linguistic level.

In the Greek and Turkish nation-building process, the place of religion is particular. Indeed, for exchanged populations, the second support of identity was religious membership. And contrary to language, this one, is transportable. Albert Bastenier speaks of religion as a 'mobile homeland'.[18] Indeed, the only part of homeland that the refugees from Anatolia brought to Greece was Orthodoxy. This religiosity, like Islam originating from Crete or Macedonia, was adapted to the new land. This adaptation was made ostentatiously. The Turkish-speaking Christians from Anatolia showed how much they were attached to Orthodoxy, and the refugees from Crete, from the Islands or from the Balkans, always demonstrated how Islamic they were, trying to prove that they were identical.[19]

When one of the identity supports is weak (language), the groups emphasise more the second support (religion). Linguistic conversion is much easier and much more acceptable for the new members of the nation than religious conversion. The compulsory exchange of populations between Greece and Turkey was an operation of amputation. But it was transformed in a few decades into an operation of transplant.

But the compulsory exchange was not complete. Thus, the so much desired homogenisation could not be carried out. In January 1923, the homogenisation of the Turkish (and Greek) population was institutionalised.[20] The Greeks of Istanbul as well as the Muslims of Western Thrace will remain as *établis* (established), having the citizenship of the state of residence. Why? The question is legitimate. It seems that, at the beginning of the discussions, the Turkish delegation opposed the maintenance of a Greek population in Turkey.[21] In his memories, Ismet Pasha recalls how he had to yield to the insistence of Venizelos and George Curzon on the question of this maintenance, which goes together with the maintenance of the Patriarchate.[22] Indeed, there was the real question. What could have been the importance, for Greece and partly for the Western powers, of the maintenance of a Greek community in Turkey, and, more so, the maintenance of the Patriarchate?[23] For the Turks, the starting point of the negotiations was to exempt the Muslims of Western Thrace from the exchange but to integrate the Greeks of Istanbul and especially the Patriarchate. Finally, the compromise solution was that both communities remained in a reciprocal way;[24] this word is important.

Thus, the Greeks of Istanbul, at least those who had lived there since 1918, had the right to be *établis*, forming a material justification of the maintenance of the Patriarchate. At the insistence of Western powers, the Turkish delegation had accepted this maintenance as long as it remained a purely religious institution. In order for the Patriarchate to deal with the internal religious affairs in Turkey, it needed a consistent Orthodox community. Besides the Greeks of Istanbul, two other communities were exempted of exchange. The small Orthodox community of the two islands situated at the entry of the strait of Dardanelles, Imbros and Ténédos also obtained this right under more confused circumstances, according to Article 14 of the Treaty of Lausanne and with a right of autonomy that was never provided. The Turkish-speaking Orthodox community of central Anatolia were included in the exchange and the Arabic-speaking Orthodox community of Antakya did not form part of Turkey until 1936.

For the Patriarchate, the exchange of populations had a double importance. Not only is it precisely this exchange that 'creates' the Greek and Turkish minorities, but moreover, some of the Greeks who remained in Istanbul, around 10 per cent were Hellenic nationals. This community of Greek citizens partly ensured the survival of the Greeks of Istanbul until the 1960s.

A minority is born of a double external process: minoration, as a quantitative process, and minorisation as a qualitative process. The conjugation of these two processes creates a tension between those who are considered in minority and thus dominated and those who are considered as a majority and thus in a dominant position. This double process is the fruit of both an external perception of the majority and an internal self-perception of the minority members. Communities such as the Greeks of Turkey or the Turks of Greece who feel threatened as groups, stick all the more to their characteristics, thus creating an 'inflation of identity'. This identity inflation is necessary to keep and reinforce the feeling of otherness. Because the two nations need this otherness in order to be defined and to remain as much as the groups in minority position, in a kind of jealousy of belonging, they use the same otherness to avoid disintegration, agitating the spectrum of a supposed acculturation. We are thus in an identity spiral in which the nationalist paradigm, like the monotheist religions, refuses dual belonging. Thus, in this vision of the world one cannot be at the same time Greek and Turkish in spite of an undeniable shared way of life and vision that one could call 'culture'.

This otherness has a double effect in the nation-making process and therefore in the reinforcement of the feeling of belonging or non-belonging. When the Turkish group thinks about the 'Greek' it sees the Other, the different one, threatening the existence of Turkishness itself. However, even if this otherness is necessary to sincere (or instrumentalist) nationalists of both groups, it becomes problematic when it is used for the minorities. In the case of minorities included to the otherness of enemy in the sense of Carl Schmitt, the entire set of characteristics lent to the group is verifiable in everyday life.

How should states identify their enemies and respond to threats? Carl Schmitt maintained that external enemies should be treated in a wholly different manner from internal enemies. Schmitt's seemingly straightforward distinction is far from obvious. His view of the external enemy as a collective of people to be opposed yet respected contains the seeds of its own destruction and collapses into his view of the internal enemy as an 'other' that must be eliminated. He implicitly maintains that it is uncomplicated to make principled spatial and temporal distinctions between enemies.[25]

This is valid for the Greeks of Turkey as well as for the Turks of Greece. This situation led to a reaction of marginalisation on behalf of the dominating group. The majority constantly demands fusion of the members of the minorities, but when those people 'exit their group' to approach, in a *visible* way (by the abandonment of the religious practices, by the use of the language of the majority, mixed marriages, ideological attitudes that conform with that of the majority, etc), this same majority takes refuge behind the most rigid aspects of its identity. Fearing the dilution of the group, they create an otherness of proximity, even stronger than the remote otherness. The individuals or groups in such a situation are thus doubly marginalised, by the majority group because the public opinion doubts their sincerity and prefers them to belong to the different group, but also by the minority because, betraying their original identity, they threaten the existence of the group. The examples are numerous, with an example being Sabetayists in Turkey. Turks have never ceased doubting the sincerity of the Sabetayists, even though conversion to Islam took place three centuries ago.

The Turks and the Greeks used and continue to use the opposite group to solidify the cohesion of the nation. In this permanent instrumentalisation, minorities are at the same time essential mirrors and *repoussoir*, foreground figures. In both cases, the nationalist paradigm uses an invaluable tool, that of holism, in other words allotting the whole of the group with characteristics incompatible with those of the majority: language, religion, physical appearance, accent, religious practice, clothing practices, food and so on. We can even see a semantic reflection of this holism in the use of the 'singular' to indicate the group in question. 'The Greek' is at the same time the Greek of Greece, of Istanbul, of Cyprus of the United States. He is identical in time and in space and represents Greekness. The same for 'the Turk': of course, he has to be a Muslim. To become a Turk in the Ottoman Empire meant converting to Islam.

The otherness of proximity functions sometimes more severely than the remote otherness. Thus, once the building of the nation is completed, the group can even remember the experience of living together with the opposite group and can express sympathy. With regard to the Greeks and the Turks, the examples are multiple. At the time of the seism of 1999, the sympathy of the Greek people went to the Turks of Turkey, but that did not result in an immediate feeling of sympathy towards the Turks of Greece. In the same framework, a huge nostalgic literature exists in Turkey that stresses the 'similarity' of Greek and Turks (same food, same music, same physical appearance and so on) without transforming it into sympathy towards the Greeks of Turkey. Otherwise, in nation building, once the utopia of nation-state seems to be close, the glances turn to the only elements that prevent its concretisation, namely minorities.

In these circumstances, what does 'human dimension' mean in international relations? Are there non-human dimensions? This book is constructed through the theoretical framework of complex interdependence.[26] This framework, used mainly in political science and international relations, makes it possible to grasp the complexity and dynamism of the relations between two states, two nations, with multifaceted societies and dynamic tensions. Not only is this bilateral relationship multidirectional, but it also follows paths contradictory to the sociological context, sometimes following irrational feelings and the maximisation of concrete interests. Thus, all aspects of Greek–Turkish relations are, at the same time, human and technical. But it's also true that by personal interest and lack of technical knowledge, I focused more on human groups, such as minorities or refugees, than on legal or financial aspects.

These groups are at the very same time actors, spectators and instruments of Greek–Turkish relations. They are included and assimilated or excluded and tolerated. This state of tolerance is centred on a spectrum of attitudes and sensitivities, ranging from 'positive hospitality' (*Wirtbarkeit*) in a Kantian sense, as well as efforts to include or exclude the group from the mainstream, to assimilation and/or elimination that reflects the societal objective: the dream of being 'among (our)selves' and having a homogeneous population that bears no distinctions. This has been the dream of nationalists in the nineteenth century and became a dream of nationalists again in the twenty-first century. Yet, due to unprecedented developments on the turn of the twentieth century, the dream of a 'pure' nation espoused by nationalists in the nineteenth century has become nearly impossible to achieve, because of several factors:

- First, denationalisation of governance, which imposed the transfer of sovereignty to supranational – political, cultural and economic – structures;
- Second, public access to transportation, which despite leading to economic and political discrepancies between the North and South also empowered transnational communities;
- Third, the shift towards micro-autonomies (regions, minorities, federate entities, Euro-regions), which continued the fomenting of infranational entities.

Nevertheless, the rise of national populist discourses and policies all over the world, and of course in Greece and in Turkey, show that it's still too early to announce the death of nation-state, which would result in majorisation of minorities (i.e., the end of dominated ethnic/cultural groups in a given nation).

The 'disenchanted universe' of Max Weber has not arrived yet, partially due to the resistance evident in most nation-states, and especially in Southeast Europe, where a 'nation' tends to employ radical measures in response to pressure of multicultural societies from within. Such behaviour by the state, as in the case of Greece and Turkey begs a question: is it possible for groups to pursue, obtain or preserve their rights for fear of reprisals by the state? More than the rights, it is in fact, a matter of 'the right to have rights', according to Arendt's terms. In other words, it is a matter of reaching a legitimacy of existence that is purely Simmelian.[27] Needless to say, in 2022 this legitimacy of existence is still controversial, or at least persists to be a subject of public discourse both in Greece, concerning the Turks of Greece and the existential question of what it means to be Greek, and in Turkey, regarding a few thousand remaining Greeks and whether the minority presents a danger to Turkish interests. Nevertheless, both nations succeeded in assimilating in three generations those who came from the other side, and their descendants are actors of reconciliation through shared collective memory.

Does 'Europeanisation' play a role in Greek–Turkish Relations? Certainly not as an actor. Both the European Union and the Council of Europe have shown they were weak international actors, but they can be considered more in the sense of an approach to human dimensions. If there is a role played by the EU, it is a negative one insofar as the 2004 Cyprus accession or the 2016 Turkey EU 'refugee deal' are catastrophic for bilateral relations. However, we may say that in the last three decades, an obvious societal Europeanisation occurred in both Greek and Turkish societies. This societal Europeanisation drove the process of legitimisation of citizens (individuals) over states and groups (minorities) over dominant structures.

The process of structural Europeanisation in Turkey and in Greece can, at best, 'normalise' the human dimensions of bilateral conflict. The question at hand is not the inclusion of these groups in the Greek or the Turkish 'nations', but that a solution is finally found to internalising their political belonging to the territorial entity by the respective nation.

However, due to the duality of the Westernisation phenomenon, legitimisation of human groups as actors (and not only instruments) is a dialectical process. On one hand, the state apparatus (bureaucracy, army) reaches the level of clarity to concede to and accept the existence of the non-state actors in international relations.

And in this context, the process of Europeanisation paradoxically goes hand in hand with a more or less sincere discourse of 'multiculturalism'. Multiculturalism is a societal fact that does not require an explicit public policy authorised by the government. In certain European states, such heterogeneity of the population is recognised and accepted by the official rhetoric as well as by public opinion, without a formulated policy being enforced by the state. In other states, like Canada, where recognition and acceptance of minorities is not easily achievable (see the Islamic family law issue[28]), public policies are designed to reinforce and facilitate the course, which Kymlicka calls 'multiculturalism'.[29] It is clear that this proactive ideology is neither shared by all members of the EU, nor specifically by Greece and Turkey. Conversely, the Greek Orthodox minority of Turkey and the Turkish Muslim minority of Greece have to realise and accept that the minority status does not have a degrading connotation. This perception of the minority status as demeaning is the heritage of both the nineteenth century's Ottoman society and the nation-state ideology. The last two decades have witnessed important transformations for these two minorities in the context of their self-perception and socio-political shifts in Europe.

As I said, nations are founded and built on victories as much as on defeats. The pains are magnified and cherished, as are successes and victories, gluing the community together with the shared pride of national heroic acts and veneration for the myth founders. Thus, Turkish as well as Greek literature is saturated with texts about national suffering. Venezis said that Greeks, as a community, build their identity on pain.[30] The Greek nation had already been built before the *Mikriasiatiki Katastrofi*, and the Turkish nation was beginning its construction during the *Kurtuluş Savaşı* (which narrates the same event from both points of view). Combined with the compulsory exchange of populations, the 1920–30 period brought a traumatic experience to both nations. As a result, the 'Other' was formed by and within Greek and Turkish nations, permanently linking up the majority with its respective minority. Apart from a collective trauma, every political, ethnic or even social group needs to have the 'Other'.

May we say, in 2023, that the 'other' of Greeks and Turks is no longer the same as it was one century ago. Only partially? Of course, the so-called refugee crisis since 2016 (re-)introduced the 'Arabic' or the 'Oriental' as the main other in both countries.[31] However, as the retransformation of Hagia Sophia into a mosque in 2020 shows, Turkey still does not consider the Greek Orthodox past as its own. It remains the 'other', a hated other sometimes, when Eris is around, an admired and loved one, *ο αδερφός μου*, when Eros dares to show his nose.

Notes

1. Greetz, Clifford (ed.), *Old Societies and New States*, London: The Free Press of Glencoe, 1963.
2. Van Den Berghe, Pierre, *The Ethnic Phenomenon*, New York: Oxford, 1981.
3. Connor, Walker, *Ethnonationalism, Princeton*, Princeton: Princeton University Press, 1994.
4. Armstrong, John, *Nations Before Nationalism*, Chapel Hill: The University of North Carolina Press, 1982.
5. Deutsch, Karl W., *Nationalism and Social Communication*, New York, London: MIT Press, 1953.
6. Gellner, Ernest, *Nations et nationalisme*, Paris: Payot, 1989.
7. Hobsbawm, Eric, *Nations et nationalismes depuis 1789*, Paris: Gallimard, 1992.
8. Schnapper, Dominique, *La communauté des citoyens*, Paris: Gallimard, 1994.
9. Renan, Ernest, *Qu'est-ce qu'une Nation? et autres essais politiques*, Paris: Presses Pocket, 1992, pp. 54–5.
10. Gellner, Ernest, *Nations and Nationalism*, New York: Cornell University Press, 1983, p. 53 and *passim*.
11. Giraud, Émile, 'Le Droit des nationalités. Sa valeur, son application', *Revue Générale de Droit International Public*, no. 31, 1924, p. 18, quoted within Pierré-Caps Stéphane, *Nation et peuples dans les constitutions modernes*, Nancy: Presses Universitaires de Nancy, p. 102.
12. Thonberry, Patrick, *International law and the Rights of Minorities*, Oxford: Clarendon Press, 1991, p. 25 *et passim*.
13. Öktem, Emre, 'L'évolution historique de la question des minorités et le régime institué par le Traité de Lausanne au sujet des minorités en Turquie', *Turkish Review of Balkan Studies*, 1996/1997, p. 62.
14. Ibid, p. 60.
15. For example, the treaty of Neuilly sur Seine of 1919 envisaged a voluntary exchange of population between Greece and Bulgaria.

16. The expression belongs to Dr Nansen, Aktar, Ayhan, 'Türk Yunan nüfus Mübade-lesinin ilk yılı', Pekin, Müfide (ed.), *Yeniden Kurulan Yaşamlar: 1923 Türk-Yunan Zorunlu Nüfus Mübadelesi*, Istanbul: Bilgi Üniversitesi Yayınları, 2005, p. 61.

17. Clogg, Richard (ed.), *Anatolica: studies in the Greek East in the 18th and 19th Centuries*, Titchmarsh: Variorum, 1996, p. 82.

18. Bastenier, Albert, *Qu'est-ce qu'une société ethnique: ethnicité et racisme dans les sociétés européennes d'immigration*, Paris: PUF, 2004, p. 233.

19. Barbina, Guido, 'Les communautés ethno-linguistique et la conscience de leur territoire', Sanguin, André (ed.), *Les minorités ethniques en Europe*, Paris: L'Harmattan, 1993, p. 59.

20. A former Turkish diplomat who perfectly reflects the official vision of the presence of non-Muslim minorities in Turkey, qualifies the presence of these minorities and the rights granted as 'debts', Akşin, Aptülahat, *Atatürk'ün Dış Politika ilkeleri ve diplomasisi*, Ankara: Türk Tarih Kurumu, 1991, p. 134.

21. Meray, Seha, *Lozan Barış Konferansı*, Ankara: Siyasal Bilgiler Fakültesi Yayını, 1973, Tome 1, p. 121.

22. Inönü, Ismet, *Hatıralar*, Ankara: Bilgi, 1987, Tome 2, pp. 130–2.

23. Arı, Kemal, *Büyük Mübadele. Türkiye'ye Zorunlu Göç*, Istanbul: Tarih Vakfı Yurt Yayınları, 1995, p. 17.

24. Akgönül, Samim (ed.), *Recpirocity: Greek and Turkish minorities. Law, religion and politics*, Istanbul: Bilgi University Press, 2006.

25. McKoy, Christopher, 'Inevitable Enmity, Inevitable Violence: Carl Schmitt on Internal and External Enemies' (19 January 2011). Available at SSRN: https://ssrn.com/abstract=1743454.

26. Keohane, Robert, Nye, Joseph, 'Power and Interdependence in the Information Age', *Foreign Policy*, September–October 1998, pp. 79–84.

    Keohane, Robert, Nye, Joseph, *Power and Interdependence revisited*, New York: Longman Classics in Political Science, 2011.

27. The problem of legitimacy is amply discussed in the work of Georg Simmel, but he fully devotes to the subject his book *The Philosophy of Money*, London: Routledge, 1990 (*Philosophie der Geldes*, Leipzig: Duncker & Humblot, 1900). For a thorough analysis of the legitimacy question in Simmel's work see: Noreau, Pierre, 'Le droit comme forme de socialisation: Georg Simmel et le problème de légitimité', *Revue française de science politique*, vol. 45, no. 2, April 1995, pp. 56–78. Simmel makes a clear distinction between granting individual and collective legitimacy to exist. The latter implies a direct correlation between fear for survival as a group and acceptance of the other. In other words, this legitimacy can be granted only if the dominant

group (i.e., the national majority) trusts that the existence of the dominated group will not threaten its own existence.

28. Razack, Sherene, 'The "Sharia Law Debate" in Ontario: The Modernity/Premodernity Distinction in Legal Efforts to Protect Women from Culture', *Feminist Legal Studies*, vol. 15, no. 1, April 2007, pp. 3–32.

29. Cf. Kymlicka, Will, Banting, Keith, *Multiculruralism and Welfare State: Recognition and Redistribution in Contemporary Democracies*, Oxford: Oxford University Press, 2006.

30. Millas, Iraklis (Hercules) 'Tourkokratia: History and the Image of Turks in Greek Literature', *South Eastern Society and Politics*, Routledge, 2006, vol. 11, no. 1, March 2006, pp. 47–60.

31. Kalogeraki, Stefania, 'Attitudes Towards Syrian Refugees During the "Refugee Crisis" in Greece', Kousis, Maria, Chatzidaki, Aspasia, Kafetsios, Konstantinos (eds), *Challenging Mobilities in and to the EU during Times of Crises: The Case of Greece*, Cham: Springer, 2022, pp. 91–111; Terzioğlu, Ayşecan, 'The Banality of Evil and the Normalization of The Discriminatory Discourses Against Syrians in Turkey', *Anthropology of the Contemporary Middle East and Central Eurasia* vol. 4, no. 2, 2018, pp. 34–47.

BIBLIOGRAPHY

Ağır, Ülkü, *Pogrom in Istanbul, 6./7. September 1955: Die Rolle der türkischen Presse in einer kollektiven Plünderungs- und Vernichtungshysterie*, Berlin: Klaus Schwartz Verlag, 2014.

Akbulut, Olgun, 'Legal Background of Autonomy Arrangements in Turkey from Historical Perspectives', Akbulut, Olgun, Aktoprak, Elçin (eds), *Minority Self-Government in Europe and the Middle East*, Leiden: Brill, 2021, pp. 228–45.

Akgönül, Samim, 'Les musulmans de Thrace en émigration' *Mésogeios*, no. 3, 1999, pp. 31–49.

Akgönül, Samim, 'The Greeks of Istanbul', *Mésogeios*, no. 6, 1999, pp. 64–106.

Akgönül, Samim, *Une communauté, deux États: la minorité turco-musulmane de Thrace occidentale*, Istanbul: Isis, 1999.

Akgönül, Samim, 'Les Grecs d'Istanbul pendant les premières décennies de la République Turque' *Deltio*, December 2002, pp. 11–44.

Akgönül, Samim, 'Religious Institutions of the Muslim Minority of Greece', Shadid, A Wasif, van Koningsveld, P. S. (eds), *Religious Freedom and the Neutrality of the State: The Position of Islam in the European Union*, Leuven: Peeters, 2002, pp. 145–57.

Akgönül, Samim (ed.), *Recpirocity: Greek and Turkish Minorities. Law, Religion And Politics*, Istanbul: Bilgi University Press, 2006.

Akgönül, Samim, *Minorités en Turquie, Turcs en minorité*, Istanbul: Isis, 2010.

Akgönül, Samim, 'The Turkish Diaspora–A Channel of Influence', *Yearbook of Muslims in Europe*, no. 14, 2021, pp. 5–14.

Akşin, Aptülahat, *Atatürk'ün Dış Politika ilkeleri ve diplomasisi*, Ankara: Türk Tarih Kurumu, 1991.

Aktar, Ayhan, *Varlık vergisi ve Türkleştirme Politikaları*, Istanbul: İletişim, 2000.

Aktar, Ayhan, 'Türk Yunan nüfus Mübadelesinin ilk yılı', Pekin, Müfide (ed.), *Yeniden Kurulan Yaşamlar: 1923 Türk-Yunan Zorunlu Nüfus Mübadelesi*, Istanbul: Bilgi Üniversitesi Yayınları, 2005.

Alexandris, Alexis, 'The Expulsion of Constantine VI: The Ecumenical Patriarchate and Greek–Turkish Relations, 1924–1925', *Balkan Studies*, no. 22, 1981, pp. 333–63.

Alexandris, Alexis, *The Greek Minority of Istanbul and Greek–Turkish Relations. 1918–1974*, Athens: Centre for Asia Minor Studies, 1992.

Alexandris, Alexis, 'Tenedos, from the Treaty of Lausanne to Nowadays', *The Forgotten Island of Tenedos*, Athens: Anatoli, 1997.

Alioğlu Cakmak, Gizem, Hüseyinoğlu, Ali, 'Muslim Turks of Western Thrace and Greek–Turkish Relations: The Troadic relational Nexus', Yürür, Pınar, Özkan, Arda (eds), *Conflict Areas in the Balkans*, London: Lexington Books, 2020, pp. 3–24.

Alogoskoufis, George, *Historical Cycles of the Economy of Modern Greece from 1821 to the Present*, Athens: Department of Economics Athens University of Economics and Business, Working Paper no. 01-2021.

Anastassiadou, Méropi, Dumont, Paul, *Les Grecs d'Istanbul et le patriarcat œcuménique au seuil du xxie siècle. Une communauté en quête d'avenir*, Paris: Les Éditions du Cerf, 2011.

Anderson, Benedict, *Imagined Communities: Reflections on the Origin and Spread of Nationalism*, London: Verso, 1991.

Andric, Ivo, *Titanic et autres contes juifs de Bosnie*, Paris: Rocher, 2001.

Apostolidis, Nikos, *Αναμνήσεις από την Κωνσταντινούπολη*, Athènes: Troholia, 1996.

Arı, Kemal, *Büyük Mübadele. Türkiye'ye Zorunlu Göç*, Istanbul: Tarih Vakfı Yurt Yayınları, 1995.

Armstrong, John, *Nations Before Nationalism*, Chapel Hill: The University of North Carolina Press, 1982.

Aydın, Mustafa, 'Between Euphoria and Realpolitik: Turkish Policy toward Central Asia and the Caucasus', Aydın, Mustafa, Ismael, Tareq Y. (eds), *Turkey's Foreign Policy in the 21st Century*, London: Routledge, 2019, pp. 211–28.

Baddoura, Rita, 'Chékri Ganem: pionnier et virtuose du verbe', *L'Orient le Jour*, no. 166, April 2020.

Baer, Marc David, 'An Enemy Old and New: The Dönme, Anti-Semitism, and Conspiracy Theories in the Ottoman Empire and Turkish Republic', *Jewish Quarterly Review*, vol. 103 no. 4, 2013, pp. 523–55.

Bafeiadis, Simos, *Ένας Πολίτης Θυμάται*, Athènes: Ekdoseis Tsoukatou, 1998.

Bahcheli, Tozun, 'Cycles of Tension and Rapprochement: Prospects for Turkey's Relations with Greece', Aydın, Mustafa, Ismael, Tareq Y. (eds), *Turkey's Foreign Policy in the 21st Century*, London: Routledge, 2019, pp. 229–36.

Balat ve Fener semtlerinin Rehabilitasyonu (Istanbul Tarihi Yarımadası), Istanbul: Fatih Municipality, European Union, UNESCO IFEA, 1998.

Bali, Rifat, *Cumhuriyet Yıllarında Türkiye Yahudileri. Bir Türkleştirme Serüveni (1923–1945)*, Istanbul: İletişim, 1999, p. 84.

Balta, Evangelia, *Beyond the Language Frontier: Studies on Karamanlis and Karamanlidika Printing*, Istanbul: Isis, 2010.

Barbera, Pablo, Casas, Andreu, Nagler, Jonathan, Egan, Patrick, Bonneau, Richard, Jost, John, Tucker, Joshua, 'Who Leads? Who Follows? Measuring Issue Attention and Agenda Setting by Legislators and the Mass Public Using Social Media Data'. *American Political Science Review*, vol. 113, no. 4, 2019, pp. 883–901.

Barbina, Guido, 'Les communautés ethno-linguistique et la conscience de leur territoire', Sanguin, André (ed.), *Les minorités ethniques en Europe*, Paris: L'Harmattan, 1993, s. 59.

Bastenier, Albert, *Qu'est-ce qu'une société ethnique: ethnicité et racisme dans les sociétés européennes d'immigration*, Paris: PUF, 2004, p. 233.

Baydar, Ertuğrul, *İkinci Dünya Savaşı İçinde Türk Bütçeleri*, Ankara: Maliye Bakanlığı Tetkik Kurulu, 1978.

Benbassa, Esther, 'Le Clandestin', *CEMOTI*, no. 28, 1999, pp. 54–5.

Benlisoy, Yorgo, Macar, Elçin, *Fener Patrikhanesi*, Istanbul: Ayraç, 1997.

Birsel, Salâh, *Ah Beyoğlu vah Beyoğlu*, Ankara: Yonca, 1983.

Bozkurt, Gülnihal, *Batı Hukukunun Türkiye'de Benimsenmesi. Osmanlı Devleti'nden Türkiye Cumhuriyeti'ne Resepsiyon Süreci (1839–1939)*, Ankara: Türk Tarih Kurumu, 1996.

Bromberger, Dominique, 'Méditerranée', *Anthropen* (2019-04-23), https://doi.org/10.17184/eac.anthropen.106.

Butler, Kim, 'Defining Diaspora, Refining a Discourse', *Diaspora, A Journal of Transnational Studies*, vol. 10, no. 2, 2001, pp. 189–219.

Cakal, Ergun, 'Pluralism, Tolerance and Control: On the *Millet* System and the Question of Minorities', *International Journal on Minority and Group Rights*, vol. 27, no. 1, 2020, pp. 34–65.

Canetti, Elias, *Crowds and Power*, London: Farrar, Straus and Giroux, 1984.

Çarkoğlu, Ali, Rubin, Barry (eds), *Greek–Turkish Relations in an Era of Détente*, New York: Routledge, 2005.

Christofis, Nikos, 'The State of the Kurds in Erdoğan's 'New' Turkey', *Journal of Balkan and Near Eastern Studies*, vol. 21, no. 3, 2019, pp. 251–9.

Cihangir, Erol, *Papa Eftim'in Muhtıraları ve Bağımsız Türk Ortodoks Patrikhanesi*, Istanbul: Turan, 1996.

Clark, Bruce, *Twice a Stranger: How Mass Expulsion Forged Modern Greece and Turkey*, London: Granta, 2006.

Clogg, Richard (ed.), *Anatolica: Studies in the Greek East in the 18th and 19th Centuries*, Titchmarsh: Variorum, 1996.

Connor, Walker, *Ethnonationalism*, Princeton: Princeton University Press, 1994.

Curtiss, John Shelton, *The Russian Church and the Soviet State 1917–1950*, Gloucester: P. Smith, 1965.

Dalay, Galip, 'Turkey, Europe, and the Eastern Mediterranean: Charting a way out of the Current Deadlock', *Brookings*, 28 January 2021, https://www.brookings.edu/research/turkey-europe-and-the-eastern-mediterranean-charting-a-way-out-of-the-current-deadlock/.

De Cloarec, Vincent, *La France et la question de la Syrie, 1914–1918*, Paris: CNRS Éditions, 2010.

Decaux, Emmanuel, *La réciprocité en droit international*, Paris: Librairie générale du droit et de jurisprudence, 1980.

Deleon, Jak, *Beyoğlunda Beyaz Ruslar*, Istanbul: Remzi, 1996.

Demir, Hülya, Akar, Rıdvan, *Istanbul'un Son Sürgünleri*, Istanbul: İletişim, 1994.

De Tapia, Aude Aylin, 'The Rums of Greek-Orthodox in Turkey', Gültekin, Ahmet Kerim, Süvari, Çakır Ceyhan (eds), *The Ethno-Cultural Others in Turkey: Contemporary reflexions*, Yerevan: Russian-Armenian University Press, 2021, pp. 163–83.

Deutsch, Karl W., *Nationalism and Social Communication*, New York, London: MIT Press, 1953.

Duman, Gökhan, 'Devletlerarası İkili İlişkilerde Azınlık Kimliği Etkisi: Batı Trakya Örneği', *Sivas Cumhuriyet Üniversitesi İktisadi ve İdari Bilimler Dergisi*, vol. 22, no. 1, 2021, pp. 379–94.

Dumont Paul, 'La période des Tanzimat', Mantran Robert (dir.), *Histoire de l'Empire Ottoman*, Paris: Fayard, 1989, pp. 476–506.

Dumont, Paul, *Mustafa Kemal*, Paris: Complexe, 1997.

Dündar, Fuat, *Türkiye Nüfus Sayımlarında Azınlıklar*, Istanbul: Doz, 1999.

Elias, Norbert, *Time: An Essay*, Oxford: Blackwell Publishers, 1992.

Erginsoy, Güliz, 'Tam ve Yarı zamanlı vatandaşlık, Gliki'den Bademli'ye Dört Kuşak', Akgönül Samim (ed.), *Images et perceptions dans les relations gréco-turques*, Nancy: Genèse, 1999.

Erikson, Erik 'Pseudospeciation in the Nuclear Age', *Political Psychology*, 1985, vol. 6, no. 2, pp. 213–17.

Erim, Nihat, 'Milletlerarası Daimi Adalet Divani ve Türkiye, Etabli Meselesi', *Ankara Üniversitesi Hukuk Fakültesi Dergisi*, vol. 2, no. 1, 1944, pp. 62–73.

Galanti, Avram, *Türkler ve Yahudiler - Tarihi, Siyasi, İçtimai Tetkik*, Istanbul, 1947.

Gautier, Théophile, *Constantinople en 1852*, Istanbul: Isis, 1990.

Gellner, Ernest, *Nations and Nationalism*, New York: Cornell University Press, 1983.

Gellner, Ernest, *Nations et nationalisme*, Paris: Payot, 1989.

Georgeon, François, Dumont, Paul (dir.), *Vivre dans l'Empire ottoman: Sociabilités et relations intercommunautaires (XVIIIe–XXe siècles)*, Paris: L'Harmattan, 1997.

Giraud, Émile, 'Le droit des nationalités. Sa valeur, son application', *Revue Générale de Droit International Public*, no. 31, 1924.

Gökay, Bülent, 'Belgelerle Struma Faciası', *Tarih ve Toplum*, no. 116, 1993, pp. 42–5.

Gönlübol, Mehmet, Sar Cem, *Olaylarla Türk Dış Politikası*, Ankara: Ankara Üniversitesi Siyasal Bilimler Fakültesi Yayınları, 1982.

Greetz, Clifford (ed.), *Old Societies and New States*, London: The Free Press of Glencoe, 1963.

Gries, Peter, Wang, Tao, 'Public Opinion and Foreign Policy: Beyond the Electoral Connection', Rudolph, Thomas, *Handbook on Politics and Public Opinion*, Cheltenham: Elgar, 2022, pp. 430–45.

Grigoriadis, Ioannis, 'On the Europeanization of Minority Rights Protection: Comparing the Cases of Greece and Turkey', *Mediterranean Politics*, Vol. 13, no. 1, March 2008, pp. 23–41.

Grigoriadis, Ioannis, 'Between Citizenship and the *millet*: the Greek Minority in Republican Turkey', *Middle Eastern Studies*, vol. 57, no. 5, 2021, pp. 741–57.

Groom, A. J., Barrinha, Andre, Olson, William C., *International Relations Then and Now: Origins and Trends in Interpretation*, London: Routledge, 2019.

Güçlü, Mehmet, 'İzmir'in işgaline tanık bir zatın kaleminden, İzmir'de neler oldu 1336/1920 kitapçığı üzerine', *Çağdaş Türkiye Tarihi Araştırmaları Dergisi*, vol. 10, no. 22, 2011, pp. 65–76.

Güler, Ali, *Pontus meselesi ve Rum-Yunan Terör örgütleri*, Ankara: Rizeliler Derneği, 1984.

Hasan, Kuruyazıcı, Mete, Tapan, *Sveti Stefan Bulgar Kilisesi. Bir Yapı Monografisi*, Istanbul: Yapı Kredi Yayınları, 1998.

Helmreich, Paul, *From Paris to Sèvres: The Partition of the Ottoman Empire at the Peace Conference of 1919–1920*, Columbus, OH: Ohio State University Press, 1974.

Hirschon, Renée, *Heirs of the Greek Catastrophe*, New York: Oxford University Press, 1989.

Hirschon, Renée (ed.), *Crossing the Aegean: Assessing the Consequences of the 1923 Exchange of Populations, Between Greece and Turkey*, Oxford: Berghahn Books, 2003.

Hobsbawm, Eric, *Nations et nationalismes depuis 1789*, Paris: Gallimard, 1992.

Hoffmeister, Frank, *The Legal Aspects of the Cyprus Problem: Annan Plan and EU Accession*, Leiden: Martinus Nijhoff Publishers, 2006, pp. 130–54.

Hüseyinoğlu, Ali, 'Rethinking Limits of Anti-Muslim Hatred and Discrimination in Contemporary Greece', *Stratejik ve Sosyal Araştırmalar Dergisi*, no. 5, 2021, pp. 1–20.

Hüseyinoğlu, Ali, Eroğlu Utku, Deniz, 'Turkish–Greek Relations and Irregular Migration at the Southeasternmost Borders of the EU: The 2020 Pazarkule Case', *Migration Letters*, vol. 18, no. 6, November 2021, pp. 659–74.

Inalcık, Halil, *Tanzimat ve Bulgar Meselesi*, Ankara: n.e., 1943.

Inönü, Ismet, *Hatıralar*, Ankara: Bilgi, Tome 2, 1987.

Kalafat, Oguz, *Türkiye'de Özel Okullar Tarihi*, Istanbul: Akademisyen, 2021.

Kalaycıoğlu, Sema, 'Türk Yunan dostluğuna gastronomik bir yaklaşım, Kokoreç diplomasisi', *Finansal Forum*, 27 January 2000.

Kalogeraki, Stefania, 'Attitudes Towards Syrian Refugees During the "Refugee Crisis" in Greece', Kousis, Maria, Chatzidaki, Aspasia, Kafetsios, Konstantinos (eds), *Challenging Mobilities in and to the EU during Times of Crises: The Case of Greece*, Cham: Springer, 2022, pp. 91–111.

Kamouzis, Dimitris, *Greeks in Turkey: Elite Nationalism and Minority Politics in Late Ottoman and Early Republican Istanbul*, London: Routledge, 2021.

Katsikas, Stefanos, *Islam and Nationalism in Modern Greece*, Oxford: Oxford University Press, 2021.

Kaya, Nurcan, 'Teaching in and Studying Minority Languages in Turkey: A Brief Overview of Current Issues and Minority Schools', *European Yearbook of Minority Issues*, vol. 12, no. 1, 2015, pp. 315–38

Kaymak, Özgür, Beylunioğlu, Anna Maria, 'İstanbul'da Yaşayan Antakyalı Ortodoksların Kendilerini Kimliklendirme Süreci ve İstanbul Rum Cemaatiyle İlişkisellikleri', Haris, Rigas (ed.), *Üç Milliyetçiliğin Gölgesinde Kadim Bir Cemaat: Arapdilli Doğu Ortodoksları*, Istanbul: Istos, 2018, pp. 71–142.

Keohane, Robert, Nye, Joseph, 'Power and Interdependence in the Information Age', *Foreign Policy*, September–October 1998, pp. 79–84.

Keohane, Robert, Nye, Joseph, *Power and Interdependence Revisited*, New York: Longman Classics in Political Science, 2011.

Kitsikis, Dimitri, 'Le projet d'entente balkanique. 1930–1934', *Revue Historique*, no. 241, 1969, pp. 115–40.

Kitsikis, Dimitri, *L'Empire Ottoman*, Paris: Presses Universitaires de France, 1985.

Köker, Tolga, 'The Establishment of Kemalist Secularism in Turkey', *Middle East Law and Governance*, vol. 2, no. 1, 2010, pp. 17–42.

Köker, Tolga, Keskiner, Leyla, 'Lessons in Refugeehood: The Experience of Forced Migrants in Turkey' Hirschon, Renée (ed.), *Crossing the Aegean: Assessing the Consequences of the 1923 Exchange of Populations, Between Greece and Turkey*, Oxford: Berghahn Books, 2003, pp. 193–208.

Kolarz, Walter, *Religion in the Soviet Union*, London: Macmillan, 1961.

Koumpli, Vassiliki, 'Managing Religious Law in a Secular State: The Case of the Muslims of Western Thrace', Yassari, Nadjima, Foblets, Marie-Claire (eds), *Normativity and Diversity in Family Law. Ius Comparatum – Global Studies in Comparative Law*, vol. 57, 2022, pp. 327–49.

Koutrolikou, Penny, 'Reading Perceptions of the 'Other' Through the Debates and Public Discourses about Islamic Religious Practices and the Presence of Mosques in Athens', Micha, Irini, Vaiou, Dina (eds), *Alternative Takes to the City*, vol. 5, New York: Wiley, pp. 125–50.

Kuneralp, Sinan, 'Les Grecs en Stambouline: diplomates ottomans d'origine grecque', Vaner, Semih (ed.), *Le différend gréco-turc*, Paris: L'Harmattan, 1988, pp. 41–6.

Kymlicka, Will, Banting, Keith, *Multiculruralism and Welfare State: Recognition and Redistribution in Contemporary Democracies*, Oxford: Oxford University Press, 2006.

Leffler, Melvyn P., 'Strategy, Diplomacy, and the Cold War: The United States, Turkey, and NATO, 1945–1952', *The Journal of American History*, vol. 71, no. 4, March 1985, pp. 807–25.

Levi, Avner, *Türkiye Cumhuriyet'inde Yahudiler*, Istanbul: İletişim, 1992.

Lévi-Valensi, Jacqueline 'La Méditerranée d'Albert Camus: une mythologie du reel', Armignani, Paul, Laurichesse, Jean-Yves, Thomas, Joël (eds), *Rythmes et lumières de la Méditerranée*, Perpignan: Presses Universitaires de Perpignan, 2004, pp. 267–76.

Lisi, Marco, Llamazares, Iván, Tsakatika, Myrto, 'Economic crisis and the variety of populist response: evidence from Greece, Portugal and Spain', *West European Politics*, vol. 42, no. 6, 2019, pp. 1284–309.

Lory, Bernard, 'Strates historiques des relations turco-bulgares', *CEMOTI*, vol. 15, 1993, pp. 149–67.

Ma Mung, Emmanuel, *La diaspora chinoise, géographie d'une migration*, Paris: Ophrys, 2000.

Macar, Elçin, *İşte geliyor Kurtuluş – Türkiye'nin 2. Dünya Savaşı'nda Yunanistan'a Yardımları*, İzmir: İzmir Ticaret Odası, 2017.

Macar, Elçin, 'The Ecumenical Patriarchate under Patriarch Bartholomew and Greek–Turkish relations', Heraclides, Alexis, Alioğlu Çakmak, Gizem (eds), *Greece and Turkey in Conflict and Cooperation: From Europeanization to De-Europeanization*, London: Routledge, 2019, pp. 129–44.

Marshall, Tim, *The Power of Geography: Ten Maps That Reveal the Future of Our World*, London: Elliott & Thompson, 2021.

Mavropoulos, Dimitros, Πατριαρχικές Σελίδες., Τό Οἰκουμενικόν Πατριαρχεῖον *1878–1949*, Thessaloniki, n.e., 1960.

McKoy, Christopher, 'Inevitable Enmity, Inevitable Violence: Carl Schmitt on Internal and External Enemies' (19 January 2011), https://ssrn.com/abstract=1743454.

Meray, Seha, *Lozan Barış Konferansı*, Ankara: Siyasal Bilgiler Fakültesi Yayını, Tome 1, 1973.

Millas, Iraklis (Hercules), 'Tourkokratia: History and the Image of Turks in Greek Literature' *South Eastern Society and Politics*, Routledge, 2006, vol. 11, no. 1, March 2006, pp. 47–60.

Moser, Pierre, *Arméniens, où est la réalité?*, Saint-Aquilin-de-Pacy: Mallier, 1980.

Mumcu, Uğur, *40'ların Cadı Kazanı*, Ankara: umag, 1990.

Murphy, Alexander B., 'The May 2004 Enlargement of the European Union: View from Two Years Out', *Eurasian Geography and Economics*, vol. 47, no. 6, 2006, pp. 635–46.

Nadje, Al-Ali, Koser Khalid, *New Approaches to Migration? Transnational Communities and the Transformation of Home*, London: Routledge, 2002.

Nichols, Theo, Sugur, Nadir, Sugur, Serap, 'Muhacir Bulgarian Workers in Turkey: Their Relation to Management and Fellow Workers in the Formal Employment Sector', *Middle Eastern Studies*, vol. 39, no. 2, 2003, pp. 37–54.

Noreau, Pierre, 'Le droit comme forme de socialisation: Georg Simmel et le problème de légitimité' *Revue française de science politique*, vol. 45, no. 2, April 1995, pp. 56–78.

Nüfus ve Demografi 1927–1990, Cumhuriyet Dönemi Istanbul istatistikleri, Istanbul: Istanbul Büyükşehir Belediyesi, 1997.

Öktem, Emre, 'L'évolution historique de la question des minorités et le régime institué par le Traité de Lausanne au sujet des minorités en Turquie', *Turkish Review of Balkan Studies*, 1996/1997.

Ömeroğlu, Aydın, *Batı Trakya Türkleri ve Gerçek*, Istanbul: Avcı Ofset, 1994.

Oran, Baskın, *Türk Yunan İlişkilerinde Batı Trakya Sorunu*, Istanbul: Bilgi, 1991.

Örs, Romain Ilay, *Diaspora of the City: Stories of Cosmopolitanism from Istanbul and Athens*, London: Palgrave, 2018.

Öztürk, Ahmet Erdi, Akgönül, Samim, 'Turkey: forced marriage or marriage of convenience with the Western Balkans?', Bieber, Florian, Tzifakis, Nikolaos (eds), *The Western Balkans in the World. Linkages and Relations with Non-Western Countries*, London: Routledge, 2019, pp. 269–88.

Papadakis, Yannis, *Echoes from the Dead Zone, Across the Cyprus Divide*, London: I. B. Tauris, 2005.

Pekin, Müfide (ed.), *Yeniden Kurulan Yaşamlar, 1923 Türk-Yunan Zorunlu Nüfus Mübadelesi*, Istanbul: Bilgi Üniversitesi Yayınları, 2005.

Pierré-Caps, Stéphane, *Nation et peuples dans les constitutions modernes*, Nancy: Presses Universitaires de Nancy, s.d.

Psomiades, Harry J., 'The Ecumenical Patriarchate under the Turkish Republic: The First Ten Years', *Balkan Studies*, no. 2, 1961, pp. 47–70.

Ralli, Angela (ed.), *The Morphology of Asia Minor Greek*, Leiden: Brill, 2019.

Razack, Sherene, 'The 'Sharia Law Debate' in Ontario: The Modernity/Premodernity Distinction in Legal Efforts to Protect Women from Culture', *Feminist Legal Studies*, vol. 15, no. 1, April 2007, pp. 3–32.

Renan, Ernest, *Qu'est-ce qu'une nation? et autres essais politiques*, Paris: Presses Pocket, 1992.

Şahin, Recep, 'Türk Devletlerinin Ermeni Politikaları', *Türk Tarihinde Ermeniler*, Izmir: Dokuz Eylül Üniversitesi, 1983, pp. 99–114.

Schmitt, Karl, *The Concept of the Political*, Chicago: The University of Chicago Press, 2007 (1932).

Schnapper, Dominique, *La communauté des citoyens*, Paris: Gallimard, 1994.

Simmel, Georg, *Philosophie der Geldes*, Leipzig: Duncker & Humblot, 1900.

Simmel, Georg, *The Philosophy of Money*, London: Routledge, 1990.

Sitaropoulos, Nicholas, 'Freedom of Movement and the Right to a Nationality v. Ethnic Minorities: The Case of ex Article 19 of the Greek Nationality Code', *European Journal of Migration and Law*, no. 6, 2004, pp. 205–23.

Sofuoğlu, Adnan, *Fener Patrikhanesi ve Siyasi Faaliyetleri*, Istanbul: Turan, 1996, p. 207.

Struve, Nikita, *Les Chrétiens en URSS*, Paris: Seuil, 1962.

Tekir, Süleyman, 'The Issue of Civilian and Military Refugees in Turkey in World War II Years', *Kafkas University Journal of the Institute of Social Sciences*, no. 23, Spring 2019, pp. 227–56.

Temel, Ahmet, 'Between State Law and Religious Law: Islamic Family Law in Turkey', *Electronic Journal of Islamic and Middle Eastern Law*, vol. 8. no. 1, 2022, pp. 68–76.

Terzioğlu, Ayşecan, 'The Banality of Evil and the Normalization of the Discriminatory Discourses Against Syrians in Turkey', *Anthropology of the Contemporary Middle East and Central Eurasia* vol. 4, no. 2, 2018, pp. 34–47.

Tesal, Reşat, *Selanik'ten Istanbul'a*, Istanbul: İletişim, 1998.

Thiesse, Anne Marie, *The Creation of National Identities Europe, 18th-20th Centuries*, Leiden: Brill, 2021.

Thonberry, Patrick, *International law and the Rights of Minorities*, Oxford: Clarendon Press, 1991, p. 25 *et passim*.

Topuz, Hıfzı, *Eski Dostlar*, Istanbul: Remzi, 2000.

Tsitselikis, Konstantinos, *Old and New Islam in Greece: From Historical Minorities to Immigrant Newcomers*, Leiden: Brill, 2012.

Tsitselikis, Konstantinos, Mavrommatis, Giorgios, *Turkish: The Turkish Language in Education in Greece*, Leeuwarden: Mercator European Research Centre on Multilingualism and Language Learning, 2019.

Tsvetana, Georgieva, 'Pomaks: Muslim Bulgarians', *Islam and Christian–Muslim Relations*, vol. 12, no. 3, 2001, pp. 303–16.

Tutel, Eser, *Beyoğlu Beyoğlu İken*, Istanbul: Oğlak, 1998.

Tziampiris, Aristotle, 'Greek foreign Polity and the Macedonian Name Dispute: From Confrontation to Europanization?', Anatasakis, Othon, Bechev, Dimitar, Vrousalis, Nicholas, *Greece in the Balkans: Memory, Conflict and Exchange*, Newcastle: Cambridge Scholars Publishing, 2019, pp. 138–56.

Ülkümen, Selahattin, *Bilinmeyen Yönleriyle Bir Dönemin Dışişleri*, Istanbul: Gözlem, 1993.

Uras, Esat, *The Armenians in History and the Armenian Question*, Istanbul: Documentary Publications, 1988.

Van Den Berghe, Pierre, *The Ethnic Phenomenon*, New York, Oxford: Bloomsbury, 1981.

Varouhakis, Viron, 'Greek Intelligence and the Capture of PKK Leader Abdullah Ocalan in 1999', *Studies in Intelligence*, vol. 53, no. 1, 2009, pp. 1–8.

Vasilios, Stavridis, *Η Οικουμενικη Πατριαρχη 1860-Σιμερον*, Athènes: Eteria Makedonikon Spudon, 1977.

Venezis, Elias, *Νούμερο 31328*, Athens: Kambana, 1924.

Xydis, Stephen, 'Toward 'Toil and Moil' in Cyprus', *Middle East Journal*, vol. 20, no. 1, 1966, pp. 1–19.

Yalçın, Kemal, *Emanet çeyiz: Mübadele insanları*, Istanbul: Bir Zamanlar Yayınları, 1989.

Yerasimos, Stefanos, 'Les rapports gréco-turcs, mythes et réalités', *CEMOTI (Cahiers d'études sur la Méditerranée orientale et le monde turco-iranien)*, 1986, no. 2–3, pp. 3–10.

Yücel, Hakan (ed.), *Rum Olmak, Rum Kalmak*, Istanbul: Istos, 2018.

INDEX

Aegean, 1, 7, 9, 12, 22, 50, 52, 53, 58, 66, 78, 86, 95, 158, 160, 161, 164, 170, 175–6, 182, 183, 184, 188

Aga, Mehmet Emin, 142, 145, 150

Ahmet, Sadık, 138–50, 153, 154, 155, 156, 165, 177

Aksu, Sezen, 170

Albania, 19, 73, 110, 126, 127, 159, 160, 167

Alexandroupolis, 21, 86, 129, 131, 141, 165

Alexiou, Haris, 170

amele taburu, 75, 113

America, 30, 35, 115, 159, 179, 181

Anatolia, 12, 16, 31, 32, 34, 36, 39, 48, 52, 58, 59, 62, 134, 190, 191

Andric, Ivo, 14

Annan, Kofi, 172–4

Antakya, 88, 89, 114, 191; *see also* Antioch

Antioch, 95, 97, 111; *see also* Antakya

Apostolidis, Nikos, 114

Arabs, 13, 15, 26–35, 88–98, 103, 114, 116, 132, 169, 177, 187, 191, 197

Armenia, 34, 35

Armenians, 15, 16, 28, 31–5, 76, 77, 87, 90, 103, 106, 119, 123, 124, 163, 169

Article 19, 133, 136–8, 153, 166

Asia Minor, 1, 4, 6, 27, 28, 31, 32, 33, 35, 36, 38, 40, 42, 48, 49, 58, 115, 189; *see also* Anatolia

Atatürk, Mustapha Kemal, 18, 30–44, 46, 51, 57, 72, 73, 74, 80, 103–8, 150

Athenagoras (Patriarch), 19, 80, 109, 167

Athens, 3, 4, 7, 9, 30, 35, 36, 39, 78, 79, 85, 107, 116, 117, 123, 131, 132, 140, 142, 143, 144, 151, 153, 154, 162, 163, 164, 169, 170, 180

Bafeiadis, Simos, 114

Balıkesir, 32, 36, 85

Balıklı, 90–2

Balkans, 12, 46, 50, 51, 111, 150, 160, 165, 190

Bartholomeos (Patriarch), 109, 167–9, 181

Beyoğlu, 18, 92

Bolsheviks, 36, 37, 40

Bozcaada *see* Imbros

Bulgaria, 5, 19, 20, 21, 27, 61, 74, 78, 110, 114, 126, 127, 129, 134, 135, 159, 165, 166

Bursa, 3, 8, 34, 37, 114, 132, 134, 135, 136

Caliphate, 29, 40, 105, 107

Canetti, Ellias, 16

Cappadocia, 189

Çakmak, Fevzi, 38

Catholics, 14, 15, 152

Cem, Ismail, 163

Çiller, Tansu, 161

Clinton, Bill, 161, 179

Council of Europe, 133, 138, 141, 147, 195

Crete, 48, 49, 50, 52, 53, 73, 189, 190

Curzon, George, 104, 191

Cyprus, 9, 17–19, 66, 67, 77–86, 93, 98, 101, 102, 139, 158, 161, 164, 168, 171–5, 181, 193, 195

Damat Ferit Pasha, 34

Davos (spirit of), 23, 141, 181

Dede, Andülhalim, 143

Demirel, Süleyman, 86, 147, 162

Denktaş, Rauf, 150, 171, 173

diaspora, 4, 8, 39, 66, 126, 127, 132–8

Dodecanese, 19, 78, 126

Echinos, 3, 4, 21, 165, 166

Emin, Sabahattin, 143

European Union, 168, 171–5, 195

Evros, 7, 136, 141

exchange of populations, 2, 3, 6, 7, 8, 12–17, 23, 42, 48–63, 66–9, 72–3, 95, 104, 107, 115, 116, 122, 126, 129, 182, 185–91, 196

Faikoğlu, Ahmet, 145, 146, 147, 149

Fener *see* Phanar

Fotios II (Patriarch), 108, 109, 110

France, 4, 22, 31, 35, 36, 38, 40, 42, 72, 124, 128

Ganem, Chekri, 16, 26–8, 40

gecekondu , 17

Georgeon, François, 13

Germany, 4, 19, 21, 54, 103, 112, 126, 127, 128, 132, 133, 140, 141, 150, 151

Gökçeada *see* Tenedos

Golden Horn, 90, 99, 114, 135

Great Britain (United Kingdom), 31, 35, 42, 82, 173, 187

Grigorios V (Patriarch), 101, 107, 108

Grigorios VII (Patriarch), 107

Gülen, Fethullah, 170, 180

Gümülcine *see* Komotini

Hacıibram, Orhan, 149

Hacopoulos, Alexandros, 134

Hagia Sophia, 1, 178

Halki theological school, 86, 95, 158, 168, 178–81

Hamza, Osman, 178
Hatipoğlu, Hasan, 140, 142
Hemşeri, Necdet, 178
Heybeliada *see* Halki

Imbros, 3, 4, 49, 63, 66, 67, 69, 73, 84,
    89, 95–8, 109, 114–16, 191
Imia/Kardak (island), 160, 161
İnönü, Erdal, 147
İnönü, Ismet, 19, 33, 38, 39, 73, 75, 82,
    103, 104, 191
Ioakim (Patriarch), 108
Iskeçe *see* Xanthi
Ismet Pacha *see* İnönü, Ismet
Istanbul Ekspres, 18, 80
Italy, 8, 21, 26, 31, 35, 36, 42, 72, 74,
    79
Izmir, 1, 3, 4, 7, 18, 39, 49, 50, 51, 62,
    79, 102

Jihad, Halil, 178

Kadıköy, 92, 107, 108, 114
Kallithea, 87, 116
Kamo, Mustafa, 178
Kanarya, Vacip, 142
Kanatlı, Şükrü, 79
Karaköy, 90
King Paul, 79
Kızılyürek, Niyazi, 175
Komotini, 3, 4, 8, 20, 79, 129, 131, 132,
    139, 140, 143, 144, 145, 147, 149,
    165, 176, 177, 178
Konstantinos VI, 107
Kosovo, 159
Köprülü, Fuat, 79
Kurtuluş, 1, 11, 18, 87, 92, 196

Lausanne (treaty and convention), 16,
    42, 49–52, 66–73, 95, 102–4, 109,
    115, 126, 130, 176, 185, 189, 191
League of Nations, 28, 71, 72, 122
Livaneli, Zülfü, 170
Lloyd George, David, 35, 40, 41
Loizidou, Tartina, 172

Macedonia, 15, 20, 50, 52, 53, 136, 159,
    160, 164, 190
Makarios, 80, 82, 93
Maximos V (Patriarch), 108
mecelle, 107
Meço, Cemali, 140, 141, 153, 177
Megali Idea, 23
Menderes, Adnan, 18, 79, 80
Mete, Ahmet, 178
millet system, 13, 15, 16, 47, 88, 102,
    103, 126, 130, 190
Mitsotakis, Konstantinos, 148
mübadele see exchange of populations
Mudros (Armistice), 30, 103
mufti, 9, 20, 22, 130, 131, 140, 145,
    150, 153, 158, 167, 176–8
muhacir, 47, 53–63, 135
Mustafa (Mustapha) Kemal *see* Atatürk
Mustafa, Hüseyin, 177

NATO, 1, 78, 79, 164
Nea Smyrni, 87, 116

Öcalan, Abdullah, 8, 161–3
Orbay, Rauf, 33, 34
Özal, Turgut, 23, 117, 133, 141, 142,
    147, 165, 167

Paleo Phaliron, 116

Pangalos, Theodoros, 161
Papa Eftim,107
Papagos, Alexandros, 78
Papandreou, Andreas, 23, 141, 161
Papandreou, Georgios, 163–5
Patriarchate, 9, 22, 28, 30, 35, 80, 81, 84, 85, 86, 92, 95, 99–113
Pera Zographeion High School for boys, 93
Pera Zographeion High School for girls, 93
Phanar, 92, 97, 98, 99, 100, 108, 167, 168
Pomaks, 7, 20, 22, 120, 126, 127, 129, 133, 146, 165, 166
Prince Islands, 92, 116
Prince Sebahattin, 29

Queen Frederica, 79

reciprocity, 66–7, 85, 89, 92, 97, 130, 131, 168, 180
Rhodope, 7, 21, 135, 148, 165
Rodoplu, Ismail, 141, 142, 143, 144, 145, 147, 149, 150, 153
Rumelili, Mustafa, 136
Russia, 103, 110, 111, 114, 162, 167, 172

Sabetayci, 50, 193
Samné, Georges, 26–8, 34, 37, 42
Saraçoğlu, Rüştü, 75, 114
Sarajevo, 14
Sergei (Patriarch), 111
Şerif, İbrahim, 144, 145, 150, 177, 178
Sèvres (Treaty), 28, 36, 37, 38, 40, 103
Simitis, Costas, 161, 162, 176

Şinikoğlu, Mehmet Emin, 177
Sirkeci, 135
Slavic, 15, 47
Soviet Union, 37, 38, 40, 74, 78, 110, 115, 167
Struma, 112
Sublime Porte, 103

Tanzimat, 47, 106, 130
Tenedos, 4, 49, 66, 67, 69, 73, 84, 89, 95, 109, 115, 116, 191
Tengirşenk, Yusuf Kemal, 38
Theodorakis, Mikis, 170
Thessaloniki, 3, 4, 7, 8, 18, 20, 50, 80, 107, 116, 132, 139, 140, 141, 142, 143
Tikhon (Patriarch), 110
trampa see exchange of populations
Tsipras, Alexis, 178
Turkish Republic of Northern Cyprus (TRNC), 171, 173
turkokratia, 11, 12, 23

Union and Progress, 28, 32, 36
United States of America see America
USA see America

vakıf, 85, 90, 91, 130, 168
Valoukli see Balıklı
varlık vergisi, 16, 75–7
Vasilios (Patriarch), 108
Venezis, Elias, 14, 196
Veniamin (Patriarch), 108
Venizelos, Elefterios, 28, 35, 36, 37, 48, 73, 74, 103, 104, 108, 191
Venizelos, Sophocles, 79
Vienna (Congress of), 187

Wealth Tax *see varlık vergisi*
Western Thrace, 7, 8, 19, 20, 21, 49, 52,
    66, 67, 68, 78, 79, 81, 85, 96, 97,
    104, 116, 129–38, 158, 164, 165,
    176, 178, 179, 190, 191

Xanthi, 3, 4, 7, 20, 131, 132, 143, 144,
    145, 148, 149, 165, 176, 177, 178

Yerasimos, Stefanos, 12
Yirmi Kura Askerlik, 113
Yılmaz, Mesut, 142
Young Turks, 26, 32, 147
Yugoslavia, 19, 79, 159
Yuvanidis, Konstantin, 91

Zolotas, Xenophon, 145

EU representative:
Easy Access System Europe
Mustamäe tee 50, 10621 Tallinn, Estonia
Gpsr.requests@easproject.com

www.ingramcontent.com/pod-product-compliance
Lightning Source LLC
Chambersburg PA
CBHW050649270326
41927CB00012B/2938